ELDERHOSTELS

The Students' Choice

SECOND EDITION

Mildred Hyman

JOHN MUIR PUBLICATIONS

Santa Fe, New Mexico

John Muir Publications, P.O. Box 613, Santa Fe, NM 87504

Second edition. Second printing February 1992

Library of Congress Cataloging-in-Publication Data

Hyman, Mildred L., 1920-
    Elderhostels : the students' choice / Mildred Hyman. — 2nd ed.
      p. cm.
    ISBN 0-945465-98-X
    1. Elderhostels—United States—Guide-books. 2. Elderhostels—
Guide-books. 3. Continuing education—Curricula. 4. Adult
education—Curricula. I. Title.
LC5471.H96 1991
374'.01—dc20   91-11505
                                                            CIP

Typeface: Sabon and Gil Sans Bold Condensed
Typesetter: Copygraphics
Designer: Marcy Heller
Cover design: Sally Blakemore
Cover illustration: Holly Wood
Printer: Banta Company

Distributed to the book trade by
W.W. Norton & Company, Inc.
New York, New York

Contents

Contents

FLORIDA

GEORGIA

HAWAII

IDAHO

IOWA

KENTUCKY

MAINE

OKLAHOMA

OREGON

PENNSYLVANIA

SOUTH DAKOTA

TENNESSEE

TEXAS

UTAH

VERMONT

VIRGINIA

INTERNATIONAL PROGRAMS

(Note: International programs often are scheduled for 2- and 3-week courses, each week in a different location. Therefore, programs are listed here by week, not alphabetically.)

CANADA

New Brunswick

Nova Scotia

Ontario

Quebec

CHINA

COSTA RICA

ENGLAND

ENGLAND/SCOTLAND/WALES

FRANCE

ISRAEL

ITALY

JAPAN

KENYA

MEXICO

PORTUGAL

SPAIN

Contents

TURKEY

Acknowledgments

I am sincerely grateful to my contributors, without whose earnest assistance this guide would not have been possible. Thanks to them, the book is an engaging mix of kudos and complaints, of congratulations and criticism. The photographs were taken by Elderhostel friends, some members of my family, and a few wannabe professional photographers.

My panel of one hundred Elderhostelers is a geographically diverse group from urban, suburban, and rural locations in some twenty-six states and one Canadian province. The panelists are all much-traveled hostelers, competent to discriminate between good and inferior programs. Many interviews were conducted face-to-face, but the majority of evaluations were solicited through the mail. These acknowledgments would be incomplete without thanking my conscientious editor who unfortunately will have to wait twenty years before she can enjoy the pleasures described herein.

Foreword

When I discovered that the text herein by my fellow Tucsonan Mildred Hyman has good descriptions about accommodations available for Elderhostelers in their travels, I was reminded of my 1976 presidential campaign. You may remember that in the early days of the campaign, my chief opponent, Jimmy Carter, a good ol' boy, ran kind of a down-home type of operation. He did things like stay in people's homes as he traveled back and forth across the country. "You've got to do that, too," said my key advisers. "It'll make you more human. Besides, we'll save a few bucks." I probably was more impressed by the second argument, but anyway, I agreed to give it a try. Now my 6'-5" frame is not easily parked, and I wound up one night sleeping, or trying to sleep, in a bed usually occupied by my host's small daughter. It was a miserable night. "No more," I told the staff the next morning. "Let Jimmy Carter have any votes he can get that way."

That's kind of an oblique way of making a point here—that *Elderhostels: The Students' Choice* would seem to be must reading for those of you who frequently travel to unfamiliar places and want to know what to expect when you arrive. Obviously, the quality of the educational experience is of top priority. But comfort is important, too. The need for a book frankly discussing Elderhostel offerings is obvious. Institutions aren't going to emphasize the shortcomings of their programs, educational or otherwise. I have a friend who went to a New England resort whose brochure said the beach was only a short walk through "field and pine." It turned out to be a horrible two-mile hike through a brier patch. Mildred says the program at my alma mater, the University of Arizona in Tucson, has teachers who are well prepared and know their subjects. But she says the accommodations "leave much to be desired." So be it. Elderhosteling will be much less guesswork to readers of this book.

Morris K. Udall
Member of Congress

Introduction

The Elderhostel organization, founded in 1975, has been called the greatest social movement of the century by *Time* magazine. Headquartered in Boston, Massachusetts, it is based on the premise that people of all ages should have access to education. Founder Marty Knowlton, a social activist and educator, patterned the program on the European youth hostel movement. Like the European model, there is no charge for membership and the organization is nonprofit. Many golden-agers would dispute the adage that life begins at forty—for them, through Elderhosteling, it begins at sixty.

Over fifteen hundred institutions in 50 states, all 10 Canadian provinces, and 40 foreign countries offer a variety of one- to three-week residential educational programs. Major universities, community colleges, music schools, conference centers, and national parks are among the ever-increasing number of host institutions. Elderhostel courses are not for credit, and, except for a few intensive study programs, there are no exams, grades, or required assignments.

Eight to ten times a year, one-half million large newsprint catalogs of educational opportunities are mailed to men and women over age sixty. This free official catalog contains a ten- to twelve-line description of each facility followed by a brief summary of the courses and a schedule of when the courses are given. This is not a great deal of information, particularly for the first-time hosteler.

The catalog contains an array of appealing opportunities, but it can be a surfeit of riches. With so many offerings, how can the novice Elderhosteler select the destination that will best meet his or her special interests and physical needs? Because the catalog descriptions are written by the host institutions, it is unlikely that their own shortcomings and weaknesses will be revealed. Some colleges, struggling to keep their fiscal heads above water, burdened by escalating costs, declining enrollments, and diminished financial aid, have turned to Elderhosteling to fill unused classrooms and dorms. These schools are not apt to be forthright about their frugal cafeterias or their inhospitable terrain. How, then, can prospective attendees learn what any given site or program "is really like"?

The need for this guide surfaced some years ago when I, too, started to Elderhostel. I found myself, like many new to the movement, cross-examining the old hands at every opportunity. Table conversation in the cafeteria, at breakfast, lunch, and dinner, revolved primarily around previous Elderhostel experiences. I took numerous mental notes but forgot the details ("All New England sites fill to capacity early in the fall foliage season"; "Santa Fe is a must for opera buffs in the summer"; "the drive up the mountain to Idyllwild is hairy"). It soon became clear that I should keep an Elderhostel journal.

I recently met a forty-year-old woman who volunteers as a docent at the Arizona Desert Museum. When I mentioned my Elderhosteling to her, she looked at me with new respect and laughed. "My trainer at the museum warned me," she said. "Tour all the little fifth-grade classes you can get, but never, never, never host a group of Elderhostelers. They know more than you do about your subject and aren't the least bit shy about telling you so."

The young woman's statement triggered the thought that Elderhostelers must return some very provocative evaluations to their host institutions, along with their room keys, at the conclusion of their stay. I thought, wouldn't those uncensored comments be fun to read! I was right. They are fun to read and informative, too. Rumors like the one voiced by the museum trainer may have given rise to the cliché opprobrium "hostile elders." But this is undeserved; for the most part, you'll find the reviews that follow frank but also tolerant. Criticism, they say, is poor stuff if it strikes no positive note.

Our need for information seems to be similar to that of the

eighteen-year-old prospective college student who selects a destination after a fact-finding campus visit, a chat with students, an audit of classes, and a stroll through the neighboring community. That high school senior has an advantage over the Elderhosteler—access to dozens of college guidebooks that list "the most popular, the most exciting, and the best." Some published college guides rate schools by cost and SATs required. Elderhosteling costs are modest, and the only SAT score necessary is your word as to your age and a desire to learn something you've always dreamed of learning, or a wish to hear again something half-forgotten.

This book, much like the underground student guides, contains candid program critiques submitted by experienced Elderhostelers for the use of the uninitiated. Most of all, this travel guide has been compiled to take the place of that campus visit. Although it would be impossible for me to determine the "best" or "most exciting" program, those adjectives have been used occasionally by the contributors. But I note the "most popular" institutions when informed about long waiting lists. Under the "Getting In" category, I warn my readers about overpopular programs and the need for early registration. However, the popularity of international destinations varies from year to year according to the changing political climate of the countries.

But early registration is not the whole answer. The most popular programs cannot be filled on a simple first-come, first-served basis for fear that Bostonians would get preferential treatment by hand-delivering their requests. Therefore, when applications exceed available space, a computer-generated lottery is held one month after the catalog is delivered to determine the accepted registrants and the waiting lists. During one summer, the national registration department received 400 applications for an Alaskan program that had space for 50. This random-selection process does not seem to be discouraging Elderhostelers, who continue to join the movement in droves. My best guess is that only a handful of destinations must be filled by lottery.

When I tried to register for an East Coast program one December, I was placed in a nonenrolled category, "wait-list and standby." My registration certificate was wrapped in a packet of goldenrod and pink form letters that explained my options and the necessary procedures. Elderhostel standby, like the airline classification of the same name, is designed for travelers free to take off on a moment's notice. This was not an option open to me, but the use of a standby process reveals the organization's efforts to solve its serious registration difficulties.

Cost is not a factor at Elderhostels—the weekly rate varies only by $10 to $20. The cost in the United States is typically $265 per week for room, board, and no more than three courses, each of which meets for one to one and a half hours per weekday. The fee includes registration, six nights lodging, all meals from Sunday evening through the following Saturday breakfast, five days of classes, and some field trips and extracurricular activities. The cost and arrangements for travel to and from your destination in the United States, Canada, Jamaica, Mexico, and Bermuda are your own responsibility.

The difficulty of traveling to and from some locations is infrequently, if ever, mentioned in the catalog. Driving alone, I have struggled with treacherous mountain roads and axle-breaking unpaved furrows so rough I would have reconsidered or made other travel arrangements had I been forewarned. In addition, lodgings vary from college dormitories to luxury hotels with private baths, from bunk beds in youth hostels to private homes in foreign countries. The variety of housing accommodations is not adequately addressed in the official catalog. Even the tableware varies from tin mess kits to silver teapots. The most common misconception among nonmembers is that Elderhosteling is not for them. They find the prospect of sharing a bathroom and eating institutional food displeasing. As you will learn in the following pages, amenities such as private baths and gourmet food are available at some destinations.

In compiling this work, I was awed by the eclectic range of programs and people. Hostelers wade through Chomskyan linguistic theory in Massachusetts, write poetry in Iowa, and debate religious philosophy in an air-conditioned classroom overlooking Mulholland Drive. The classrooms are not all indoors; hostelers also photograph Alaskan glaciers and spot bighorn sheep in virgin forests. Nor do the classes appeal only to philosophy scholars. Elderhosteling attracts people with the time and intellectual curiosity to know the woods and wilderness firsthand and to study and value the flowers, fauna, birds, and forests. These environmentally concerned Elderhostelers worry about leaving their grandchildren and great-grandchildren a diminished world whose natural beauty and vitality have been exploited.

Not only do the intellectual and social interests of hostelers vary but their physical needs are also diverse. The sixty-year-old, still active in a career, has needs unlike those of a septuagenarian or an octogenarian. The difference is that of a generation—the sixty-year-old born in 1928 has few memories in common with the ninety-year-old born in 1898 before President McKinley was shot. Everyone over age sixty is not exactly a contemporary.

The dissimilitude of programs prevented me from designing a system to rank Elderhostels. When it was suggested that the book be subtitled "The Best and the Worst," it was okay with me, but it was not okay with many Elderhostelers. Most of my fellow members proved to be a proud, protective lot. I was told, "There are no worst." I always had to promise anonymity and occasionally had to repeat my inquiry to elicit specific criticisms from my contributors. I often said, "Think of yourself as a not-young woman traveling alone, or a newcomer to the movement. Which destinations should you avoid?" Not surprisingly, the same complaints were echoed over and over about the same institutions. In preparing this revised edition, I was pleased to note that many of the most disliked destinations are no longer in the Elderhostel business.

Favorites were easy to spot. I asked contributors to submit evaluations of a few of their most positive and most negative experiences; of the possible thousands of destinations, I found the same schools named repeatedly. Included herein are the results of that unscientific selection. You will find many direct quotes from Elderhostelers who have returned to the same host institution four and five times. Yes, the quotes are subjective but no more so than you'll find in any other insider's travel book.

I did not design a system to rank programs, but a man who did, a man "hooked on Elderhostel" who ranked his fifty-five experiences on a scale of one to five, shared his chart with me. All of his number one favorites are also praised by the panelists. The man, probably a statistician or actuary before retirement, mails his chart and newsletter to Elderhostel acquaintances.

This book was not developed as a "kiss and tell" exposé, a "let's-accept-the-host's-hospitality-then-give-'em-a-black-eye" sort of inside scoop, even though some institutions seem to deserve a shiner. But please remember that the deficiencies may have been corrected since publication. I urge readers to call the Elderhostel director at the site before registering to determine if the problem reported herein has been rectified. Despite all my years of research and efforts to update the facts, things change. The educational institutions that host Elderhostel programs are not static. Institutions grow and change: universities can clean their dormitories and hire new chefs, and, conversely, they can go downhill and cut back existing services; railroad companies and airlines may cancel unprofitable stops. One Elderhostel addict noted unhappily that when she registered for a third year at a favorite destination, she was told the school van that had formerly met her at the airport would not be available this year. She was advised that she should try to share the $22 taxi ride from the airport to her dormitory.

I've tried to avoid a dull, mathematical comparison of places and services but have included some numbers that seem relevant. For instance, I note the size of the school: huge University of Arizona with 37,000 students has a campus environment vastly different from the University of New England with 600 undergraduates. I have also indicated the altitude of many sites. A physician warned me that the decreased oxygen of high elevations may cause pulmonary or cerebral edema in some elderly folk.

As egalitarian as Elderhostel purports to be, it nevertheless has developed its own social stratification based on the number of hostels attended. Except for this one infraction, the populist philosophy seems to work. Snobbery of any stripe is discouraged. The retired ditchdigger rooms with the retired bank president, and the former manicurist stands in the cafeteria line with the former school principal. With less than 20 Elderhostel notches on my gun, I have roomed with a former magazine editor, a retired dancer, and a former nonprofit executive. I have square danced with a telephone lineman, scooped ice cream with a retired farmer, listened to opera with a college administrator, and photographed a Hohokum burial site with a retired nuclear physicist. But information about former careers and curriculum vitae just trickles forth over bowls of chocolate pudding.

While gathering material for the book, I conducted a face-to-face interview with a married couple who had experienced a particularly dismal hostel. After commiserating with the unhappy pair, I asked, "Did you complete your postsession evaluation form honestly? That's your tool for calling the administration to task." The woman replied angrily, "No, because I knew the program director would just toss our evaluation into the round file, since she was responsible for our displeasure." I pressed, "Then why didn't you forward your complaints to Boston headquarters?" The husband sighed. "We didn't want Boston to penalize us regarding future requests. Put us down as cranks. We've been on a couple of waiting lists."

Since publication of the first edition of *Elderhostels: The Students' Choice*, I find myself cast as the Ralph Nader or "Fight Back" Horowitz of the movement and therefore receive lots of unsolicited mail. Correspondents write of complaints to national headquarters that go unanswered, of lack of staff to handle medical emergencies, of program directors formerly "wonderful, now spread too thin," as well as of experiences that are much better than the reviews printed in my book. Every letter has been answered, the complimentary as well as the grouchy ones. And, more important, every one of those destinations has been reevaluated, many new ones added, and all programs updated.

Those letters called my attention to another need—additional information for the single traveler. My new "Going Solo" category is in response to angry stories about cliquey couples who caused someone's "first and last" Elderhostel or touching comments such as "I'm newly widowed and always lonely in a crowd." I asked my panelists to rate destinations as to their suitability for singles on a scale of one to five, five being highest. I further requested statements to support the rating. The issue evoked some very thoughtful responses and encouraged many couples to examine their own social attitudes more critically. Not every site is so evaluated because my reviewers either chose not to answer the question or gave me too brief a response to allow a fair assessment. Therefore, I have compiled a few factors that make destinations work well for singles. Generally, it is easier to meet people when couples are the exception rather than the rule, when dining arrangements are not isolating, when pleasant communal rooms are handy, when the site is accessible by public transportation, and when competent, caring, cordial program directors are on the scene. In general, I believe Garrison Keillor's "shy persons" would fare better in the more regimented environment of international programs.

Introduction

I have tried to report all programs faithfully and hope this work will be appreciated by couples as well as singles. By shopping carefully for their destinations, readers will be able to separate the wheat from the chaff and increase their odds of having a truly rewarding experience. I hope this opinionated journey reads like a dialogue with a friend.

DOMESTIC PROGRAMS

ALABAMA

Gulf Shores—University of Southern Alabama

Courses of Study: Ecology of the Dunes; Birds and Sea Creatures; Historical Highlights; Creative Writing from A to Z; Climb Your Family Tree, Introduction to Genealogy; Explore Special Features / Creatures of Gulf Coast Area

Quality of Instructors: Very interesting specialists are brought in for each lecture. Some of the topics covered are shrimp, oysters, the oil industry, birds, and hurricanes.

Environment: This Elderhostel is located in a resort area on the Gulf of Mexico. The swampy bayous of the Mobile delta provide a winter refuge for waterfowl, while the white, sandy beaches and mild weather provide a winter refuge for "snowbirds" from the north.

Near Mobile one can still find stately antebellum homes decorated with wrought-iron balconies and white Doric columns. These plantation homes are hidden at the end of long, gracious driveways roofed with huge shade trees.

Housing: Elderhostelers are housed in a two-story resort motel in rooms with private baths. In addition, there's an indoor heated pool, a hot tub, and a fitness center, all overlooking the Gulf of Mexico.

Food: Lunch and dinner are served by waiters in a dining room, breakfast is cafeteria style. The southern menu of hominy grits for breakfast, corn pone, black-eyed peas, collards, and turnip greens was not enthusiastically received.

Unique Attributes: Everything—classes, meals, and lodging—is in the same resort complex, so very little walking is required. The beaches are clean and not very crowded, ideal for surf casting. Thousands of tourists annually follow the Azalea Trail and visit the Bellingrath Gardens where moss-draped oaks overhang the shores of the Fowl River.

Shortcomings: There were some complaints about the menu, but the complaints were outnumbered by praise for the facilities.

Going Solo: This is not recommended for "shrinking violets" because most enrollees are couples who drive to the site. Nonetheless, the resort is self-contained, so it rates a 3, a maybe.

Getting In: I believe early reservations are essential.

Getting There: Automobile is the best bet, but one can fly to Mobile or Pensacola, Florida, then rent a vehicle. There is limited bus service.

ALASKA

Anchorage—Alaska-Pacific University

Courses of Study: Natives of Alaska; Nature Study and Hikes; Habitats and Natural History; Alaskan Art; Geology and Man

Quality of Instructors: My reviewers, some twenty-five individuals, found the instruction excellent. I also received a few comments of "outstanding professors" and one comment of "good delivery."

Environment: This wooded, attractive campus is located in the center of Anchorage, a city of 300,000 people. The air is clean and clear, and the people in Alaska's largest city are friendly. The campus has wonderful walking trails and also offers easy access into town by public bus. One athletic couple said the highlight of their week was renting bicycles and exploring the lovely public parks where they saw peonies the size of grapefruit.

Housing: The dormitory accommodations are adequate, with the usual shared bathroom facilities. Buildings in Alaska are constructed to retain the heat, so interiors can be uncomfortably hot in May (heaters on) and cold in August (heaters off).

Food: The food is good but without frills. It is served cafeteria-style with a salad bar.

Unique Attributes: The director is a superb coordinator and sees to every detail. She is applauded unanimously. Wildlife can be seen on afternoon field trips to nearby mountains; an optional glacier tour offered on Saturday is a wondrous extra-cost event. One can see glaciers that look like ice sculptures and others that resemble blue rivers of ice. My reviewers wrote, "A never-to-be-forgotten experience!" "Moose roam the campus!"

The bars stay open until 5:00 a.m. in this macho state. And do not forget all those extra hours of daylight because of Alaska's proximity to the Arctic Circle. Reading about it is not the same as experiencing this delightful phenomenon.

Shortcomings: Much like in New England, the weather can be foggy and cold in August and rather hot in June. A woman from the Southwest, accustomed to temperatures of over 100 degrees, was amazed to find Anchorage so hot. She also advised bringing your longjohns for the glacier tour. "Alaska is big and so are its mosquitoes, and what's more, they have lots of them!"

Anchorage is a classic example of a program revisited and re-evaluated after a caring, competent coordinator came on board. Please, all of you Elderhostelers who howled "how dare you," remember it is the duty of a thorough travel writer to report the discomforts as well as the pleasures.

Going Solo: The program is well designed for single travelers, and many do participate. All the single women were housed in one area of the dormitory, and the entire group dined and went on field trips together. There were also some evening activities planned. In addition, Elderhostelers meet other participants on the plane en route to Anchorage and share taxis to the campus. This can be a great way to break the ice.

Getting In: In spite of the expensive airfare, the Anchorage programs have become, according to my reporters, "very popular." They are frequently filled by computer lottery as described in the introduction.

Getting There: Anchorage can be reached by frequent flights of regularly scheduled airlines. Northwest, an old-timer in the old-timer business, offers a 10 percent discount or a coupon book to all passengers at least 62 years old. Delta and United do the same. All three airlines fly to Anchorage.

Fairbanks—University of Alaska

Courses of Study: Mining for Gold; Photography; Big Game Hunting; Useful Plants; Alaska Politics; Introduction to Alaskan Ichthyology

Quality of Instructors: Excellent.

Environment: Fairbanks stretches for 8 miles along the muddy Chena River in the interior of Alaska, with a winter climate much colder than Anchorage. The town sprang up when gold was discovered in the region in the 1800s. One can still find examples of pioneer gold mining saloons in this frontier settlement. Paddle wheelers ply the shallow waters of the river, and sled dogs can be seen romping across the snow.

The university is situated 5 miles west of downtown Fairbanks and offers a spectacular view of 20,320-foot Mount McKinley, the highest point in North America.

Housing: College dormitories can be hot in June. The management should provide fans.

Food: Hostelers are served three unimaginative square meals a day.

Unique Attributes: The campus lies in the fertile Tanana Valley where, in spite of the short growing season, farmers plant a variety of crops. Reindeer graze in the fields, and the campus is ringed by hundreds of snow-capped mountains. Photographers have over 21 hours of sunlight in the summertime, and hostelers have 35 miles of trails and plant and animal research farms to explore.

Shortcomings: Elderhostelers arriving by plane cannot bring fans or bedlamps. These minor items are the only complaints.

Getting In: No problem reported.

Getting There: Air and rail are preferred, although one wag suggested dogsled. The Alaska railroad has glass-domed cars that run between Anchorage and Fairbanks. This might be a wonderful way to view the interior of the state.

Homer—Kenai Peninsula College/ Kachemak Bay Branch

*(Week 2 of a 2-week program with Sitka—
Sheldon Jackson College)*

Courses of Study: Human and Natural History of Kachemak Bay. (At Sitka, the courses are Ravens and Rubles; Natural Resources of the Tongass National Forest; Life of Southeast Alaska's Seas and Shore)

Quality of Instructors: Excellent and enthusiastic. The National Park Service personnel are much admired—"interested, spirited, and well qualified."

Environment: Homer lies at the tip of the Kenai Peninsula, on the shore of Kachemak Bay, in the southeastern part of the state. A salmon fishing center, Homer is a community of just 2,209 people. The town offers breathtaking views of the mountains and glaciers across the bay. The coast of Kachemak Bay is cut by steep-sided inlets called fiords. Because of its waterfront location, Homer enjoys milder temperatures than inland Alaska. If you're lucky, you may see moose wandering through town in the spring.

Housing: The accommodations require some adaptability and a sense of humor. "Neither comfortable nor adequate in Homer, but we made do." An extreme room shortage due to the popularity of the program forced three singles into a room designed at best for two.

Food: In Homer, participants eat all meals at local restaurants. "Two excellent and two poor restaurants."

Unique Attributes: One reviewer, an avid veteran of ten hostels on the international circuit, rated this overall adventure an A. "At last, a two-week Alaska program with possibilities," she sighed. (Another two-week program combining Denali National Park and the University of Alaska at Fairbanks is now offered.) One is taken by bus or boat to see as much of this enormous state as possible. The indescribable beauty of the land, the waterways visited, the interesting excursions, and the concern and dedication of the program coordinators make the experience gratifying and fascinating.

Shortcomings: The living quarters in Homer are too small and too cramped, but it is such a small, primitive town it may well not have anything better to offer. "One must be a competent walker for this program, though several individuals with canes managed very well."

Going Solo: Very suitable. Two of the important factors for the comfort of singles are present: a caring, conscientious coordinator and daily bus and boat excursions as a group.

Getting In: My reviewer is just one of many individuals who were eagerly awaiting a two-week Alaska program "with great possibilities."

Getting There: It takes some perseverance to get to this program from the East Coast, even by plane. The college will meet attendees at the airport for a small fee. Alaska has huge car-carrying ferries that ply the waters from Seattle, Washington. The Kodiak Island ferry connects Seward, Kodiak, Homer, Valdez, and Cordova.

Juneau and Aboard MV *Matanuska* — University of Alaska

Courses of Study: Politics of Alaska; Sea Mammals; Forest Lands; Alaskan Literature; Inside Passage, Southeast Alaska, and the Tongass National Forest

Quality of Instructors: Very professional. "How could they miss with such fascinating subjects in such a spectacular setting?"

Environment: Juneau, the capital of Alaska, lies in a strip called the Panhandle, the southeasternmost part of the state. The mountains of the Coast Range jut sharply out into the Pacific Ocean and form a lush rain forest. Sparkling glaciers dot the coast, and the action of thousands of glaciers has formed long inlets called fiords.

Housing: Hostelers stay in a fine hotel in Juneau and a stateroom on board the ship, where two-berth inside cabins have private baths.

Food: Adequate in the hotel, but much too much on shipboard!

Unique Attributes: The MV *Matanuska*, a ship in the Alaska marine highway system, is a floating campus for seven-day or ten-day voyages exploring the fabled Alaskan Inside Passage. My reviewers participated in an eight-day experience, four days in Juneau and four days on shipboard. The "breathtakingly spectacular scenery" was noted, as was the fact that the classes on shipboard were made more interesting by the attendance of native Alaskans.

Shortcomings: The MV *Matanuska* is a small ship and has small staterooms.

Going Solo: Because of the prearranged group airfare, many Elderhostelers meet on the plane. They share cabs to the hotel and must share staterooms on the ship. An ideal setup for solo travelers.

Getting In: My reviewers were wait-listed but moved up to an enrolled category in time to make all the necessary travel arrangements.

Getting There: My reviewers flew to Seattle, then boarded an Air Alaska flight on which group discount fares were prearranged.

Sitka—Sheldon Jackson College

(Week 1 of the 2-week Homer program)

Courses of Study: Literature of Oral Tradition; Chemistry in Southeastern Alaska Environment; Cultural Diversity; Alaska's Booms and Busts; Alaska Wildlife; Forest Succession, Will Sphagnum Moss Take Over?

Quality of Instructors: Good to excellent.

Environment: Sitka means "the best place" in the Indian language. The city is a salmon-packing center and a paradise for fishermen. It was once the capital of Russian America; Alaska, at its westernmost point, is only 54 miles across the Bering Strait from Russia. Sitka is also a center for the Tlingit Indians. The Sheldon Jackson campus is situated in an island-dotted harbor just 4 blocks from downtown. It overlooks the Pacific Ocean and has a backdrop of rugged snow-topped mountains.

Housing: Comfortable dormitory rooms; no complaints.

Food: Quantity and quality are good.

Unique Attributes: The Sitka National Monument contains an old Indian stockade where Tlingit Indians made their last stand against the early Russian settlers. There's also a fine exhibit of totem poles. The Sitka session includes a boat and bus tour of the area.

Shortcomings: The professors do not talk down to the Elderhostelers or simplify their scientific presentations. This fact is viewed as a plus by some attendees and a shortcoming by others. Watch out for rain in Sitka (which doesn't interfere with scheduled programs). One panelist requested more time to take in museums.

Getting In: Like most Alaskan programs, this one is popular.

Getting There: Limited access by air. A pleasant way to travel the coast is by the Alaska state ferry system. The schedule is complicated and changes frequently. Fares are also subject to change. Reservations are required for on-deck passage or for vehicle space.

ARIZONA

Cordes Junction — Arcosanti /
The Cosanti Foundation

Courses of Study: Arcosanti, Man and the Environment; Arcosanti, an Urban Laboratory; Zen Buddhism at Arcosanti

Quality of Instructors: Dedicated experts-in-residence teach geology, land use, architecture, cosmology, and Zen. The lectures are augmented with slides, films, and hands-on experience.

Environment: Arcosanti is a relatively isolated, unfinished urban laboratory sixty-five miles north of Phoenix. It is the design, planned habitat, and vision of brilliant, radical architect Paolo Soleri. Domed concrete structures in various stages of completeness sit on the crest and side of a spectacular mesa. Experimental solar greenhouses and a working forge (kept busy casting Soleri bells) are also part of the complex.

Cordes Junction is located halfway between Phoenix and Flagstaff. The 3,800-foot altitude creates a climate brisk and sometimes snowy in winter and pleasant in the summer.

Housing: Elderhostelers stay in twin-bedded rooms with private baths in a small motel-like building at the base of a steep hill. The quarters are spartan and a tough climb from the dining area. Individual gas space heaters are welcome on chilly nights. A recent workshop attendee has pledged the gift necessary to convert this structure into a greenhouse by enclosing it within a plastic membrane. The greenhouse will make the unit cooler in the summer and warmer in the winter.

Food: Adequate, but no choice of menu, served in a small, dramatic atrium cafeteria. The meals have been improved since last reviewed with a menu that is now more appropriate to needs of seniors. Fresh fruit is available round the clock. Members of the resident staff operate a bakery on an upper level of the visitors

Visitor center café, Arcosanti, Arizona

Silt casting, Arcosanti

center and the tantalizing fragrances of fresh baked bread and cinnamon cookies fill the dining room each morning.

Unique Attributes: One of the thought-provoking activities scheduled at Paolo Soleri's futuristic city is a weekly picnic in the Boschetto where visitors and staff share thoughts, experiences, and readings about world hunger. The picnic is but one of several dialogues Elderhostelers have with Signore Soleri during which he shares his imaginative philosophy and complex concept of arcology. The glossary of key words and ideas distributed to attendees is helpful to the scientifically unsophisticated. "One of the most unusual and informative weeks I've ever spent in Elderhosteling." "Definitely a program for the intellectually curious."

Guided nature hikes to Indian ruins, Hohokam burial grounds, and petroglyphs are conducted by exceptionally talented geographers, historians, and naturalists, but they're for robust hikers only. A 25-meter outdoor pool offers *agua fria* for the brave hostelers.

Shortcomings: Arcosanti is a construction site in use, and therefore the terrain is very rugged; stairs and gravel paths make it a challenge. The campus coordinator's letter is very clear and warns attendees about the rough dirt road that leads into the property: it is a 3-mile axle-breaking stretch, somewhat improved since our last visit. A communal room is needed for between and after-class socializing; until then, you'd better bring a radio, a good book, and knitting to while away long evenings in your neat, recently constructed, bare-bones motel room.

Getting In: Arcosanti can only accommodate twenty Elderhostelers, so getting in is rather difficult, but Mary Hoadley, a fine, on-site campus coordinator, ambitiously operates programs for 20 weeks a year.

Getting There: This destination is accessible only by automobile or by bus from Phoenix or Flagstaff to Cordes Junction. The program coordinator will arrange to meet the bus at Cordes Junction.

Douglas—Cochise Community College

Courses of Study: Field Study of Birds; Chiricahua Mountains; Writers of the Purple Sage, Western Fiction; Painting with Pastels

Quality of Instructors: Excellent. One reviewer, an ardent "birder," said the ornithologist was one of the best of the many with whom she has studied.

Environment: Douglas is a historic rural community in southeastern Arizona. It is bounded by the Chiricahua Mountains on the west and northeast and Mexico on the south. The 4,500-foot elevation provides pleasant daytime temperatures and breezy nights. This area was settled by Indian tribes and traversed by the Spanish conquistadors.

Housing: In the historic old Gadsden Hotel.

Food: Served in a very good college cafeteria with sufficient choices. Hostelers bus their own trays.

Unique Attributes: Douglas is part of an important flyway and is located at the edge of several habitats. Enrollees will find themselves just a feather away from a hummingbird or within beak distance of a desert hawk. The focus of the course is to teach recognition and principles of identification. Two very comfortable, air-conditioned vans with bathroom facilities are used for the day field trips. The instructor entertains the group with a slide show every evening.

Shortcomings: Field trips can be hot, so don't forget comfortable walking shoes, sunscreen, hat, thermos, and binoculars. The organizers do not take advantage of their proximity to Mexico, so there are no field trips across the border.

Going Solo: Not a great choice since there's little to do after classes if one is alone. My avid avian who was so favorably impressed by the ornithologist said, "Thumbs down. This is not a destination for solo travelers."

Getting In: Not a problem.

Getting There: Bus service is sporadic at best. Douglas is not easy to reach without a car. One can fly to Tucson and rent a car for the 120-mile drive.

Flagstaff—Northern Arizona University

Courses of Study: Southwest Archaeology: The Spanish Southwest; The Anasazi Indians; The Grand Canyon: The World's Greatest Natural Wonder; Planet Earth; Native American Culture in Northern Arizona

Quality of Instructors: All instructors receive an excellent-to-superb rating.

Environment: NAU has a large, beautiful campus in the heart of northern Arizona sightseeing territory. Flagstaff is the crossroads, the jumping-off place to see the red rocks of Sedona, a few miles south, and Walnut Creek Canyon to the east. Located in the Coconino National Forest at an elevation of 7,000 feet, Flagstaff is a homely little city, an ugly duckling surrounded by lovely swans. Approached from either end, the main street is a forest of neon-lit motels and fast-food emporiums.

Arizona has twenty Indian reservations; two of them, the Hopi and Navajo reservations, are an easy drive from Flagstaff. Visitors are welcome to drive to the old Hopi pueblo villages on top of the mesas, but guests must be discreet. Photographing, taping, or sketching of rituals may be forbidden. Spectators should be respectfully dressed; no shorts or halter tops are permitted because some of the performances, such as the Kachina dances, are religious in nature.

Housing: The major source of complaint at the Flagstaff campus seems to be the housing. Several groups of Elderhostelers housed in a commercial motel 2 miles from school were disappointed with rooms that were clean but needed repairs to plumbing, among other things. "Our very old dorm at the northerly edge of the campus," another couple said, "was inexcusable. It was like a disreputable army barracks." Other attendees reported comfortable, adequate accommodations in school dormitories or in a motel just a ten-minute walk from campus.

Food: Meals served in the college cafeteria are good to excellent, but more attention could be paid to housekeeping details. One motel only serves breakfast; another offers three meals a day, with a waitress-served fixed menu. The menu, just for the Elderhostel group, is published at the beginning of the week.

Unique Attributes: The school has a beautiful campus building that contains an Olympic-size swimming pool, but one reviewer noted that the program was so full she didn't have time to enjoy the pool. The program is very well organized. The leaders arrange an icebreaking get-together the first evening and enough evening activities to forge some group cohesiveness. "The weather is divine. Cool every night in the summer. The students are very friendly and the local museum is a must!" The visit to the Lowell Observatory (where Pluto was discovered) is an unusual learning experience. "I saw the rings of Saturn," exclaimed one hosteler.

The all-day trip to the Grand Canyon is the highlight of NAU's program. Every American should at some time in his or her life stand at the top of that great precipice and marvel at the silent beauty of the Colorado River snaking through the valley below. A Phoenix couple has just spent a fortune to revive the steam train track from the South Rim of the Grand Canyon to Williams, 30 miles west of Flagstaff. The train runs across 64 miles of Kaibab National Forest to the historic station at Grand Canyon Village.

Shortcomings: Check on your housing accommodations before you register. NAU has not been offering Elderhostel programs as long as some schools, so the staff is still ironing out the wrinkles. Morton Hall dormitory is a half-mile walk from the cafeteria. This is not a problem if you bring your own automobile.

Getting In: This is a very popular program, so it is essential to register early.

Getting There: Flagstaff has an airport and a Trailways bus terminal for traveling north or south. It is also on the east/west mainline of the Amtrak Railroad. But to enjoy the sightseeing to its fullest, an automobile is a necessity.

Nogales — University of Arizona

Courses of Study: Border-related subjects; The Autumn Birds of Sonoita Creek; Spanish for Travelers; Hands Across the Border; Memoir Writing; Music of the Southwest

Quality of Instructors: Varies, from excellent down to barely adequate.

Environment: Nogales is a small, bustling, commercial city on the Mexican border. It lies in the midst of dry, southwestern hills and gullies that have a most unusual, stark, parched beauty. The hotel is a short walk from the border, enabling attendees to wander at will into Old Mexico to sightsee and shop.

Housing: This Elderhostel provides excellent accommodations in the centrally located Americana Hotel.

Food: Excellent food is provided in the hotel dining room. Many authentic Sonoran dishes, of course.

Unique Attributes: The entire event is well run and well organized. Finding an elevator in the hotel is a nice surprise. This is a particularly good hostel for individuals curious about Mexico but not quite ready to spend a week on the other side of the border. Nogales, Mexico, provides an interesting contrast to its sister city in Arizona. The Mexican city is a bustling tourist mecca where crowds of Americans flock to purchase handmade huaraches and pottery; Nogales, Arizona, is a homely little industrial center whose streets are lined with small motels, factories, and gas stations.

This Elderhostel provides a special opportunity to discuss first-hand the problems of United States and Mexican relations.

The Hands Across the Border session is led by bilingual instructors, so one can be totally immersed in Mexican art, food, and music.

Shortcomings: Nogales is best reached by private automobile. Getting there by bus is a trifle awkward. The bus driver is not prepared to let passengers disembark in front of the hotel. Double check with the bus company before loading your suitcase onto the vehicle.

Getting In: No one reported problems.

Getting There: Accessible only by private automobile or public bus from Tucson.

Phoenix — Grand Canyon University

Courses of Study: Hohokam Cultural History; Native Americans of the Southwest; History of Arizona Gold; Flora and Fauna of the Desert; Don't Pet the Cactus; Arizona's History

Quality of Instructors: Reported as average to exceptional.

Environment: The college is located in the heart of Phoenix, a sprawling southwestern metropolis with palm tree-lined boulevards. The city has a downtown of modern glass-walled sky-scrapers and neighborhoods of white stucco, Spanish-style residences with terra-cotta half-roofs, surrounded by groves of fragrant citrus trees. Phoenix just spirals out into the desert until its growth is halted by a ring of mountains. The college has easy access to all city buses, and the college buildings have handicap access.

Housing: This program is held in a commercial facility that has double occupancy rooms with private baths.

Food: No one complained about the plain food.

Unique Attributes: Very well planned extracurricular activities are scheduled. Arrangements are made for Elderhostelers who wish to take advantage of concerts, shows, and other entertainment that can be reached on public buses. Be careful to check the schedules, as many buses do not run after 6:00 p.m. or on Sundays. There are many reasonably priced Mexican restaurants and many after-hour activities.

One field trip is offered with this program. The choices are the Art Museum, Frank Lloyd Wright's Taliesin West, or the Heard Museum. By all means see the Heard Museum of Anthropology and Primitive Art, with its spectacular Kachina doll and Indian art collection, and Taliesin West.

Elderhostelers are welcome to use the school's heated swimming pool. A devoted following of hostelers compulsively returns year after year because of the landscape and because Phoenix enjoys 300 sunny days per year.

Shortcomings: The major complaint repeated over and over was that the program is "hard to get into" during the winter months. Beware: The average high temperature from June through August is 103°. May and September are almost as bad. I also received this impassioned gripe from a hosteler: "No buses run on Sundays, many buses stop service after 6:30 p.m., and the central bus line shuts down completely at 9:30 p.m." Getting around without a car is expensive.

Getting In: This is a popular winter destination. Grand Canyon University Elderhostel program has a long waiting list every January and February.

Getting There: Phoenix has an international airport served by most major airlines and has good interstate bus service.

Prescott—Yavapai College

Courses of Study: Grand Canyon: A Sense of Place; Arizona History; Spanish Language; Southwest Indian Artifacts; Exploring Red Rock Country; Diagnosing and Analyzing Current Events; Ranchers-Cowboys, the Myths

Quality of Instructors: Most of the teachers are lively and interesting. I also received one report of an excellent professor and another rated as thorough.

Environment: Prescott is a historic old town located in pine-clad mountains 100 miles north of Phoenix. From the city, one has a panoramic view of forests of pine, ash, walnut, and cherry. The climate is cool and comfortable at this elevation of 5,300 feet. The campus is not particularly attractive: "rather ordinary," according to one couple. At Yavapai, environmental studies are an essential component of the curriculum and undergraduates do extensive fieldwork.

Housing: Elderhostelers stay in a variety of accommodations depending on the courses selected and the time of year. On-campus dormitories have small rooms with private baths, an inducement for many participants. Some sessions use a motel with private baths close to the campus. One couple found it "second rate." The Hassayampa Hotel, the "jewel of Old Prescott," has recently been restored to its former grandeur and is used for lodging, meals, and classes for some sessions.

Food: The meals at Yavapai are prepared by a concessionaire and could be improved. "No better and no worse than most," wrote one couple. There is a good salad and dessert bar. Meals are served in the student center cafeteria at hours convenient for the preparers and the student athletes, not for Elderhostelers. No one complained about the meals served at the Hassayampa Hotel.

Unique Attributes: The field trips to the Grand Canyon and Sedona / Oak Canyon are wonderful and are included in some programs. A broad variety of entertainment, slide shows, music, and so forth, is arranged for evenings. Prescott is an old mining town and contains some interesting landmarks. Like Flagstaff, it is ideally located for a trip to watch the daylight change and play on some of Arizona's natural wonders—the red rocks of Sedona and the grand cliffs and plateaus of the Grand Canyon. Summer weather is delightful; the days are pleasant and the nights chilly. Springtime, however, can be cold and wet, as one reviewer reported, and this is ski country in the winter.

If it is not included as a field trip, one should take a side excursion to Jerome State Historic Park. Jerome became a ghost town in 1953 when the last copper mining operation closed. All that remains of a bustling mining town are a few residents peddling historical mementos.

Shortcomings: A car and a driver with leisure time to spare is necessary to thoroughly enjoy this experience.

Going Solo: Not great for single hostelers. Public transportation is limited and limiting. The motel arrangement discourages interaction among the attendees.

Getting in: Yavapai has the distinction of being among the twenty most popular Elderhostel host institutions. To meet the demand, they now offer winter off-campus programs at nine locations. These unusual locations include a Hopi mesa, a lodge on the rim of Marble Canyon, Peach Springs near the bottom of the Grand Canyon, a golf resort, and a hotel adjacent to Montezuma Castle. Many hostelers, drawn by the high peaks and low oxygen, retrace their steps to the same spot each year.

Getting There: Prescott is best reached by private automobile. To fully enjoy the nearby sights and parks, a car is recommended, although the area is served by tour buses and by Golden Pacific Commuter Airlines. Some of my reviewers flew to Phoenix and rented a car for the two-hour drive north.

Surprise—Rio Salado Community College

Courses of Study: Writing for Fun; Sketching in Perspective; Conquering the Great Plains; Water the Great Resource; Current Issues in U.S. Foreign and Domestic Policy; The Healing Power of Humor

Quality of Instructors: My reviewers wrote that, in general, the teaching did not compare with the instruction received at Elderhostels hosted by major universities.

Environment: This Elderhostel is held in an adult education center, one of many operated by Rio Salado Community College. The center, a self-contained resort with an urban atmosphere, is located between Sun City and Sun City West, both retirement communities.

Housing: "Terrific." All participants are assigned apartments in the Sun Ridge complex. The apartments are equipped with kitchens and laundries, everything one can need.

Food: Splendid. All meals are served in the Sun Ridge dining room with a complete choice of menu.

Unique Attributes: The housing and dining are much more elegant than at most Elderhostels. There are heated pools, spas, and recreational and exercise facilities. Shops, restaurants, and golf are nearby but must be reached by automobile. The field trip to Desert Caballeros Western Museum at Wickenburg is very worthwhile.

Shortcomings: This is a new program in a new facility, so wrinkles are still being ironed out. The director is unfamiliar with the job. The building is still under construction, so noise and plaster dust can be troublesome.

Going Solo: This program offers single rooms on request. The dining room hostess seats the Elderhostelers together whenever possible, thus enabling solo travelers to become acquainted with the group. Rio Salado attracts a friendly group, but one of my reviewers said she was "trapped during free time without a car." On a scale of 1 to 5, she rated this one a 3.

Getting In: This one's a sleeper. I imagine it will get more play next winter.

Getting There: Fly to Phoenix, then take a local cab or airport transportation van to Surprise.

Tucson—University of Arizona

Courses of Study: Arizona, the Land and Its Diversity; History of the American West; Anthropology and You; Missions of the Southwest; Pioneer Jews of the Southwest; Space, Time, Matter, and Energy; Conversational Spanish

Quality of Instructors: The teachers are well prepared and know their subjects. The teaching assistants who conduct the classes held at the motel are less heartily endorsed.

Environment: The university is spread over an urban campus with approximately 37,000 students and is located in the center of a southwestern city of 405,900 inhabitants. The predominant architectural style of Tucson is pink, Spanish adobe topped with a flat roof and red tile trim. The smooth stucco facade of the homes and old office buildings creates a perfect surface for reflecting the multicolored prisms of red-orange southwestern sunsets. The sun belt city sits in a valley ringed by five ranges of splendid purple mountains, but the main two thoroughfares of the city are a tasteless jungle of billboards and vulgar strips of commercialism.

Housing: The accommodations for the Elderhostel program leave much to be desired. Various motels have been used, one reported as having all motel services but in an unsavory, inconvenient neighborhood. Another "downtown" Elderhostel motel has a commanding view of a used car lot! None are within walking distance of the university campus.

Food: The food is good and the selection excellent in many of the school cafeterias. Expect to find many Mexican dishes—chimis, tacos, and guacamole—since Hispanics comprise 29 percent of the city's population. A few evaluators groused about the long

University of Arizona, Tucson, campus (Photo: Barbara L. Silvers)

lines in the cafeterias; however, a pair of Elderhostel devotees were very miffed when they had to eat all their meals in the motel with a fixed menu limited to a single entrée. In their view, one of the outstanding features of the Elderhostel experience is the opportunity to have informal dialogue with students in the cafeteria and while walking on the campus between classes.

Unique Attributes: Tucson is a sprawling city, but the campus is centered around a spacious green mall where students in shorts hang out in the bright winter sunshine. "I loved the landscaping on the campus and in town. Lots of palm trees and saguaros and many varieties of cacti." The dry desert climate and sunshine draw large numbers of Elderhostelers to Tucson in the winter. A few miles to the south one can visit Indian reservations and a Tucson landmark, the serene and beautiful 300-year-old Spanish mission, San Xavier del Bac. All U of A Tucson Elderhostel weeks include a trip to the Arizona-Sonora Desert Museum, one of the greatest natural habitat and education demonstration museums in the world.

Elderhostelers may be lucky enough to encounter a few real cowboys in high-heeled boots and broad-brimmed Stetsons strolling or riding horseback through town. Numerous working ranches can still be found just a few miles from the center of the city, and some programs include a cowboy cookout at a dude ranch. This adventure is in sharp contrast with the new Arts District being developed in downtown Tucson. A diverse array of galleries, shops, exhibits, and music are making the downtown come alive at night.

Shortcomings: There were numerous complaints about the pre-planned meals being served at the motel and the attendees being bused to see the university. The inconvenient, undesirable location of the motel was noted repeatedly. One veteran of Elderhosteling in Tucson noted an inconsistency in staff organization. She wrote that preparation ranged from good to poor on succeeding visits: "too many canceled projects and no evening plans." One couple also noted that they had never before participated in a program with 100 attendees. A class of 50 is too large when the acoustics are imperfect and the hearing ability of many of the students is likewise.

Going Solo: This destination should work well for singles. Excellent public transportation is available, enrollment is so large the preponderance of couples does not matter, the motel dining arrangement is nonisolating, and hostelers spend a great deal of time socializing poolside in the sunshine.

Getting In: The Tucson Elderhostel can accommodate a large group, so admission doesn't seem to be a problem. No programs are scheduled during the desert summer heat, which can, on occasion, feel like the interior of a blast furnace.

Getting There: Tucson has an international airport that is served by thirteen major airlines. There are Greyhound and Trailways bus terminals and an Amtrak railroad station. In addition, multi-lane macadam highways lead in and out of town.

Tucson—YWCA

Courses of Study: History of the Southwest; Conversational Spanish; Birds of Southeastern Arizona; Arizona Astronomy; Southern Arizona, the Land of Mañana

Quality of Instructors: Mixed. One who "held the group spellbound" to a couple of "not very inspiring."

Environment: This hostel is held in a very nice motel amidst a commercial strip of restaurants. The area is primarily residential. The architecture of the motel, restaurants, and shops all reflect a taste of the old west.

Housing: "More comfortable than most." Many single attendees can be housed alone in large double rooms or suites.

Food: A caterer prepares a fixed menu that is served in the motel dining room. It is a poor menu. Most lunches are served picnic style on the field trips.

Unique Attributes: The housing is much more elegant than most college dormitories. This program is primarily a sightseeing adventure. Mexico is just one hour south of Tucson, and the city boasts a fine planetarium, Indian missions to the south, natural canyons to the east, and in February, the world's longest unmechanized rodeo. And giant saguaro cacti grow 50 feet tall in the wonderful winter sunshine!

Shortcomings: The program can be poorly organized, with canceled classes and last-minute trip changes. Hostelers have too much free time to loaf on the deck of the motel swimming pool. My reviewers were in classes of forty, uncomfortable in the motel communal room.

Getting In: The large classes enable the YWCA to fill all registration requests.

Getting There: See the travel information for the University of Arizona, Tucson.

CALIFORNIA

Carmel Valley Village—Hidden Valley Institute of the Arts

Courses of Study: Dance, a Lifelong Love; Steinbeck, His Home and Work; Chopin, the Music and the Man; A National Elderhostel Chorale; The Great Sounds of Gospel Music; Beethoven, the Music and the Man

Quality of Instructors: Unusually talented instructors include gifted musicians, dancers, and literary experts.

Environment: Carmel is situated south of the Monterey Peninsula and Pebble Beach, at the foot of rolling hills near the Pacific Coast. It has long been a center for artists and writers and has a whimsical style of architecture. Many tourists flood the area year-round. Settled by Spanish and Mexican colonials, the area now attracts the well-heeled, who build elegant mansions overlooking the surf. The Institute is located in a beautiful spot at the foothills of the Santa Lucia mountains. It offers promising young talent in music and dance an opportunity to study and perform in a supportive atmosphere.

Housing: The dormitory rooms are spartan and unscreened and the bunk beds "not very comfortable." Rooms are equipped for high school-age kids. The facility is a 20-room single-storied building designed for double occupancy.

Food: Meals are served buffet-style in a dining lounge. They are always adequate, with many fresh greens. Elderhostelers scrape and stack dishes for the kitchen crew.

Unique Attributes: The 300-seat theater and dance studio used for student seminars is very appropriate for the Elderhostel programs. The area teems with wonderful sightseeing opportunities: the Steinbeck country of Salinas County, the Monterey Bay Aquarium, the beautiful San Carlos de Borromeo Mission, the windswept shoreline, and Carmel's beach of clean white sand. One Elderhosteler exclaimed, " I saw sea otters saved from the Alaskan oil spill."

Shortcomings: All off-campus sightseeing arrangements must be made among the Elderhostelers themselves. Only one field trip is included in the program. "Quite a lot of time is left to oneself, good for some and bad for others!" "No television available, which may be good, may be bad!"

Getting In: There may be some waiting on lists, but this institution hosts many Elderhostels. Perhaps a date change will get you in.

Getting There: A car is obviously the best way to get to Carmel, but one can use Greyhound to Monterey, then local transport to the gate. Amtrak trains call at Salinas, and connecting flights to Monterey may be obtained in either San Francisco or Los Angeles.

Claremont—Pitzer College

Courses of Study: Gay and Lesbian Studies; Sexuality Through the Ages (In the past Pitzer has done other intensive studies with a single focus; Japan was the most recent of these Elderhostel courses.)

Quality of Instructors: All are outstanding regular faculty at Pitzer College. One of my much-traveled reviewers selects a list of "top ten" professors every year. Three Pitzer instructors made the list. "I've been to many Elderhostels, but you don't always have as talented a crew."

Environment: Claremont is located in Los Angeles County between Los Angeles and San Bernardino. Los Angeles and Hollywood are just 45 minutes away by car but light years away in feeling. Pitzer is a beautiful, small college campus, the least traditional of a group of five schools known as the Claremont Colleges. Even the buildings at Pitzer are unusual—modernistic octagons.

Housing: Dormitory rooms with a bath between each pair. There are washbasins in each room. The lodgings are very comfortable.

Food: Excellent food with a good variety; several entrées to choose from. Salad bar, fresh fruit, and ice cream are available every day.

Unique Attributes: This innovative course shatters biases and myths. Pitzer, in preparation for an undergraduate course in gay / lesbian studies, tested this curriculum on Elderhostelers. A troubling finding shows that homophobia is on the increase in this country. Twenty-two hostelers registered for this program in June 1990 and concluded the week with very positive feelings. The bold group—gays, lesbians, heterosexuals married and unmarried and married without spouses, and parents and relatives of homosexuals—was varied in its sexual orientation but shared views and experiences openly. The courses ranged from homosexuality in ancient Greece to child custody battles of lesbian mothers today.

The college representative is very supportive of the Elderhostel program and may repeat the course because of the sympathetic reaction of the attendees.

Shortcomings: None reported by an Elderhosteler on his fifty-first hostel program.

Going Solo: This one earns the highest rating because travel to and from the campus is easy, there are few, if any, safety problems on campus, single rooms are available if you wish, and "everyone is made to feel welcome."

Getting In: Not difficult now. May not be so in the future.

Getting There: Easy auto and air accessibility. Ontario airport is only minutes away.

Fresno — Wonder Valley Ranch / California State University at Fresno

Courses of Study; Japan, Enemy to Friend; Sierra Foothills; Vaudeville Revival; Middle East Politics

Quality of Instructors: A talented group of specialists conducts the courses. "Georgie Taps," an old-time vaudevillian tap dancer brings that era to life, and an Egyptian tackles the highly controversial subject of Middle Eastern politics.

Environment: The area is strictly rural with a small town nearby. Wonder Valley Ranch is a private children's camp in the summer, so it hosts its Elderhostelers in the winter. Wonder Valley is the sixth sunniest spot in the United States.

Fresno is the geographic center of the state and lies in the heart of its agricultural production. The State University with 17,000 students also operates a farm and an arboretum.

Housing: Elderhostelers stay in double rooms with private baths in rustic cottages. It's the luck of the draw whether one wins a new facility or lands in one of the older ones.

Food: The menu is varied and portions plentiful.

Unique Attributes: This hostel enjoys a great aura of camaraderie. "A daily 5:00 p.m. happy hour with a cash bar does much to foster the gemütlichkeit." The facilities are able to accommodate as many as 75 hostelers comfortably. An early morning hike, or aerobics class, is offered daily for early rising, energetic attendees. So many evening activities are planned that sometimes several activities may take place simultaneously. My reviewers chose this as their favorite site after several years of hosteling.

Shortcomings: Hilly terrain; can be unexpectedly cold in February.

Going Solo: My reviewers were all couples, but they believed this was a great destination for solo travelers. The singles they observed were "all fun-loving, extroverted types."

Getting In: This destination can accommodate an unusually large group.

Getting There: Fly to Fresno airport. The management will meet planes for a fee.

Idyllwild—Idyllwild School of Music and the Arts (ISOMATA)

Courses of Study: Enjoying Choral Music; The Secret of Exercise and Relaxation; Raku Pottery; Myth, Legend, and Fairy Tale in Russian Music; Earthquakes and Volcanoes; An Exploration of the Musical Stage; Contra Dancing

Quality of Instructors: Opinions varied regarding the instruction at ISOMATA. All of my panelists enjoyed the cordial atmosphere and enthusiasm of the teachers, but their teaching ability was somewhat less admired. "Virginia, the program director, is an interesting, charming woman, the greatest," wrote an Idyllwild booster.

Environment: Idyllwild is located in a beautiful pine forest on the crest of the San Jacinto mountains, 110 miles east of Los Angeles. There is a quaint little touristy village nearby; otherwise, the school is isolated. If you love the rich remoteness of the woods or were an avid summer camper as a child, the sights and sounds of Idyllwild may fill you with nostalgia. The school is a residential arts academy with classes in music, dance, drama, and the visual arts.

Housing: Elderhostelers sleep in modern log cabins, some with private and some with shared baths. The cottages are scattered in the woods a short walk from the cafeteria. The main lodge, used for all day and evening activities, is a brief climb uphill from the cafeteria. Some of the cabins have very pleasant communal rooms with wood-burning fireplaces, cozy spots for marshmallow roasting, or cocktail hour nibbling and socializing. There is also a brand-new dormitory with private baths, but only the first of its two floors is air-conditioned.

Food: The cafeteria is also reminiscent of summer camp. Plain, well-prepared food is served. "When the kitchen staff was short-handed, our Elderhostelers pitched in with the cooking and serving."

Unique Attributes: The folk-singing and dancing attract an informal, fun-loving crowd. Because the site is so self-contained, Elderhostelers must, for the most part, create their own evening entertainment. "Contra dancing, a cross between square and line dancing, was such a hit we added extra sessions every night."

The mile-high secluded location tends to mean the weather is unpredictable. "A late winter snowstorm blanketed the site with soft whiteness and buried the man-made paths and footprints," reported one couple. "It was breathtakingly beautiful."

Another couple found themselves at Idyllwild one February during six days of rain. Even though their ardor was dampened, would-be artists and photographers made pictures of raindrops. They enjoyed it so much, they returned the following year. Try to schedule your visit while students are in attendance, too. Some fortunate Elderhostelers were treated to piano performances, vocal concerts, and a dance recital.

Shortcomings: The road up the mountain from Palm Springs is hairy; there are few, if any, guardrails and many sharp switchbacks. It is not for the timid, especially in the winter. A less treacherous but longer alternate route is available up the mountain. If you are driving alone, make inquiries first. Bring your boots, earmuffs, and rain gear. The hills are steep between cafeteria, lodge, and cabins.

Going Solo: Though frequented by many couples who are veterans of three and four visits to Idyllwild, it is very suitable for active single travelers. The self-contained environment of the site and the congenial ambience of the cottages makes this a particularly appropriate destination. Only "getting there" might dissuade one from registering.

Getting In: No problems reported, though this program received enthusiastic hurrahs.

Getting There: No public transportation is available to this lovely secluded site.

Los Angeles—University of Judaism

Courses of Study: Ten Commandments; Poets in Search; Paths to Jewish Belief; Ethics of the Fathers; The Shabbat, What Is It About?; Broadway Bound

Quality of Instructors: Varying degrees of skill. Several brilliant rabbis, a museum curator, and other less competent instructors teach the Elderhostel program.

Environment: The university, which has a student body of just 201, has a metropolitan setting on a hillside on Mulholland Drive with a beautiful view of the San Fernando Valley. It sits in an exclusive westside residential neighborhood of Los Angeles, with access to all the city pleasures.

Housing: The dormitories are luxurious and air-conditioned. Most rooms have private baths. "The new twin-bedded dormitories are the best Elderhostel accommodations I've experienced," wrote one veteran.

Food: I was unable to obtain a consensus regarding the food served. Some comments were: "The dining atmosphere and food are tops." "The well-stocked salad bar is great for dieters!" "Among the best of all my years of Elderhosteling." However, an experienced couple who had attended fourteen Elderhostels said, "The need to serve kosher food strains the budget of the kitchen managers and therefore the menu is limited."

Unique Attributes: The University of Judaism provides a superb cultural and religious experience with thought-provoking programs. The school is a scholarly oasis in the middle of a city of fancy cars, movie stars, and mansions. Elderhostelers can enjoy the special treats of Los Angeles: Chinatown, sushi bars in Little Tokyo, Universal Studios, and the fantasy of Disneyland. The Elderhostel staff is very warm and helpful.

Shortcomings: Los Angeles has terrible smog. One has to risk life and limb on the crowded freeways to go anywhere. Both the brown haze and the traffic can be an unnerving experience for out-of-towners. But there are long waiting lists. One veteran felt "the atmosphere in this program is not conducive to getting to know other Elderhostelers." This was echoed by another couple who agreed that the administration is greedy. While revisiting the site for a fourth time, they found a disappointing diminution of services. "Two hundred enrollees at one time strain the facilities, and mechanical equipment breaks down. We felt like sardines," they said.

Going Solo: As noted under "Shortcomings," the large number of enrollees diminishes group cohesiveness. However, if you are very outgoing, this site might work well with a requested roommate. But I cannot categorically recommend that procedure since I've heard reports of some very unhappy pairings.

Getting In: These are very popular programs given in a favorite destination, so the classes fill up fast. "Always oversubscribed," wrote one Elderhosteler. "We had to wait two years before getting accepted on the third try." "We were sixty-fifth on the waiting list but kept trying," wrote another would-be student. The University of Judaism is frequently filled by lottery (described in the introduction) even though it now has the capacity to house 200 Elderhostelers at one time.

Getting There: Los Angeles is a city easily reached by all forms of public transportation. The train to the West Coast is a superliner with a glass-enclosed double-decker observation car. Call 1-800-USA-RAIL for reservations, and remember to ask for your senior citizen discount.

Marin County—Green Gulch Farm

Courses of Study: Zen

Quality of Instructors: Excellent, all members of the Zen community.

Environment: Green Gulch Farm is located in Marin County, just north of San Francisco. This is an ongoing commune, located in a secluded valley within a mile of the Pacific Ocean and light-years from the cosmopolitan diversity of San Francisco. Persons living there practice Zen, grow much of their own food, and share the daily chores of living.

Housing: A new Japanese-type building in which each two bedrooms share a bath. The Guest House also boasts a wood-burning stove.

Food: Excellent vegetarian cooking. Kitchen facilities and snacks are available day and night in each housing unit.

Unique Attributes: Elderhostelers live, work, and study a 2,500-year-old art in a Zen community. Meditation practice several times a day is followed by lectures on the life of Buddha and informal discussions on "The Community and Its People." The elaborate tea ceremony is demonstrated.

One Elderhostel week coincided with a silent week, during which community members eat in silence. Elderhostelers were given the option to eat with the community or "eat and talk." All chose to eat in silence.

Because of the intimate living conditions and the small size of the class, the Elderhostel group has nightly discussions around the wood stove. They discuss religion in general and Zen in particular—a most congenial and provocative Elderhostel experience. Working in the garden, kitchen, temple, or workshop is encouraged but not mandatory for Elderhostelers. "My breathing-meditation-stretching practices (learned at my EH Zen experience), when followed faithfully, help me to attain a small sense of well-being and inner peace."

Shortcomings: Definitely none reported.

Going Solo: All people are very welcome at Green Gulch, with or without a partner. The only drawback would be the difficulty of traveling to the site.

Getting In: Easy.

Getting There: Fly to San Francisco and use public transportation that is available at the airport. It is a fairly easy drive to Green Gulch Farm. If you can combine this hostel with a sightseeing visit to San Francisco, all subway and surface transportation systems in the city offer attractive senior citizen fares, even the cable cars. San Francisco is one of the stops on Amtrak's glass-domed "Superchief."

Quincy—Feather River College

Courses of Study: High Sierra Astronomy; Basque Sheepherders of the Sierra Nevada; Geography of the Feather River Watershed; Tall Timber Country; 49'er Gold Rush; Square Dancing; Natural History Photography

Quality of Instructors: A caring group of naturalists and specialists lead the field trips and make the classroom presentations.

Environment: The location in the High Sierras is spectacular. The area has a rich heritage of gold mining and timbering. The nearest town is Quincy, a village of just 6,000 people. This program is designed for Elderhostelers seeking an escape into the hushed beauty of the mountains, where the summits are swathed in clouds. But the site is just 90 minutes from Lake Tahoe.

Housing: Elderhostelers are housed in private apartments.

Food: A nice variety of nutritious meals are served.

Unique Attributes: If you're interested in searching for feathered friends and identifying wildflowers, this is the place for you. One hosteler wrote, "One hundred sixty-two species of birds should intrigue any bird fancier." Hostelers receive lots of tender loving care and go on many bus trips. Feather River is a wildlife paradise. This hostel provides physical, rather than mental, stimulation. The college has tennis courts and jogging trails for athletically minded attendees.

Shortcomings: There isn't any public transportation to Quincy, so plan on getting there by private car.

Getting In: No problems reported.

Getting There: Feather River can only be reached by car, as noted above.

Redlands—De Benneville Pines

Courses of Study: Super Sensuality; Mythology: Campbell and Jungian Psychology; Native American Religions; Buddhism for the Non-Buddhist; Art of the Renaissance and Beyond; Writing, Basic Dynamic Devices

Quality of Instructors: Usually excellent; one interviewee said, "Two out of three were very good, while the third, a last-minute substitute, was not qualified."

Environment: This Unitarian Universalist church retreat center, snuggled in the pines of the San Bernardino National Forest, at 6,800 feet elevation, is just 25 miles from Redlands. The mountainous site has bears and barking dogs that entertain the hostelers at night. It is "a real mountain retreat, grade A. Secluded in the woods and beautiful." Lovely footpaths wind between the cabins and classrooms.

Housing: Hostelers share rustic, heated cabins with shared bathrooms. Bring your sleeping bag for use on the double-deck bunk beds. Quarters are somewhat cramped, "just a grade D."

Food: Family-style meals are served in a spacious lodge that has a lovely sun deck. A three-time alumnus of De Benneville Pines said, "The excellent food is one of the features of this popular spot." "A highly praised vegetarian menu."

Unique Attributes: Wonderful trails for hiking in the mountains. A jacuzzi, a swimming pool, and a nearby lake add to after-class enjoyment. The beautiful location and the friendly atmosphere are this program's greatest assets. This conference center has developed a loyal following who "just love the place."

Shortcomings: Very rocky footpaths and rustic cabins make this an Elderhostel best attended by sure-footed, nonluxury seekers. "Participants should be in good health and vigorous."

Going Solo: Rated a 3.5 and a 4 by two single travelers, because of De Benneville's informal, friendly ambience and caring staff. It lost points because it is frequented by couples who make this an annual excursion.

Getting In: No problem, probably because of the site's relative inaccessibility.

Getting There: One can fly to the Ontario airport and rent a car for the hour drive. The De Benneville staff will meet planes at Ontario for an additional charge. The highway from Redlands is excellent.

Riverside—Loma Linda University

Courses of Study: Vegetarian Cooking; Infant Heart Transplants; The Christian Centuries: Art, Architecture, Philosophy, and Literature; Journey Through Musical America; Film Criticism and Appreciation: Fun Facts and Fitness

Quality of Instructors: Very good, good-natured, and devoted.

Environment: Riverside is the navel orange capital of the United States. In 1873, a resident obtained cuttings of a new type of orange, a mutation developed in Brazil. These cuttings were the beginning of huge navel orange groves. Riverside is in southern California, an hour from Los Angeles and its beaches and mountains. Loma Linda is a small, Seventh Day Adventist university with strong emphasis on medical and health-related programs.

Housing: The air-conditioned college dormitories have shared-bath suites.

Food: Vegetarian, Seventh Day Adventist lacto-ovo style. No complaints. An excellent, wide variety of choices are offered.

Unique Attributes: The classes at Loma Linda are particularly interesting. Loma Linda Hospital is used when appropriate, and a visit to the marina at San Pedro is included.

Shortcomings: A serious amount of walking is required over hilly terrain to the dining hall and to classes. Remember, no alcohol or smoking permitted on this campus.

Getting In: Easy.

Getting There: Riverside is near San Bernardino if one is arriving by bus, train, or plane. There is public bus service to the college.

San Clemente — San Clemente American Youth Hostel

Courses of Study: Ocean Life; Southern California History; Are We Alone in the Universe; Pen and Brush, Sketchbook to Watercolor; Coastal Wetlands, Birds and Marine Life

Quality of Instructors: Energetic, enthusiastic young people with affection for the land, the oceans, and all the wildlife found therein. "Expert outdoor educators."

Environment: This Elderhostel program is held in an international youth hostel with a very informal atmosphere. Lots of backpacking youngsters coming and going make this environment lively and interesting for Elderhostelers eager to swap stories with the young hostelers. San Clemente is a charming southern California town that lies halfway between Los Angeles and San Diego on the Pacific coast.

Housing: Separate men's and women's dormitories with bunk beds and communal baths. Dormitories hold twenty plus persons. "Not for light sleepers."

Food: Judged to be satisfactory to excellent. Elderhostelers help with the clean-up.

Unique Attributes: With a car, one can visit either San Diego or Los Angeles, both of which have innumerable attractions. The San Clemente library, beach, and fishing pier are within walking distance of the youth hostel. All of the young staff are very agreeable and helpful.

This program is not designed for Elderhostelers searching for fancy furnishings and slick service, but serious birders and whale watchers should find plenty of memorable experiences. Don't forget to bring your binoculars!

Shortcomings: "The sleeping quarters are noisy, KP is not too much fun, and Elderhostelers are bused to their class locations."

Getting In: No difficulty.

Getting There: The preferred method of enjoying the California coast is by private automobile, but both San Diego and Los Angeles are easily accessible by all forms of public transportation.

San Diego—Grossmont/Cuyamaca Community College

Courses of Study: Gold, Grapes, and Robes—All in San Diego

Quality of Instructors: Fair.

Environment: The city of San Diego, spread between forested hills and the Pacific Ocean, remains one of the most appealing of American travel destinations. Their zoo has 3,400 animals and exotic plants exhibited in a spectacular natural setting of ravines and canyons, the aquarium is famous, and Sea World features killer whales, performing dolphins, and sea lions. The city's lovely beach area and marina are renowned, and the harbor includes many shore installations of the U.S. Navy. The college is located in El Cajon, San Diego's next door neighbor.

Housing: Elderhostelers stay in a very good motel with private baths, a ten-minute bus ride from the college.

Food: "Food runs the gamut from barely edible to a gastronomic disaster."

Unique Attributes: San Diego is situated just across the border from the booming Mexican town of Tijuana and offers an unusual opportunity for Elderhostelers to learn about the problems of maintaining social, economic, and political harmony between our two countries. The specific problems of undocumented workers slipping through the "Tortilla Curtain" and the evils of drug traffickers are better understood after program field trips. Expeditions to a San Diego winery, a mission, and a museum are included in the course. The climate of San Diego is balmy year-round.

Shortcomings: The Elderhostel is not in San Diego as advertised. Attendees without cars have to rely on public transportation to enjoy all of San Diego's attractions. "Connection with the college is invisible."

Getting In: No problems reported, although San Diego is a very popular tourist destination.

Getting There: San Diego can be reached by bus, airplane, or Amtrak, but an automobile is essential during your stay because of the remote location of the campus. If you rent an automobile, don't forget to ask for your senior citizen perks.

Santa Barbara—
Mount Saint Mary's University

Courses of Study: Personality Principles of Balance and Wholeness; History of the California Missions; The American Indian Experience; Spring Wildflowers of Santa Barbara; The Self-Healing Power of Happiness; The Enneagram

Quality of Instructors: The sisters and priests of St. Joseph of Carondolet conduct very fine classes. "Always excellent," wrote a three-time participant in Mount St. Mary's program.

Environment: The Elderhostel program is held at the Franciscan Renewal Center adjacent to the Old Mission of Santa Barbara. The center is located just 3 miles from the Pacific Ocean. Santa

Barbara is spread along the Pacific Coast in an area known as the California Riviera. The town is beautiful and the gardens renowned. It is situated 100 miles northwest of Los Angeles on one of the most scenic oceanfront drives in the United States. Pacific Coast Highway skirts along the shore, overlooking sheer cliffs and rock formations. Despite the large University of California campus there, Santa Barbara does not have a particularly intellectual atmosphere. Suntanned students in shorts loll on the beach and toss Frisbees in the air while luxurious yachts sparkle in the yacht basin.

Housing: Elderhostelers are given nice simple rooms with central showers and communal baths down the hall. Singles are available upon request.

Food: Good, plain, unpretentious fare is served.

Unique Attributes: The Mission of Santa Barbara, sometimes called the "Queen of the Missions," is famous for its twin towers. The brown-frocked brothers conduct tours of the facility. Santa Barbara is a favorite southern California resort town with miles of beaches on its south-facing shore. The town sits between the cobalt Pacific Ocean and a range of pale purple mountains. It has preserved its Spanish heritage with distinctively Mediterranean architecture: red tile roofs cover white stucco storefronts, and costly mansions are secluded in the mountains, with just their red rooftops peeking through the trees. One reviewer wrote, "A car is not necessary to enjoy this program. Public transportation is readily available to many local scenic and historic sights." Some hostelers report that living on the mission grounds is unique and delightful.

Shortcomings: None reported.

Going Solo: All participants receive a warm, cordial welcome. The sensitivity of the sisters and priests and spiritual atmosphere of the mission give this program a 5-out-of-5 rating.

Getting In: Despite Santa Barbara's proximity to Los Angeles, the program does not seem to be heavily oversubscribed. Waiting lists, yes, but no disappointments reported.

Getting There: Santa Barbara can be reached by all forms of public transportation, although a private car is recommended if one wishes to enjoy the scenic splendors of the oceanfront drive. The very busy international airport has frequent service from all parts of the country.

Santa Cruz—Bosch Baha'i School

Courses of Study: World Peace; World Religions; Issues of the '90s; Values; Redwoods in the Springtime; Environmental Issues; Freeways

Quality of Instructors: Instructors are carefully selected from throughout the country. They are outstanding, as a rule, and occasionally just good.

Environment: Santa Cruz is a seaside year-round resort on the coast south of San Francisco. The county has 29 miles of beaches, innumerable restaurants, and a busy beach boardwalk. The school, however, has a secluded, retreat-style setting among the oaks and towering redwoods of the Coast Range just 15 miles north of Santa Cruz.

Housing: Offered in rustic, heated cabins that accommodate singles, doubles, or triples. Each has its own bath.

Food: Excellent food is tastefully prepared and served family-style in a dining hall nestled in the woods.

Unique Attributes: The school staff and program manager offer a very warm welcome. Marty Knowlton, the founder of the Elderhostel movement, lived here for several months—serving coffee and doing clean-up work. The retreat includes a new meeting hall and an unheated, outdoor swimming pool. Dining facilities and classrooms are a short walk from the cabins. One of my reviewers has been to Bosch Baha'i six times in three years! "Because of the meaty courses," he said. This is not a sightseeing Elderhostel. Class-related discussions and programs fill the evenings.

Shortcomings: Without a car, one is confined to the campus.

Going Solo: This destination would be judged perfect except for the difficulty of access. Once there, however, all attendees are made welcome and encouraged to participate.

Getting In: There seem to be sufficient cabins to meet the demand.

Getting There: One can get to the site by public transportation, but "it takes a while." This is a really remote site so the drive can be a challenge despite good, clear directions that are mailed in the preattendance packet.

Santa Cruz—Mount Madonna Center

Courses of Study: Yoga and the Community

Quality of Instructors: Outstanding to good. All are members of the Yoga community.

Environment: A secluded community of 100 practicing Yogas of all ages, the retreat and conference center of 335 mountaintop acres is surrounded by a redwood forest and overlooks Monterey Bay. There is a lovely small lake for swimming and hiking and jogging trails. Santa Cruz is a resort that lies on the craggy coast south of San Francisco. It boasts 29 miles of public beach and is well known as an arts and crafts center and as the home of an annual fly fishing invitational.

Housing: Elderhostelers stay in a dormlike structure with shared baths. A choice of single or double rooms is offered.

Food: Outstanding vegetarian food is served, much of it raised in the center's own gardens. "Great home-baked bread!"

Unique Attributes: Elderhostelers each have a personal meeting with the Yoga guru. This is indeed a unique way of learning Yoga practices—breathing, exercise, and meditation—and Yoga psychology. One may become as much a part of the community as desired. My reviewers were eager that this program be included in the book; this was not their first visit to Mount Madonna. This program "helps one to understand the mysteries of life and the universe." This program is designed for hostelers seeking subjects of more than routine interest, willing to do some serious soul-searching.

Shortcomings: One is confined to the campus without a car. This is definitely not a "sightseeing" Elderhostel. Alcohol is not allowed on the site. These are not necessarily drawbacks.

Going Solo: The small classes create a sense of intimacy, and singles are made to feel a part of the community as well as a part of the Elderhostel class. The only problem is the remoteness of the site.

Getting In: Easy. This is a highly specialized program, not for everyone.

Getting There: Accessible by automobile only. One can, however, fly to San Francisco and rent a car.

Santa Paula—Tokyo International College

Courses of Study: Discover Your Town; Gems and Minerals; Insider / Outsider, the Japanese; Traveler's Japanese; Traditional Japanese Arts and Crafts; Japan Today; Look at American Theater

Quality of Instructors: "Good, thought-provoking." Classes are taught by professors of Asian-American studies, local individuals drawn from the academic resources of the community, and Japanese artisans.

Environment: Santa Paula, "the Citrus Capital of the World," lies close to Ventura, a little north of Los Angeles. Ventura is a busy modern city that once was a small Spanish mission. Santa Paula is a quiet, slow-paced little town with an atmosphere reminiscent of days gone by. A former stagecoach stop, it looks as though time has stood still.

This program, sponsored by the City Parks and Recreation Department, strives to create a "folk school" learning environment.

Housing: Elderhostelers live in a turn-of-the-century, restored three-story hotel that does not have an elevator. All rooms are double occupancy with private baths. "It looks European," my reviewer wrote.

Food: Meals are served in the dining room of the hotel. Very satisfying food is nicely served.

Unique Attributes: Ventura offers all the seaside activities of sailboating, ocean swimming, cruising, fishing, and just plain beachcombing.

Classes, lodging, and meals are all offered in the Glen Tavern Inn, in a situation somewhat unique among Elderhostels. My reviewers thought it important to learn more about the philosophy, attitudes, language, and mores of our newest economic competitors. "Learn about Japan from the Japanese," they said.

Shortcomings: None.

Getting In: No problem. Not yet a popular program.

Getting There: All forms of public transportation are available—bus, train, and plane.

Saratoga—Institute for Jewish Studies

Courses of Study: The Role of the Priest in the Bible; Religion and Politics in the Second Temple Period; Jewish Mysticism

Quality of Instructors: Professors from the University of California, Berkeley, and Stanford University. "Scholars of very high quality."

Environment: This Elderhostel is hosted at Camp Swig, a youth camp sponsored by the Union of American Hebrew Congregations. The camp is located 4 miles out of Saratoga on Highway 9, one hour south of San Francisco. The region is lovely and hilly, the camp is set high among the redwoods, and the campus sports a fig tree with ripe figs. The facilities include a swimming pool, many small cabins, tennis courts, a campfire circle for cookouts and bonfires, and a nice community building for classes and eating. "The setting is dynamite. . .cool nights and warm days," said one enrollee.

Housing: In individual cabins with two cots and a chest of drawers in each room. Each pair of rooms shares a bathroom.

Food: Familiar food is served family-style. Quality is excellent and quantities are ample, though kosher food rules are observed.

Unique Attributes: The director, Yoram Kolerstein, rents Camp Swig for these Elderhostels under the auspices of the Institute. The atmosphere and general camaraderie is joyous and friendly, the number of participants at capacity, and the instruction unparalleled. "For any hostelers interested in the history of the Old Testament, I would recommend it unconditionally to Jews and non-Jews alike. Of the 48 hostelers there with us, there were only three who were not Jewish." "If the earthy smell of the forest turns you on, and you are not put off by moldy shower curtains, this one's for you." Coming or going, one can browse the artsy-craftsy boutiques of Santa Cruz or San Jose.

Shortcomings: Grounds need some manicuring, and cabin interiors need some housekeeping. "Because of the complaints, I believe the problems will be remedied before the next Elderhostel."

Going Solo: Very suitable because of the self-contained camp setting and general camaraderie. "One-fourth of our group were singles, and they were given single rooms as requested. They enjoyed everything, no 'shy persons' among them."

Getting In: My reviewers applied early but were wait-listed for several weeks.

Getting There: The precourse packet of instructions is very helpful, and the director is most accommodating. Amtrak has a station in San Jose if you wish to enjoy the spectacular coast of California, or Yosemite and the High Sierras, in armchair comfort.

Squaw Valley—Olympic School Academy

Courses of Study: Flora and Fauna; Lake Tahoe History; Watercolor; Geology of the Lake Tahoe Basin; Photographing Family and Friends

Quality of Instructors: "Excellent." Many instructors are naturalists concerned with maintaining the delicate balance of the ecosystem.

Looking down Squaw Valley to hiking trails and ski lifts (Photo: Mary Helfrich)

Emerald Bay, Lake Tahoe (Photo: Mary Helfrich)

Environment: "Glorious!" Mr. Packard of Hewlett Packard is trying to save this gorgeous 6,200-foot mountain setting from development. Squaw Valley is just 4 miles from Lake Tahoe, on the Nevada border; it was the site of the 1960 Olympics. In the winter, Squaw Valley is a famous ski center.

Housing: Pretty special. The buildings, built in 1985, include two- and three-person rooms, each with a private bath. But there are bunk beds, and one may have to sleep in an upper berth when the classes are crowded.

Food: Unusually good. "They even serve 'egg beaters' at breakfast for individuals on low cholesterol diets."

Unique Attributes: The school's proximity to Lake Tahoe is a plus. Tahoe is one of the most magnificent mountain lakes in the world. It is surrounded by ponderosa and cottonwood forests and boasts splendid wildflowers. During the summer Shakespearean plays are offered by the water's edge. The programs make excellent use of their location; field trips include a boat ride on Lake Tahoe and a trip to the ski center (and a ride on a ski lift), old mansions, and the Donner Museum.

Shortcomings: This can be thunderstorm country in the summertime. Because of the high altitude, it gets very cold at night and in the early morning.

Going Solo: This site attracts many single attendees, sometimes as many as 50 percent of the group. There's lots of bridge playing at night and other internal entertainment. One reviewer described a high-spirited amateur performance of Shakespeare.

Getting In: No problems.

Getting There: The school is only 15 miles from the Reno Airport, but one must arrange his or her own transportation from airport to school. If you'd like to try the comfortable convenience of Amtrak, there is a station in Reno.

Yosemite National Park—Yosemite Institute

Courses of Study: Yosemite's Beauty in Late Summer; Explore the Beauty of Yosemite: An Intergenerational Experience; Yosemite's Majesty in Winter

Quality of Instructors: An expert group of naturalists sensitize Elderhostelers to the pleasures of enjoying without destroying.

Environment: The 1,200 square miles of breathtaking beauty that comprise Yosemite National Park are situated 200 miles east of San Francisco. "Beautiful! Can't be beat!" said one attendee. Go in the spring to enjoy the torrential, crystal-clear waterfalls, the grandiose mountains with mammoth peaks and pinnacles, or El Capitan, the largest single block of granite on earth. Yosemite, our first national preserve, was consciously designed 100 years ago to protect our wilderness. It is a complete mountain paradise.

Housing: In June, the accomodations are somewhat rugged—they are wooden, canvas-framed, unheated cabins (twin-bedded, no singles) with rest rooms and shower houses nearby. But one can reserve rooms with private baths at the lodge for a small extra charge. In July and August, Elderhostelers stay 16 miles away in rough bunkhouses with mattresses supplied but no linens. In September, however, Elderhostelers are housed in wooden, heated cabins. These also have rest rooms and showers nearby. Elderhostelers help clean their sleeping quarters, kitchen, and bathhouse.

Food: Excellent food is served in the Yosemite Lodge cafeteria, breakfast and dinner only. Lunch is eaten in the field.

Unique Attributes: Elderhostelers go on all-day hikes where they learn to tread gently, observe carefully, and listen intently. Some of the highlights of the program are visits to the Mariposa Grove of giant sequoias, dinner at the elegant, 63-year-old Awahnee Hotel (extra cost), and viewing the soaring domes of granite and listening to the thunderous sound of the waterfalls. Photo opportunities are provided along the way. Evening programs address environmental topics and the management of our national parks.

Yosemite Institute, Yosemite, California (Photo: Mary Helfrich)

Shortcomings: This program is designed for the outdoor hosteler, and participants must be in good physical condition. The hikes range from easy to moderate. Rain and snow arrive late in October, but the weather in the park can be very capricious. It can get pretty muddy near the cabins, so protective footwear is recommended, particularly if you hike 5 miles a day over a wet, snowy, winter trail. One reviewer wrote, "Tent city is noisy at night, but hopefully, after hiking all day, you will sleep anyway."

Getting In: No problem reported.

Getting There: Take the dramatic automobile drive over one of the four roads that lead into the park, located about a four-hour drive east of San Francisco. It is possible to get a public bus to Yosemite in Merced, California.

COLORADO

Colorado Springs—La Foret

Courses of Study: A Healthy Earth; Tricultural Art of the Southwest; Creative Outdoor Photography; Ecology of the Rocky Mountain Front Range; Colorado Facts and Fiction; Colorado Gold

Quality of Instructors: A team of caring ecologists and specialists "do a great job."

Environment: La Foret, a lovely facility in the Black Forest of Colorado, was built in the 1920s. It is a serene rustic campsite surrounded by towering blue spruce. All of the buildings afford a spectacular view of the reddish granite of Pike's Peak, Colorado's most famous year-round snow-topped mountain. The peak towers 14,110 feet above sea level, but the Ponderosa Lodge and

Photographing wildflowers, La Foret, Colorado (Photo: Bill Behrends)

other buildings at La Foret are at an altitude of 7,500 feet. The air in the mountains is dry, crisp, and invigorating.

Housing: Elderhostelers are housed in comfortable four-bedroom, two-bath, one-story cabins. The cabins have central rooms with fireplaces and are heated.

Food: Good, stick-to-the-ribs meals are served in the modern dining lodge.

Unique Attributes: Delightful side trips are arranged to the Garden of the Gods and the Air Force Academy. The Garden of the Gods is a fantastic wilderness park of strangely shaped red rocks amid gnarled junipers. La Foret attracts hostelers who enjoy searching for the delicate beauty of columbines and larkspur and identifying the sounds of obscure bird species. Expect to have many evening discussions about preserving our natural environment and halting man's careless exploitation.

Shortcomings: La Foret is best reached by private car.

Getting In: No problems reported.

Getting There: The drive from Denver to Colorado Springs enables one to taste and see the best of Colorado's mountain summits. The Trailways bus stops in Colorado Springs, and Peterson Field accommodates regularly scheduled airlines.

Durango—Sonlight Christian Camp

Courses of Study: Colorado Rocky Mountain Ecology; Colors Come Alive in Stained Glass; Navajo Weaving; Trout from Hatchery to Frying Pan; Geology of Colorado's 14,000-Foot Peaks; Narrow Gauge Railroads of Southwest Colorado

Quality of Instructors: One reviewer reported two out of three instructors were outstanding.

Environment: The camp is located a short distance from the nearest town in the San Juan mountains 60 miles east of Durango. Durango is a natural gateway to one of the most scenic sections of Colorado, an area that includes prehistoric ruins. The San Juan mountains have jagged white-topped peaks and almost vertical cliffsides. The town was originally settled by Spanish prospectors, then became a mining and smelting center. It is now a mecca for summer tourists and winter skiers.

Housing: Elderhostelers sleep in modern log facilities that have open, multi-bed, carpeted dormitories. The accommodations are upstairs. There are communal toilets and showers. Men and women are housed separately.

Food: Nice home-cooked meals are served, and there's a weekly cookout.

Unique Attributes: The informal atmosphere at this hostel is very congenial. Interesting side trips are arranged and evening activities planned. Temperatures in and around Durango have been known to plummet from comfortable days in the seventies to near-freezing at night. Remember to bring proper attire. "Hikers in our group claim to have spotted deer on the trail and golden eagles overhead." Some special Colorado wildflowers are the Indian paintbrush, red and blue columbines, and wild geraniums. Evenings are spent debating the beautiful versus the useful.

Shortcomings: To make the most of the experience, one needs a private car and a driver with time to spare. With a car one can visit Indian reservations to the south and Mesa Verde National Park, with its ancient cliff dwellings, 36 miles to the west. Visits to the cliff dwellings require a strenuous climb; the very high elevations (up to 8,500 feet) may adversely affect some persons.

Going Solo: The family-style meals and separate male and female sleeping quarters make this destination particularly attractive for single travelers. The atmosphere is congenial and communal.

Getting In: No problem reported.

Getting There: Durango can best be reached by private car, but it does have a small airport serviced by America West and several other commuter airlines. The Trailways bus company also serves Durango.

Old Keystone Village—
Keystone Science School

Courses of Study: Cross-Country Skiing; Survival in Winter; Aspens in Autumn; Stalking the Wild Mushroom; Alpine Ecology; Rocky Mountain Bird Ecology

Quality of Instructors: Excellent natural science and skiing instructors minister to the needs of the Elderhostelers.

Environment: Keystone Village is situated in a picturesque mountain valley at an elevation of 9,200 feet. The historic old village, 75 miles west of Denver, is an 1880s mining town in the Arapaho National Forest. Keystone Resort is one of Colorado's leading ski areas with a gondola, nine chair lifts, night skiing, and apres-ski amenities. The U.S. Ski Team trains on the north peak of Keystone Mountain. Among Colorado's high summits the air is dry and invigorating.

Housing: The sleeping accommodations are newly built log dormitories that accommodate two persons per room with a shared bathroom. Staff provide wood heat when required.

Food: Very good, satisfying meals are served in the dining / meeting hall. Participants must assist in clean-up.

Unique Attributes: Excellent lessons are provided, with splendid opportunities for cross-country skiing and snowshoeing. Participants build a survival snow house. Cross-country skiing is very strenuous, but the technique is easy to master. In the Rockies, cross-country skiing is particularly rugged because of the terrain and the altitude.

Sharing ski lessons and close sleeping quarters can force sudden friendliness on a group of strangers. This program is for Elderhostelers who are in excellent physical condition and willing to accept rough and rugged, not-so-posh accommodations. This one is for the "top of the mountain" (not the "over the hill") crowd. The field course on birding includes daily walks, banding, identifying, and recording data. The Alpine Ecology course includes a one-day climb above 12,000 feet.

Shortcomings: The newly constructed housing facilities removed the only shortcoming of this destination. Bring your binoculars in the summer, and remember that cold weather can be stressful.

Getting In: No problems reported.

Getting There: Keystone is best approached by private automobile, but public transportation by bus, train, and chauffered van from Denver's Stapleton Airport is also possible.

CONNECTICUT

Ivorytown — Episcopal Conference Center

Courses of Study: Conquering the Art Museum — Paintings in Context with Their Times; The Outdoor Classroom; Personality

Types and the Creative Management of Change; American Interiors and Furniture; New Frontiers of the Mind; Divine Reality: Learning to See Life in a Spiritual Context

Quality of Instructors: Excellent teachers with superior skills present the material to an attentive audience.

Environment: "Beautiful. Six hundred fifty acres of gorgeous woodland on a mile-long lake, yet only 75 miles from New York City." Connecticut, the next smallest of the New England states, is home to some of the country's most prestigious schools. Its small towns have charming village greens and white steepled churches dating from the early 1800s. The northward march of spring in New England starts in Connecticut when crocus and daffodils peek through those persistent mounds of snow.

Housing: "Fine. Rustic bungalows with good beds. Immaculately kept."

Food: "Delicious—not gourmet but tasty, with generous portions." Meals are served family-style in a central dining hall.

Unique Attributes: Ivorytown is located midway between New Haven and New London. The presence of Yale University makes New Haven an educational and cultural center, whereas New London is a center for submarine and military maritime installations. New Haven boasts the Yale Art Gallery, a fine Museum of Natural History, and a symphony orchestra.

Episcopal Conference Center caters to many groups in addition to hosting seven months of Elderhostels. The management is efficient and experienced with church retreats, school groups, seniors, and young people. Their director is "an amazing man with an infectious spirit." The intensive art program includes well-planned field trips to nearby museums in comfortable, large vans.

Shortcomings: "All the buildings are sprayed with a deodorant disinfectant that is too strong and most unpleasant."

Going Solo: This is a great destination if the number of couples does not exceed the number of singles by too large a margin. All the elements are present which strengthen a program's suitability for singles—single rooms, cozy fireplace-equipped lounges, experienced on-site management, and a site easily accessed by public transportation.

Getting In: This one is a snap in the late fall after all the leaf-lovers have been and gone.

Getting There: It's a pleasant automobile drive from New York City, Boston, or suburban New Jersey areas. The Connecticut coast can be reached by land, sea, or air. Amtrak and commuter trains both stop in New Haven, and the director will meet trains with the van.

New London—Connecticut College

Courses of Study: Psychological Portraits of American Presidents; Dante's Inferno; Country Dances of New England; Keeping the World Safe in the Next Century; The Joy of Listening to Choral Music

Quality of Instructors: An excellent faculty offers an intellectual adventure.

Environment: Connecticut College, located in the city outskirts on a very pretty campus overlooking the eastern entrance of Long Island Sound, is at the mouth of the Thames River. The college is a small, intimate school with only 1,600 students. The setting is charming and relaxed, with rolling hills and sweeping lawns and Gothic stone buildings. New London, an old whaling town, is just a short hop away from Rhode Island, which makes it an ideal starting place for an automobile tour of New England.

Housing: Elderhostelers are housed in adequate single dormitory rooms.

Food: Although there is no choice of main course, the meals are rated as good to okay. The kitchen staff are particularly helpful in adjusting the menu to the needs of special diets.

Unique Attributes: Connecticut's program is well managed by the director. She schedules a few enjoyable extracurricular activities such as a concert in the campus chapel, a boat ride on the Thames, and square dancing. The college has a superior swimming pool with open swim periods convenient for the hostelers. With an automobile, one can visit an aquarium, an arboretum, and an art museum as well as stroll the decks of restored tall ships and great whaling ships at the Mystic Seaport Museum. New London is also the home of the U.S. Coast Guard Academy and houses a United States submarine base.

Shortcomings: The only complaint I received was from a hypercritical couple who requested ice machines on every floor of the dormitory. A nice touch, but hardly a necessary amenity in college dormitories!

Getting In: The Connecticut College program is very popular because of New London's location on the coast midway between our eastern metropolises of Boston and New York. Early registration is absolutely necessary.

Getting There: New London can be reached by all forms of public transportation as well as by private automobile on the network of superhighways. The New York-to-Boston Amtrak stops there, and Trumbull Airport in Groton serves Groton-New London. The nautically inclined may arrive by boat.

West Hartford—St. Joseph's College

Courses of Study: Aran Isles Forever; One World of Many Religions; Emergence of the Female Detective Writer; American Popular Song; Our Mysterious Mathematical World

Quality of Instructors: All of the college professors received an excellent rating.

Environment: St. Joseph's College has a quiet, green, landscaped campus with lots of trees and a lovely relaxed atmosphere. West Hartford, a prosperous, well-kept suburb of the city of Hartford, combines the pleasures of urban and suburban living.

Housing: The accommodations are typical college dorms with communal bathrooms down the hall, but St. Joseph's dorms are "white glove" clean. Single rooms are available if desired.

Food: The meals are very good. A sincere effort is made to please the guests and to serve a healthful array of foods.

Unique Attributes: The geographic location of West Hartford seems to be St. Joseph's primary draw. Some of my reviewers wrote about sightseeing through Connecticut on the way to school, then continuing to other Elderhostels in New England. Other panelists described trips to Tanglewood, the summer home of the Boston Symphony Orchestra and the Jacob's Pillow dance festival. Unlike many Elderhostel institutions, St. Joseph's permits registration for two consecutive weeks, an ideal arrangement if one wishes to tour the Berkshires during the midsession weekend. Drive north on Route 91 to explore the Connecticut River Valley or head west to the Lee / Lenox area for wonderful music and summer theater. The Mark Twain House in Hartford is a popular tourist attraction, and West Hartford is replete with top-quality shopping.

Shortcomings: In the official Elderhostel catalog, St. Joseph's brags about its rave reviews. I did receive positive feedback as noted above, but I also heard that the lack of air-conditioning in the dormitories can be a serious nuisance in July. Also, the air-conditioners in the classrooms only work erratically, and the evening-scheduled programs rated only a fair. "Tell the folks they'd better bring their own fans!" one of my contributors wrote.

Getting In: No problems reported.

Getting There: One has plenty of choices of transportation to Hartford—Bradley International Airport in Windsor Locks, Amtrak, and motor coach—although your own car is preferable.

DELAWARE

Dover—Wesley College

Courses of Study: Ecology, Bay to Bay; Reel Literature, Books into Movies; Eastern Europe and the USSR in the 90s; Whodunit: Architecture as History; Wellness

Quality of Instructors: Generally very good.

Environment: Dover, a city of 32,500 people, is the county seat and the capital of the state of Delaware. This small city has wide, elm tree-lined avenues and broad green lawns, surrounding red brick, Williamsburg-style state buildings. The land is flat coastal plain, just one hour from Atlantic beaches or the Chesapeake Bay. Nearby are the 8,800 acres of the Prime Hook National Wildlife Refuge where flocks of snow geese and ducks gather in the fall, shore birds gather in the spring, and shiny ibises scavenge and wade in the shallow waters.

The college campus is nice and compact; everything is close at hand, particularly convenient in foul weather. The school serves just 662 undergraduates and is affiliated with the United Methodist church.

Housing: Very clean air-conditioned dormitories, with less admirable bathroom facilities. Except for the dormitory entrance steps, the facilities are okay for the physically handicapped.

Food: Varied, abundant, and well prepared. "Give them a couple of stars."

Unique Attributes: Campus coordinator, instructors, and staff are all friendly and helpful. The program is full, with "lots to do in your spare time," and all facilities are air-conditioned. Lovely buffet dinners are served at the beginning and end of the week with linen tablecloths, napkins, and flowers. The college president, vice-president, teachers, and spouses all attend these gracious events.

Rent an aluminum canoe to visit the swampy woods and marshes of Prime Hook. You might spot some monarch butterflies or some of the 240 species of migratory birds that seek refuge there.

Shortcomings: This is a relatively new host institution. My reviewers complimented their hosts: "Overall they did an excellent job."

Going Solo: Rated a 5 out of 5. Single rooms are available, the atmosphere is very cordial, and access is very easy over superhighways.

Getting In: No waiting lists as yet.

Getting There: Dover lies right on the main north-south highway, an easy drive from many major cities on the East Coast. Expect heavy beach traffic in the summer. Greyhound buses are available, or one can fly to the Philadelphia airport and rent a car.

DISTRICT OF COLUMBIA

Washington — Howard University

Courses of Study: Branching Out with Genealogy; Writing the Story in You; Botany for Everyone

Quality of Instructors: "Affable and full of their subject." Teachers are oriented toward black genealogy and history.

Environment: This 89-acre main campus of Howard University's five campuses is located on the northwest side of Washington, D.C. It is a friendly, beautiful campus with classic Jeffersonian buildings as well as some examples of very modern architecture. Howard, our nation's preeminent black university, promotes a liberal arts education for its 14,500 undergraduates.

Housing: Female Elderhostelers stay in Bethune Hall, a relatively new women's dormitory. Suites of seven single rooms have one shower room per suite. The building has an elevator and air-conditioning. Men are housed in dormitories with similar seven-room suites.

Food: Catered, adequate cuisine is served in the nearby dining facility. Howard students rate it "terrific." Unlike many college cafeterias, there is no ice cream or frozen yogurt available.

Unique Attributes: My reviewers thought it important to critique Howard University's first Elderhostel. Two white women were part of a group of seventeen, with two men and thirteen black women. The staff work very hard to make it a pleasant and well-monitored experience. A student "girl guide" is assigned to the group, on duty 24 hours a day. Field trips to the school's own TV and radio stations and to the Frederick Douglass home in Anacostia are part of the program.

Shortcomings: It is best to stay on campus with the group, since the school is located in a low-income, high-crime section of the city. Washington is no longer a safe city for strolling alone, so "bring extra dollars for taking taxis to off-campus excursions."

Going Solo: The rooms in Bethune Hall are all singles, so we're giving this one a "very suitable." Single women will have lots of company for card playing or whatever. My reviewers thought single men would probably want to pair up and try the city's night life.

Getting In: The program is too new to have any problems yet.

Getting There: Fly to National Airport, as Dulles is too far away. Amtrak and Greyhound both offer frequent service to the city. The remodeled Union Station is worth a visit.

Washington —
The George Washington University

Courses of Study: Great Decisions 1990; War and Peace; Healthy Life-Style; Oral History and American Childhood; American Cinema of the 1930s; Religion and Healing

Quality of Instructors: They received rave reviews of "Excellent," "Outstanding," and "Magnificent!"

Environment: This small university is located in the heart of Washington, near Pennsylvania Avenue and the State Department. The campus occupies 20 blocks of downtown D.C., within walking distance of the Lincoln Memorial and the Vietnam Memorial, "and from there everything else is within eyeshot." One can also walk to the White House and the Kennedy Performing Arts Center. The George Washington University is a private, nonsectarian school serving 6,000 full-time undergraduates and emphasizing adult education.

Housing: Everglades Hall, a high-rise resident facility at the corner of H and 22nd streets has rooms that usually accommodate three students. Elderhostelers are housed as doubles, with "lots of room" and private baths. Air-conditioning units are provided in all sleeping quarters.

Food: The University Student Center cafeteria has a great variety of excellent food served in a huge dining area. "Taco salads are great."

Unique Attributes: This is a great university in the middle of our nation's capital. "Can't beat it for sightseeing!" The staff helpfully encourages attendees to observe the business of government and tour museums, but my reviewers could not tear themselves away from the absorbing classes. Plenty of staff people on duty to help as needed.

Shortcomings: The school does not make arrangements for "stayovers," but my reviewers found a nice, reasonable hotel nearby. "Remember to walk in multiples after dark."

Going Solo: All the classrooms and eating places on campus are easy to find and within a comfortable distance. Dormitory capacity is 47, so the group is large enough to have a good number of solo travelers. "Singles should do well. Give it a 5."

Getting In: I've been told early registration is essential. My panelists were accepted from a waiting list.

Getting There: Fly to National Airport, not Dulles, and take a taxi. Taxi fare is high in this city, but there's a good Metro system, too. Greyhound and Amtrak also have convenient service to this city.

FLORIDA

Brooksville—University of Southern Florida, Chinsegut Hill

Courses of Study: Wildlife Across Florida; Florida Folk Art; America's Battlefields; Eight Stages of Life

Quality of Instructors: "Top-notch." All the university professors present the material in an interesting fashion.

Environment: The Elderhostel program is held at the Educational Conference Center, part of a research center of the USDA, pleasantly located 55 miles north of Tampa near the Gulf of Mexico. The center sits in a green forest in the Florida uplands, a region that is only 200 to 300 feet above sea level, but breezes from the Gulf relieve the summer heat.

Housing: Elderhostelers are housed in four-bedroom, two-bath cabins that are very clean, comfortable, and air-conditioned.

Food: The meals are served in the multipurpose center and are very good.

Unique Attributes: The climate on the Gulf Coast of Florida is less humid than the Atlantic side, and the elevation is higher. Both coasts, of course, are lovely in the winter. This facility is a Department of Agriculture cattle breeding station. The main building, the Manor House, is an 1842 historic dwelling. The classroom facility used for the Elderhostel program is new and comfortable. Tampa is a cigar-making and shipbuilding center, although tourism is the major industry of the state. Tampa is home to the much-visited theme park, Busch Gardens, winter festivals, and a thriving arts community. One might also combine a week at Brooksville with a visit to Walt Disney World in Orlando.

Shortcomings: The humidity in Florida can be brutal in the summer with or without the breezes from the Gulf. Walking shoes are required for the rough terrain.

Getting In: All Elderhostel programs in Florida are popular during the winter months. Early registration is recommended.

Getting There: The Brooksville program can be reached by either public transportation or private car. Buses, planes, and trains go to Tampa, but Brooksville does not have an airport.

Gainesville—University of Florida

Courses of Study: The Many Sounds of the Organ; Human Uses of Animals in Prehistoric Times; Eastern Bloc Countries; Relating Pesticide Use to Water Quality; Filmmaking from the Silent Era to the Present

Quality of Instructors: "Film professors' knowledge of the subject is extraordinary, and field trips are conducted by individuals actually doing the research."

Environment: Gainesville, a city of 125,000, is a livable college town in north central Florida. The large, beautifully landscaped campus is located in the center of the city. It is well groomed by a crew of groundskeepers. The university has lots of recent construction to accommodate its 34,000 students.

Housing: Elderhostelers are housed in an air-conditioned hotel operated by the student union.

Food: The usual college fare is offered; Elderhostelers are allocated an allowance for each meal. The dining room is also part of the hotel.

Unique Attributes: The housing and dining arrangements are unusual for Elderhosteling, and the program coordinators are always available and helpful. The University of Florida has a reputation as a party- and sports-loving school, and the students are frequently found playing volleyball or sailing and water-skiing on nearby lakes.

Shortcomings: No extracurricular evening activities are planned.

Getting In: No waiting lists reported.

Getting There: Pleasant access by automobile. Delta and US Air fly to Gainesville, and Amtrak's New York to Miami line stops in Jacksonville, which is about 50 miles northeast of Gainesville.

GEORGIA

Atlanta—Simpsonwood Conference and Retreat Center

Courses of Study: Architecture; U.S. Presidents; Indians in Georgia; Aqua-aerobics; Southeastern Indians; Psalms; Art, Developing a Feel for the Fine Arts; Flora, the Southern Piedmont

Quality of Instructors: The Elderhostel teachers are, for the most part, very serious educators.

Environment: The conference center is located 10 miles from Atlanta on 239 acres stretched along the banks of the Chattahoochee River. The atmosphere is "very cool, quiet, and reserved." As a Methodist retreat center it purports to have a reflective, restful ambience. The countryside is gorgeous; in the springtime, the fragrance of magnolia and dogwood fills the air. Some classic antebellum homes can be found in the outskirts of the city. The climate of Georgia is balmy, and the rich, red soil nourishes the thousands of acres of cotton.

Housing: Elderhostelers stay in a brand-new lodge that is heated and air-conditioned. Each room, with its private bath, has two double beds. There are no radios or TVs in the building, but the nicely appointed rooms have a view of the surrounding woods.

Food: Simple fare is prepared by the chef and served in a dining room. "Sometimes inspired and sometimes just adequate." "No one would starve." An inoffensive nonsectarian blessing precedes each meal. Peaches, peanuts, and pecans are plentiful.

Unique Attributes: Atlanta, Georgia's largest city, has a plethora of performing arts. Four wonderful evening activities are included in the Elderhostel program: theater, ballet, and the Atlanta Symphony are among the choices. These outstanding field trips, if taken independently, would be very expensive. Elderhostelers are bused to all off-campus activities in an unusually comfortable, air-conditioned motor coach.

Shortcomings: My reviewers felt short-changed by some first-time instructors and reported a bit of grousing about the just-adequate food. "Expected more."

Going Solo: An especially nice program for singles because the director has, in addition to her normal duties, established a system of hosts and hostesses. Elderhostelers are trained for the jobs and take their responsibilities seriously. The hosts and hostesses (2 for each group) are accessible day and night and encourage participation in a variety of evening activities. "Single guests receive much attention at Simpsonwood."

Getting In: In spite of its uncomplicated access, this program is not usually oversubscribed, but early registration is suggested.

Getting There: The administration of Simpsonwood provides transportation from Hartsfield-Atlanta International Airport, one of the country's busiest. Arrangements can probably be made for pickup if one arrives by bus or train. Easy access by car.

George T. Bagby State Park—Lake Walter F. George Lodge and Conference Center

Courses of Study: Victorian Architecture; Indian Lore; Georgia's Western Frontier; Geologic Phenomena; Hole in One

Quality of Instructors: Professional athletes and knowledgeable local authorities lecture as required.

Environment: This is a lovely rural area with quaint little towns nearby. The Elderhostel is held in a beautiful state park about 60 miles south of Columbus, on a 45-acre lake. "Wonderful retreat for walking, bird-watching, and canoeing." And how about casting a fly into that lovely lake?

Housing: Excellent, in a brand new air-conditioned motel-like facility.

Food: Meals are served restaurant style. Expect lots of Southern specialties: black-eyed peas, corn pone, and key lime pie.

Unique Attributes: This is a lovely new facility with an "eager-to-please" faculty. The excellent field trips and pleasant surroundings compensate for the lack of serious intellectual courses. "Thoroughly enjoyable." One couple wrote that they drove up to Warm Springs one afternoon. "The Little White House is a wonderful experience."

Getting In: A new program in a new facility. Not yet on the "biggest hits" list.

Getting There: Pretty inaccessible, except by automobile.

Jekyll Island—South Georgia College

Courses of Study: Eugenia Price, Georgia Author; Presidential Trivia; Acting and the Theater; James Joyce's Dubliners; Dynamics of the Barrier Islands; History of Coastal Georgia

Quality of Instructors: A mature, high-quality team of teachers commute from the college to the motel.

Environment: Six miles out in the Atlantic Ocean lies the small barrier reef of Jekyll Island. It is connected to the mainland by a causeway. This winter resort is owned and operated by the state of Georgia; two-thirds of the island is kept in its undeveloped natural state, and one-third is maintained as a wildlife preserve. The Elderhostel is held in a commercial facility, with the ocean and a beautiful beach at the front door.

Housing: Not-so-luxurious, two-bedroom condos that contain a living room, a kitchen, and bath facilities.

Food: A good restaurant with prescribed meals. I received many complaints about the lack of choices. "Inflexible," wrote one panelist.

Unique Attributes: Lovely mild winter climate prevails on this millionaire's retreat. The island boasts fancy oceanfront hotels and 63 holes of golf. Enjoy salt air and sunsets or ride a bicycle along the miles of beachfront. One couple wrote, "Beautiful golf courses and no honky-tonk. The entire island enforces a 30-mph speed limit."

Shortcomings: The Elderhostel coordinator is uncaring and rarely participates in activities. "The motel has seen better days." One group of hostelers were indignant at being served banana sandwiches as a field trip lunch!

Going Solo: Just okay. Access only by automobile and poor organization are problems, but many evening activities in an isolated setting are usually appreciated by single travelers. "Not for shrinking violets," one panelist wrote.

Getting In: Obviously, many Elderhostelers pay serious heed to the Georgia farewell "Y'all come back. Do ya' hear?" This destination is one of the most popular in the United States. I'm sure it is filled by lottery. Register early.

Getting There: A scenic drive over major thruways. One might fly or ride Amtrak to Savannah or to Jacksonville, Florida, then rent a car.

Toccoa—Georgia Baptist Assembly

Courses of Study: Southern Songs; Native Americans Unique to Northeast Georgia; Landscaping Flowers and Shrubs for the South; Folk History and Culture of Appalachia; Life in the Forest; Wellness

Quality of Instructors: A well-qualified team of instructors is found at the Assembly.

Environment: Eighty-five miles northeast of Atlanta at the edge of the Appalachians, this quiet site is on a remote, uncrowded, 200-acre mountain lake. The 1,000-acre forest is described by one of my reviewers as "lots of trees." Toccoa is located in the mountains on an old stagecoach route.

Housing: Elderhostelers reside in very good air-conditioned motel-like rooms with private baths. Rooms for the handicapped are also available.

Food: The buffet-style meals rate a "very good." "Authentic Southern cooking."

Unique Attributes: Lake Louise is a beautiful place for fishing or swimming. The program includes bus trips to scenic and historic sites, one of which is the Chattahoochee National Forest. This secluded camp, with large, comfortable classrooms and sleeping quarters all in the same building, appeals to nature-loving Elderhostelers.

Shortcomings: There is no public transportation to or from this site, and the location is several miles from any stores. One is totally isolated without an automobile.

Going Solo: Access is difficult, but once there, singles should fare very well. Toccoa is a very small, safe city, the site is compact, and a well-lit covered walkway leads from the dormitory building to the dining area.

Getting In: No problems reported.

Getting There: Amtrak has a station in Toccoa, but bus and plane connections are poor. Atlanta is the nearest airport, 85 miles away.

HAWAII

Honolulu—University of Manoa

Courses of Study: The Illuminated Life, an intensive, two-week course

Quality of Instructors: The professors are exemplary.

Environment: This Elderhostel program is conducted on a 35-acre campus covered with a wide variety of exotic plants. Public bus service runs from the campus, on the outskirts of Honolulu, to all of the recreational, cultural, and business centers of the metropolitan area. Hawaii is a favorite tourist destination for people on the mainland. The course title, a reference to the well-known Socratic quotation, establishes the depth and serious mood of this particular Elderhostel.

Housing: The student dormitories are beautiful round buildings but are poorly maintained. The lack of air-conditioning in the dormitories can make sleeping very uncomfortable at times.

Food: My reviewers rate the university cafeteria as just fair.

Unique Attributes: A clinical psychologist guides students through this course on the psychology of personal growth. Workshops and small-group-sharing experiences fill the mornings, while the afternoons are left free for touring the island. Evenings may be spent on homework assignments. This special workshop includes intergenerational experiences, as Elderhostelers and regular college students meet, attend lectures, and do exercises together.

Shortcomings: Although the tradewinds do blow, summer temperatures in Hawaii range between 85 and 93 degrees.

Getting In: All of the attendees reported this as a "most interesting" Elderhostel experience. All Hawaiian programs are very popular.

Getting There: Honolulu can be reached by all major airlines or by a leisurely cruise ship from Los Angeles or San Francisco.

Oahu—Brigham Young University

Courses of Study: Ocean and Man; Volcanoes; Polynesian Culture; Discover your Roots; Pearl Harbor and the Beginning of WW II; Michener's Hawaii, Fact and Fiction

Quality of Instructors: The teachers are very good; interaction with the students is encouraged and very pleasant.

Environment: Hawaii is the only one of our United States with a truly Oriental flavor. The campus is located amid the tropical beaches and majestic mountains of Oahu. The school is right next to the Polynesian Culture Center, where there are exhibits of many Hawaiian carved god figures and other sacred spirits.

Housing: The accommodations are fine. Elderhostelers stay in the Laniloa Lodge with double rooms and private baths.

Food: An amazing variety of attractively prepared fresh fruits and vegetables is offered. Native and Oriental-style dishes are featured.

Unique Attributes: Field trips for on-site learning are well designed and organized. Elderhostelers participate in an authentic Polynesian luau and a Hawaiian show and buffet. The Brigham Young Hawaiian campus offers one an opportunity to meet students from over 56 countries. Upon arrival in Hawaii, all visitors are greeted by people who place leis around their necks. This custom, using naturally perfumed flower garlands, is a native gesture of love.

Shortcomings: None reported. Because this is a church-related school, smoking, alcoholic beverages, coffee, and tea are not allowed on campus.

Getting In: No problems reported.

Getting There: Most major airlines serve the Hawaiian islands. To ease the exhaustion of travel, Honolulu International Airport has a mini-hotel where one can shower and sleep for 8 hours.

Waikiki — University of Hawaii at Manoa

Courses of Study: Hawaii's Useful Plants; Hawaii's Marine Environment; Hawaii's Poetry, Chants, Music, and Dance; Hawaii's Changing Landscape; A Look and Learn Introduction to Hawaii

Quality of Instructors: "Great! Interested in the subjects and interesting to students."

Environment: This unique state is filled with friendly people, warm temperatures, lush vegetation, beautiful scenery, and lots of beaches. The native Hawaiian population is a fascinating mix of Polynesian, Chinese, Japanese, Caucasian, and Filipino. Honolulu is a strange mix of concrete and coral with borders of sand and coco palm trees. Unfortunately, the lovely white sand beach of Waikiki and the view of the ocean are generally obliterated by the towers of high-rise hotels.

Housing: In a modern but modest hotel. My reviewers like the TV and good maid service. There's also elevator service, air-conditioning, and scenic views.

Food: Hostelers are pleased with all the choices and with the abundance of fresh fruits. If you are mad about macadamias, the nuts are much less expensive on the island than on the mainland.

Unique Attributes: The classes, field trips, bus passes, and organization of this program received rave reviews. With the two-week program, attendees have eight afternoons or mornings free to explore and visit gardens, swim beneath waterfalls, and study the exotic heritage of the people. The Honolulu anthurium nursery is a not-to-be-missed wonder. Displayed are 1,700 varieties of orchids—pink, purple, green, yellow, striped, and potted.

The most beautiful unspoiled parts of Hawaii are the outer islands. The smoldering volcanic peaks and coral reefs of Kauai, Maui, Molokai, and the big island of Hawaii are not yet crowded with hotels and tourists. One can still find plantations of sugarcane and pineapple fields. Heavy rainfall (Mount Waialeale on Kauai is one of the wettest spots in the world) makes the vegetation unbelievably lush.

Going Solo: "Give it a 5." Easy bus access to many points of interest, congeniality of many group field trips, and attentive, well-organized staff.

Shortcomings: The expense of flying to Hawaii does not seem to deter Elderhostelers from enjoying this program.

Getting In: This is a very popular destination, but, to date, the Hawaiian universities have managed to meet the demand for space.

Getting There: Most major cities on the mainland have nonstop jet service to Honolulu. Aloha.

IDAHO

Rexburg—Ricks College

Courses of Study: Llama-packing in the Grand Tetons; Natural History of the Teton Region; Fire Opals of Idaho; History and Economy of the Snake River Valley; Theology of the Mormons; Canoeing on Lewis and Shoshone Lakes

Quality of Instructors: Instructors are unusually knowledgeable, helpful, and pleasant.

Environment: Rexburg is a clean, attractive small town in Idaho's historic Snake River Valley, an area founded by fur traders and gold miners. Yellowstone National Park and the snowy peaks of the Grand Tetons are just 90 miles away across the border in Wyoming. The valley lies in a white pine forest, its roads bordered with handsome bushes of mock orange and views of the Snake River twisting through the woods.

Housing: Elderhostelers are housed in very modern student apartments that contain two bedrooms, a bath, a sitting room, and a kitchen. The apartment complex also has laundry facilities.

Food: Meals are reported to be plentiful and tasty, with a good variety of choices.

Unique Attributes: Ricks College is a two-year school run by the Mormon church. Certain standards of dress and conduct are expected of everyone on campus. Smoking and drinking of alcohol are prohibited; even coffee and tea are not served. Evening activities available on this beautiful campus include swimming, bowling, and music concerts. The distances between buildings are convenient and comfortable for walking. Field trips take Elderhostelers along quiet paths away from the tourist routes, as they search out hot springs, geysers, or raw opals.

Some courses are laboratory workshops that require the use of equipment and instruments, and field trips are rugged. One is a five-day canoe trip with 5 to 7 miles of paddling each day. The llama pack trip is another adventure not for the lily-livered hosteler. Participants hike 3 to 5 miles per day at 8,000-foot elevations with day packs on their backs.

Shortcomings: No weaknesses reported.

Going Solo: This is a great destination for the robust outdoors person.

Getting In: Idaho is not a particularly popular vacation destination, but the Ricks College courses frequently have waiting lists. One of my reviewing couples was accepted from a waiting list. Courses have limited capacities, so early registration is advised.

Getting There: Ricks College can be reached by bus or plane, but private automobile permits extra sightseeing while driving to and from the campus.

IOWA

Fort Dodge—Iowa Central Community College

Courses of Study: Scandinavian Myths and Legends; News, You Don't Have to Take It Sitting Down; Writing from Inside Out; East Meets West, Arts of Asia; East Meets West, the Economy; East Meets West, Oriental Culture and Customs

Quality of Instructors: Excellent.

Environment: Fort Dodge, a town of just 30,000 friendly people, sits in the center of the world's richest farmland, as well as in the middle of Iowa between Sioux City and Waterloo. While speeding across the prairie, one is reminded of the farm in the famous Grant Wood painting. The neat barnyards and large square houses are common throughout the state.

Housing: The dormitories are adequate, and there is no supplemental charge for singles.

Food: The college fare, with plenty of fresh fruits and vegetables, is given an excellent rating. The cafeteria has a down-to-earth menu.

Unique Attributes: The campus features tennis courts, golf and swimming nearby, and a warm, cordial ambience. The atmosphere is academically easygoing. Most small towns in the Hawkeye State hold annual food festivals celebrating the Dutch, German, Norwegian, or Czechoslovakian heritage of their people.

Shortcomings: My reviewer participates in an annual Elderhostel at Fort Dodge. In her view this comfortable campus has no shortcomings.

Getting In: This is not an oversubscribed destination.

Getting There: Driving in Iowa is very easy. One can also fly to Des Moines and rent a car or take an interstate bus to Fort Dodge.

Iowa City—University of Iowa

Courses of Study: Two-week intensive workshops in short fiction, poetry, or memoir writing

Quality of Instructors: Three members of the famous Writers' Workshop are selected each summer to work in the Elderhostel pro-

An evening at the theater, University of Iowa, Iowa City

grams. Most literary critics believe these young graduate students to be the cream of the crop. All the instructors are insightful and conscientious. "Tops!" "Gets better every year."

Environment: The small town college atmosphere is almost perfect. The Iowa River leisurely flows through the 1,880-acre campus with buildings on both shores connected by charming footbridges. "It's River City from the *Music Man*." Students can be seen paddling canoes along the river, and families of noisy ducks provide a pleasant diversion while walking to and from classes. The campus architecture is a charming mix of old and new buildings, all flanked by broad green lawns.

Housing: Modern dormitories are comfortable and convenient to all campus activities, classrooms, and the cafeteria. Single rooms and typewriters are available for a modest additional cost. Single

Poet's workshop, University of Iowa, Iowa City (Photo: Mae Woods Bell)

rooms are "large enough to swing a cat." Free refrigerators and extra pillows are provided. Try to get a river view if you can. All rooms have individual air-conditioning units, and the buildings have elevators.

Food: During the years, there has been some belt-tightening in the kitchen, but the cafeteria still ranks among the top handful in the Elderhostel movement. The menus frequently have too many temptations for calorie counters, but nutritious selections are also available. "Watch it! Food is excellent and overeating comes easy!" One reviewer wrote, "They even fixed grits for me!" The cafeteria is a large, friendly, not quiet, dining area where round tables encourage Elderhostelers to have stimulating conversations with the large, international body of students.

Unique Attributes: This is not a laid-back, get a little local culture, hostel. For the most part, participants are serious writers or would-be writers. The course includes heavy reading and writing assignments and small classes of peers critique one another's work. One invaluable program component is one-on-one student-teacher conferences scheduled once or twice during each workshop. Some teachers even prepare written critiques of students' work. The annual publication of a book of short stories and poetry written by workshop attendees is the frosting on the cake.

Do you remember the exchange of dialogue in the movie, *Field of Dreams*? "Is this heaven?" asks Shoeless Joe. "No, it's Iowa," replies Ray Kinsella. I know a bunch of over-age-60 writer wannabees who would agree with Shoeless Joe. They arrive weighed down with rejection slips and doubts and, after two weeks, fly home on wings of courage and confidence.

The state Elderhostel coordinator is "unflappable," wrote a six-year veteran. She plans for participants to enjoy all the university offerings at no additional cost: good theater, symphony concerts, ballet, and weekend day trips. Daily van service is provided for those attendees who cannot manage the distance to class or other activities.

A five-year veteran wrote, "How lucky we are! I'll continue to reapply each year because I love the experience, the people I've met, and the personal development. Late night readings of my own work is one of the unique pleasures that brings me back year after year."

Shortcomings: Iowa can be humid in the summer, but with free transportation and room air-conditioners, the humidity is a minor discomfort. The program coordinator is now responsible for all the many Iowa Elderhostels. On my fifth visit, I found her stretched too thin by her huge job, but my reviewers assure me that she was her former attentive, friendly self in 1990.

Going Solo: Unusually appropriate. Almost all participants come as singles, with the married writers leaving their spouses at other hostels or at home. As a rule, writers are introverted individuals and need single rooms for late night sessions with their muse, but the soul-baring experience of critiquing one another's work creates intimacy. Many veterans, including myself, attended their first Iowa workshop as total strangers and by the end of two weeks had made lifelong friends. This may not hold true for the Memoir Writing course that is frequented by couples who wish to prepare memoirs for their grandchildren.

Getting In: Very early registration is a must. The classes fill to capacity very quickly. If you are frozen out by registering too late, as I was one year, take comfort in knowing that the wait will make the experience all the more rewarding one year later. It also pays to telephone the site director. Occasionally there are last minute cancellations that have not yet been reported to Boston.

Getting There: Iowa City is easily reached by automobile if you like to drive. Bus is available, and Cedar Rapids is served by several airlines. The limo driver from Cedar Rapids to Iowa City is a joyful local booster! The limo costs $27 round-trip.

Iowa City—University of Iowa

Courses of Study: Four-week intensive writing workshop in the novel

Quality of Instructors: Excellent. Teachers are graduates of the Iowa Writers' School, which turns out prize-winning authors.

Environment: Iowa City is a charming university town with tree-shaded streets and mature perennial gardens. It has earned its title as the Athens of the Midwest, with politically active students, upscale bookstores, trendy boutiques, and plenty of charming college bistros with checkered tablecloths and hanging greenery. In a state historically parsimonious in its support of public higher education, the university receives a large percentage of the state's tax dollars.

Housing: Students are housed in spacious enough rooms in high-rise dormitories directly across the street from the college cafeteria. The dormitories have individual room air-conditioners and elevators and are ideally situated for strolling to downtown shops, parks, museums, theaters, and indoor swimming pools. This large university has ten dormitories, making it possible for most undergraduates and all Elderhostelers to live in college housing.

Food: Sure, it's steamtable cafeteria food, but the quantities are unlimited and the choices almost infinite. Even finicky eaters should manage well here. Subsequent visits revealed a slight tightening of the choices, but it's still superior to many college cafeterias.

Unique Attributes: This program offers an opportunity to spend four weeks with a group of your peers, all of whom are serious about their writing. Walking to class along the banks of the Iowa River or feeding the ducks seems to stir the writer's imagination, and the livable quality of Iowa City seems to foster the introspection writers need. Comments from reviewers were, "Some surprisingly good writers. We may see some of them in hardcover yet!" "An intellectual bargain with a great bunch of people who have lived long enough not to be intimidated by professors." Iowa City has too many irresistible distractions; classic films at the Bijou for movie buffs, science lectures, the Iowa Symphony, a light opera company, traveling ballet troupes, and evening readings of the works of resident poets and authors.

Shortcomings: Several reviewers found the four-week session too long and felt that their work was short-changed by the depth of the critiquing.

Getting in: The four-week novel writing program is not as heavily oversubscribed as the two-week writing programs.

Getting There: See the University of Iowa evaluation of two-week programs.

Mount Pleasant—Iowa Wesleyan College

Courses of Study: History of the Midwest Railroad; American Repertoire Theater and Tent Shows; Rural Life in the Midwest; Our Heritage, American Musical Theater

Quality of Instructors: Excellent.

Environment: Mount Pleasant is a rural community, located in the midst of our country's breadbasket. Bordered by the Mississippi on the east and the wide Missouri on the west, Iowa has rolling green hills of rich farmland. Homes in town have old-fashioned dooryard gardens where sweet peas climb taut strings and trellises of blue columbines and snapdragons lean against the white frame walls.

The college, with just 400 full-time students, is the oldest coeducational institution west of the Mississippi. It is a private liberal arts school affiliated with the Methodist church. All of the early colleges in Iowa were church-supported schools. Iowa Wesleyan has a pleasant campus of old red brick buildings that dot the wide green lawns.

Housing: Elderhostelers are housed in very adequate college dormitories.

Food: "Better than many college cafeterias." Food is excellently prepared.

Unique Attributes: Mount Pleasant is the site of the largest steam celebration in America, "The Old Threshers and Settlers Reunion." The extracurricular offerings receive raves from an Iowa Wesleyan following of loyal fans who are sorely disappointed that the school schedules so short an Elderhostel season.

Shortcomings: None.

Getting In: No waiting lists reported.

Getting There: Take the train, bus, or an easy automobile drive. Amtrak has a feeder line to Mount Pleasant from its main station in Ottumwa. There are lots of interesting folks traveling on trains, or one can catch up on some reading.

Ottumwa—Indian Hills College

Courses of Study: Ceramics; Archaeology; Watercolor

Quality of Instructors: "Great watercolor artist / teacher makes everyone feel successful, and the archaeology professsor gives excellent lectures on the history of the Iowa Indian tribes!"

Environment: The wooded campus of Indian Hills College, formerly a religious school for women, is beautiful. Carpets of green grass surround lovely little lakes, and the land is not "nearly as flat as we've been led to believe." Ottumwa is in southern Iowa, an area noted for its prime farmland, corn, hogs, and soybeans.

Housing: Elderhostelers share college dormitories with very courteous and thoughtful students. Communal bath facilities are down the hall.

Food: "Excellent. No complaints," was the enthusiastic response of one panelist.

Unique Attributes: "The best of ten Elderhostels attended," wrote a woman from California. In addition to enjoying the well-organized and well-planned extracurricular activities and classes, my reviewer found the campus had a charming feeling of uncrowded space and the state of Iowa a surprising sense of sophistication.

Advanced music students perform in a concert that exhibits their talent and training. "This, too, is charming," she wrote. Grant Wood is one of Iowa's most famous native sons. Arrangements are made for the Elderhostel class to have individual photographs taken of themselves standing behind cardboard life-size figures of the Grant Wood farmer and his wife, replicated from his painting *American Gothic*. (I hope the money supports an art museum.)

Shortcomings: Ottumwa is not an easily reached destination.

Getting In: My reviewer made early reservations, so she had no difficulty being accepted.

Getting There: The best method of going to Ottumwa is by railroad: the main Amtrak line going both east and west still stops there. Take the California Zephyr or the Desert Wind, but be aware that passengers are finding it very difficult to book sleeping accommodations as the popularity of overnight train travel increases.

KENTUCKY

Corbin—Otter Creek Park

Courses of Study: A Natural Escape (a multidisciplinary approach to the study of natural science)

Quality of Instructors: Young and enthusiastic naturalists whose ardor and high spirits are contagious.

Environment: The park is a 3,000-acre tract of forest, abandoned farms, and caves adjoining the Ohio River. Elderhostelers can enjoy the solitary space of woods and water and think about preserving the delicate balance of our ecology and these finite resources.

Housing: Participants stay in a modern, air-conditioned, creek-stone lodge with private baths, daily maid service, and superb views of the Ohio River.

Food: The meals served in the park restaurant are excellent in both quality and quantity.

Unique Attributes: The park offers great forest and meadow areas for the field study of plants and animals as well as the opportunity to watch the barge traffic rolling on the Ohio River. Evenings are filled with special courses and demonstrations such as free-form basket weaving, wool carding, and making dyes of native plant materials. Interesting side trips are arranged to the historic Doe Run Inn and the Gatton Museum of Artillery at nearby Fort Knox, the repository of America's gold reserves. The park is only 30 miles from Louisville, the home of the Kentucky Derby. It is 100 miles from Mammoth Cave, an incredible network of caves featuring rows of white stalactites.

Shortcomings: None reported, even though the park has not been offering Elderhostel programs for very many years. A private car is needed for transportation.

Getting in: No difficulties reported.

Getting There: The park is only accessible by private car, although the Louisville Standiford International Airport is served by all major airlines.

Cumberland Falls State Resort Park— Union College

Courses of Study: Natural History and Field Study; Appalachian Culture and Folklore; Geography and History of Appalachia

Quality of Instructors: The teachers from the college in Barbourville are very good. Demonstrations of handmade musical instruments and foot stompin' mountain music are excellent.

Environment: The woodlands of the park glow with beautiful yellow aspens in autumn, and the steep sides of the pass shimmer with the pale pinks of mountain laurel and rhododendrons in the spring. Cumberland Falls is known as "The Niagara of the West." Cumberland Gap is a natural pass through the Appalachians used by the pioneers on their way to settle the west. Railroads now run through the pass, and it has become the site of a national park. Daniel Boone blazed his "Wilderness Trail" through the Cumberland Gap, which straddles the Kentucky / Tennessee border.

Housing: DuPont Lodge is a deluxe lodge run by the state of Kentucky. The double rooms are very nice, with two double beds and private baths.

Food: Excellent food is served in a beautiful dining room overlooking the Cumberland River.

Unique Attributes: Cumberland Falls is renowned for its "moonbow," a beautiful physical phenomenon created by moonlight filtering through the mist of the falls. The park is surrounded by a very depressed area of Appalachia. Elderhostelers can see and hear about the abject poverty and hardships of life in the mountains, in addition to discussing the history of corruption and the economics of the area.

Some Elderhostel programs include explorations of mysterious and "scary" caves. Other programs have field trips to the site of the famous Scopes trial, where Clarence Darrow and William Jennings Bryan argued the teaching of Darwin's theory of evolution. The park is located a short distance from the Lincoln Museum, a collection of 25,000 objects devoted to the great president. Alumni of Cumberland Falls recommend this program for senior seniors; the hiking, walking, boating, and swimming are all pleasantly accessible.

Shortcomings: Some reviewers believed the class of 50 Elderhostelers too many for an optimum learning experience.

Getting In: The Cumberland Falls fan club suggests very early reservations.

Getting There: The network of federal highways through this part of Kentucky is excellent.

Melbourne—St. Anne's Convent/ Thomas More College

Courses of Study: Our German Heritage; German Musical Traditions; German American Heritage in Cincinnati Area

Quality of Instructors: Very good practicing artists and musicians teach the program.

Environment: Melbourne lies just across the Ohio River from Cincinnati, 15 miles away. The peaceful wooded ambience is delightful and unusual. The program is held in the convent where the institutional scenes of *Rain Man* were filmed. The nuns are very friendly and gracious hostesses.

Housing: Elderhostelers stay in small but adequate single rooms. The whole program takes place within the confines of the one-elevator building.

Food: "Outstanding." Old-fashioned, home-style German fare is served, with wonderful hot breads and wurst.

Unique Attributes: "Sister Bertha, the director, alone is worth the trip." The evening programs are most unusual and interesting; they include a German dance group, a choral group, a dinner tour, and a visit to the Oldenburg Brewery. My reviewers found this a favorite among years of Elderhosteling.

Shortcomings: None.

Going Solo: "A great place for lone hostelers. Everything is done to make one feel at home." The small size of the group, the single rooms, and the sequestered nature of the site are all elements that enhance the destination for singles.

Getting In: Very difficult because this special program is only given one week each year and is limited to 25 participants.

Getting There: Cincinnati has all forms of public transportation, an international airport, a bus terminal, and Amtrak. Members of the convent will meet all hostelers arriving by public transportation.

Morehead—Morehead State University

Courses of Study: Appalachian Festival and Appalachian Culture; Kentucky Ballads; The Mountain Voice; Traditional Mountain Dancing

Quality of Instructors: Well-qualified people from the area, retirees, heads of foundations, and musicians augment the excellent university faculty.

Environment: Morehead, a rural community of 7,200 inhabitants, is situated in the hills along the Licking River in the heart of the Daniel Boone National Forest, 65 miles from Lexington. Kentucky is called the "Bluegrass State" because of the dusty blue blossoms of the grass. It also has lovely rolling meadows and pastures. The university, with 4,500 students, has a well-known planetarium and operates its own radio station.

Housing: "Pretty luxurious." Elderhostelers reside in air-conditioned suites; each two rooms share a private bath.

Food: "Merely adequate; little variety or nutritional planning. Obviously the college is trying to make money."

Unique Attributes: There is mountain entertainment noon and night and demonstrations of country music and instruments. A huge exhibit and sale of area crafts is held. This is a lively, fun-filled hotel. Visits to local places of interest are optional and are scheduled on a fee basis.

Shortcomings: There are very steep hills, and a great deal of walking is required. The weather can be very hot in Kentucky in the summer. A class of 92 enrollees is too large for learning but fine for the demonstrations.

Going Solo: My reviewers give it a 4 out of 5. "Everyone is friendly and cooperative, but the single traveler must make some personal effort to mix."

Getting In: This is a very popular program. Even with 92 spaces available, early registration is suggested.

Getting There: The university will send a bus to meet attendees at the airport in Lexington. Morehead is close to major highways.

Pleasant Hill—Shaker Village

Courses of Study: Shaker History and Culture; Appreciating Our Heritage through the Decorative Arts; Kentucky Images through Literature and History; Salvaging the Past

Quality of Instructors: As needed, courses are taught by Shaker Village staff and guest lecturers, contemporary Kentucky authors, antiquarians, or members of the University of Louisville faculty. The approach is very serious.

Environment: The setting is most unusual. It is a 2,250-acre site just 25 miles south of Lexington. Elderhostelers live in restored Shaker buildings and study the Shaker beliefs as well as those of other unusual religious groups, including the myths of the mountain people. Shaker Village has been designated a national landmark. The mild temperatures of this area of Kentucky encourage tobacco farming and the breeding of horses.

Housing: "The best of many Elderhostels I've attended." The rooms, with private baths, are those used for tourists in season and are furnished in reproductions of classic Shaker furniture.

Food: Elderhostelers are treated to traditional Kentucky food, a very good but unusual style of cooking. "Beaten biscuits and hickory smoked ham!"

Unique Attributes: In Kentucky, people still live close to the land, a fact that relates to the subject of some of the courses. The village is a living tribute to the beauty and simplicity of the Shaker culture; and the hands-on experience brings to life the facts, the ideas, and the forces that shaped these religious tenets. This sect has dwindled to a handful of members living in New England, who weave their own fabrics and spin wool. The society was noted for fine farms, industry, and ingenuity. Their lovely furniture is now prized as collectors' items.

Shortcomings: None reported.

Getting In: This is a popular destination and therefore requires early registration.

Getting There: Lexington has a major airport with direct and connecting flights from all over the United States. Fly in and rent a car, or take your own car if you have the time and energy to meander over the back roads of Kentucky.

MAINE

Bangor — Husson College

Courses of Study: Maine Writers; Maine Art, from Pink Flamingoes to Andrew Wyeth

Quality of Instructors: One superb professor was given an A plus and one just a passing grade.

Environment: Bangor, the third largest city in the state, is situated on the Penobscot River northeast of Waterville. Inland Maine is heavily wooded and boasts a very invigorating climate. The winters are long and cold, fall is hunting season, spring is for fishermen, and summer is for the tourists.

Husson, one mile from downtown Bangor, is a relatively new, small, independent college. Only 21 years old, it has 484 full-time undergraduates enrolled. The school specializes in teacher and business training. The size of the student body doesn't preclude the presence of some lively night spots and off-campus hangouts.

Housing: Very good, modern, attractive dormitories.

Food: A varied menu is served in a cheerful commons.

Unique Attributes: Of seventeen Elderhostels, my reviewers selected this site as the most efficiently organized program. "Coordinators are outstanding." Take a drive up the river to Old Town and watch the craftsman construct sleek Old Town canoes, or visit the Penobscot Indian Museum.

Shortcomings: Relatively new to Elderhosteling, the coordinators scheduled two classes, each 4 hours long—too long. The problem will be remedied before next summer.

Going Solo: Singles fare well at this destination because of the splendid management. No one should get lost in the shuffle.

Getting In: This one is not yet on the favorite destination list.

Getting There: National and regional airlines fly into Bangor International Airport. There are also intrastate flights from the coast of Maine operating in the summertime. Greyhound operates daily service to Bangor.

Biddeford—University of New England

Courses of Study: The American West through Artist's Eyes; Galileo, the Not-So-Young Upstart; Mozart Operas; Beacons of the Maine Coast; A Revisit to the Thirties and Forties; Southern Maine Coast—Past and Present

Quality of Instructors: Opinions varied from excellent to not too well prepared.

Environment: The University of New England is a small independent school located in the outskirts of Biddeford on the Saco River. The school has an enrollment of just 600 career-minded students and a campus spread over 122 acres. Biddeford, with its sandy beaches and sea breezes, sits in the low coastal region on the ocean 20 miles south of Portland and just 2 hours drive from Boston. Nearby are the popular holiday seaside resorts of Old Orchard and Kennebunkport.

Housing: Elderhostelers stay in typical college dormitories with shared bath facilities.

Food: The food is excellent—lots of salad, juices, fresh fruit, and wholesome main dishes.

Unique Attributes: The Elderhostel leadership is very conscientious. The new student center has excellent facilities for physical fitness and health. The laid-back atmosphere of Maine encourages creativity; many artists and writers have established colonies and retreats on the islands and inland lakes. The ocean-side shopping streets of Biddeford are filled with art galleries and quaint craft shops.

Shortcomings: Several reviewers agreed that the range of subjects taught was too broad, but they liked meeting Elderhostelers with varied backgrounds and interests.

Getting In: No problems reported.

Getting There: Biddeford can be reached by expressways, interstate buses, or plane to Portland.

Brunswick—Bowdoin College

Courses of Study: Autobiography; Southeast Asia; Present European Politics; Environmental Geoscience; Human Personality and Ultimate Reality; International Environmental Law

Quality of Instructors: The academics are top-notch, the courses serious, and the Elderhostelers intellectually curious.

Environment: Brunswick, a small town close to Casco Bay, is situated on Route 1, just 27 miles northeast of Portland. The town of 20,000 people, an old fur-trading post, now caters to the college, the state's oldest institution of higher learning. Founded in 1794 and named for the then governor, Bowdoin counts Longfellow, Hawthorne, and Admiral Robert E. Peary among its distinguished graduates. The school challenges its 13,500 students and enjoys a reputation for excellence.

Housing: "First class." Elderhostelers stay in single bedrooms attached to sitting rooms in Coles Tower, a sixteen-story residential building that is equipped with an elevator.

Food: It is said that students enroll at Bowdoin for the food, reputed to equal that of a four star restaurant. My reviewers, unaware of this hoopla, rated the cuisine "superb."

Unique Attributes: An Elderhostel junkie described Bowdoin as one of the best of many hostels attended. This is a first-class institution located ideally for touring the rugged midcoast area of Maine. Harriet Beecher Stowe lived in the Stowe House on Federal Street while writing *Uncle Tom's Cabin*. If visiting Bowdoin in July, you might take the 16-mile drive to Bailey's Island Tuna Tournament. You might see someone pull in a 700-pound giant bluefin. And don't miss L. L. Bean, the country gentleman shopper's mecca; open 24 hours a day.

Shortcomings: None.

Going Solo: Among my panelists was a single man who gave Bowdoin a 5 out of 5. "The single rooms, with adjacent sitting rooms, is an arrangement conducive to after-class socializing," he wrote.

Getting In: Extremely difficult. Expect waiting lists or a lottery.

Getting There: Portland is served by all forms of public transportation, but a car is a necessity if one wishes to enjoy any excursions.

Bryant Pond—Maine Conservation School

Courses of Study: Birds, Bugs, and Botany; The Maine Woods; Flowers, Forests, and Folklore

Quality of Instructors: A group of experts who care passionately about the outdoors.

Environment: The school is located in a bucolic setting on Lake Christopher, a lovely wooded lake surrounded by tall white pines. The campus is nestled in the foothills of the White Mountains with an atmosphere both rugged and relaxed. Inland Maine is sparsely settled, but all those trees have made the state a leader in papermaking, toothpick manufacturing, and the Christmas tree industry. Winters in Maine are harsh and snowy, but the sunny summers are filled with tourists, small country fairs, and craft shows.

Housing: Accommodations are in log dormitory cabins with communal baths. Some reviewers rated the housing as inadequate; others accepted the rustic quality of the barracks.

Food: The meals are poor. "Skimpy food served on metal messkits with no extras and no seconds."

Unique Attributes: The setting is very beautiful and lends itself to the study of nature. Elderhostelers are invited to meander up mountains, slog bogs, and wade in cool creeks. Life in rural Maine moves at a slow pace, and the laconic Yankees live close to the land, much as the early settlers did. During the drive to Bryant Pond one journeys through tall pine forests and agricultural areas where the dominant crops are potatoes and blueberries.

Shortcomings: If nostalgic for the bygone imperfections of Boy Scout or Girl Scout camp, this adventure is for you. Be prepared to rough it for a week.

Getting In: No difficulties reported.

Getting There: Accessible only by private car. My panelists suggest that you avoid the monotonous interstate highways and follow backcountry roads to Bryant Pond.

Camden—Figaro Sailing Program

Courses of Study: Sailing, Seamanship, and Coastal Studies; Flora and Fauna of the Maine Islands; Cooking and Nutrition in the New Age

Quality of Instructors: Excellent, especially the first mate.

Environment: "Anchors aweigh." The Atlantic Ocean—you can't beat it!

Housing: Aboard a small, 51-foot yawl that accommodates six Elderhostelers and a crew of six. With a limited number of single and double berths on board, hostelers traveling alone may be assigned to share a double berth.

Food: Simple but hearty strictly vegetarian vittles are served on board.

Unique Attributes: Elderhostelers live aboard a sailboat and sail to a different island each day, after embarking from the picturesque harbor of Camden. A voyage under sail has a uniquely exhilarating element of risk. Elderhostelers learn sail handling, trimming, anchoring, and coastal navigation. They try beachcombing on uninhabited islands and study the flora and fauna.

This Elderhostel is truly an adventure. It requires skill and endurance to learn how to conquer the winds and currents, to battle tides, and to steer a course through twisting channels in all kinds of weather. The sea is a strict disciplinarian.

Shortcomings: The quarters are very crowded. If the weather is very cold or wet for an extended period, the close quarters would probably be too confining.

Going Solo: Lone travelers shouldn't hesitate to try this exhilarating activity, but remember the quarters are small and you may have to share a double berth.

Getting In: No problem reported, though it's hard to believe the program doesn't have long waiting lists.

Getting There: Camden can be reached by bus, plane, or private automobile.

Portland — Westbrook College

Courses of Study: Masterpieces of French Art; The Piano in Contemporary Music; How to be Comfortable with Computers; Human Development, Stages in Loving; Strange People and Exotic Places

Quality of Instructors: Very sincere, particularly the concert pianist who performs as well as lectures.

Environment: The campus is located on the quiet, tree-shaded streets of Portland, a famous old fishing port. Its piers abound with craggy-faced fisherman hauling in lobsters, clams, and cold-water fish. Portland is an often-used jumping-off place for touring inland Maine and for driving up the rockbound coast where one can find busy beaches cheek-to-jowl with pricey waterfront homes. Artists and writers find creative inspiration in the rugged coast and in the spirited individuality of the people.

Housing: Adequate.

Food: College cafeteria-style. Lots of wonderful blueberries and fresh fish.

Unique Attributes: The Joan Whitney Payson Gallery on the campus is a little gem of a museum used as part of the art class. Portland offers a variety of cultural opportunities: a resident theater company, an art museum, a symphony orchestra, and a contemporary dance company. The Portland String Quartet is renowned throughout the country. Situated on the coast, Portland is an ideal location for relaxing on the pier to watch lobster boats being loaded with traps or to admire the skilled shipbuilders, who still build seaworthy vessels by hand.

Shortcomings: None. Westbrook has been offering Elderhostel programs for the past ten years, and the administration has become very proficient.

Getting In: No problems reported.

Getting There: Portland is a major city and is easily reached by plane, train, or interstate bus.

Presque Isle—University of Maine

Courses of Study: Body Recall (a nonstrenuous, gentle exercise class); China's Changing Face; Computer Workshops; Introduction to Canoeing; Forestry in the North; The Soviet Union and the Soviet State

Quality of Instructors: All of the teachers are excellent. The exercise instructor makes the workout "good fun," and the other professors are outstanding.

Environment: Presque Isle, located in the northeast corner of Maine bordering New Brunswick, Canada, is a small town in the heart of potato farm country. The University of Maine's branch campus, a four-year coed institution for 1,285 undergraduates, is walking distance from the town.

Housing: Elderhostelers stay in two-person dormitory rooms with common bath facilities.

Food: The cafeteria menu is very good, plentiful, and of considerable variety. Breakfast starts with fresh doughnuts every morning, eggs cooked to order, and a cereal bar. Other culinary treats at Presque Isle are an ice cream machine and a well-stocked dessert bar.

Unique Attributes: The field trips are particularly interesting—the geologic formations, basket weaving at the Micmac Indian Reservation and school, the planetarium, and the visit to Grand Falls, New Brunswick. Informal picnics, on the field trips and at a private camp on a northwoods lake, tend to create a congenial hostel group. The campus has tennis courts, a fitness center, and a renowned, old summer playhouse.

An Allagash wilderness canoe trip is offered for very physically fit hostelers. Some portaging and white water canoeing is required. Nights are spent in tents along the waterway.

Shortcomings: "None," commented my panelists. They didn't mind the very hilly terrain of the campus.

Getting In: "A breeze—it was our first choice."

Getting There: My panelists drove up the coast of Maine, but one could reach Presque Isle by Greyhound or Trailways bus.

Waterville—Thomas College

Courses of Study: International Politics and Arms Control; Presidential Politics and the Media; Creative Awareness; Computer Studies; Drama, the Jewish Mystique; I Can Draw Anything

Quality of Instructors: The instructors are excellent. In addition to professors from the college, courses are taught by experts in the various fields.

Environment: Thomas College offers hostelers a serene setting. The landscaped campus for just 832 students is situated in the outskirts of the town along the Kennebec River. Waterville is the entrance to the Belgrade Lakes region—glistening lakes surrounded by woodlands filled with dark evergreens and slender white birches.

Housing: Elderhostelers have ground floor, private rooms with baths in a motel-like building.

Food: Very good classic college fare is served in an appetizing fashion.

Unique Attributes: The program is very well organized and operated. The extracurricular events are particularly interesting; hostelers go to the theater in the restored 1902 Opera House and visit the Player Piano Museum. Waterville is just an hour's scenic drive through the uninhabited reaches of the state from the rockbound coast. Maine is the largest of the New England states and distances are extensive between the inland cities. North and west of Waterville one can still find backcountry roads that follow lovely winding rivers.

Shortcomings: No faults were found in the Waterville program.

Getting In: The waiting lists have become very long at Thomas College. One reviewer had to try three times before acceptance.

Getting There: Waterville has limited commuter plane service from Boston but very good interstate bus service.

MARYLAND

Baltimore—Peabody Institute of Johns Hopkins University

Courses of Study: A Survey of Jazz; The Mythology of the Wagner Ring; William and Henry Walters as Art Collectors; Preludes, Melodies, and Le Ballet; Great Violinists, Great Violin Concertos; Piano Music of the 20th Century; History of Opera

Quality of Instructors: Because Peabody is a favorite destination for so many Elderhostelers, I received numerous evaluations of this program. Ratings of instructors ranged from distinguished to first rate to talented to just fair. One respondent wrote that he had learned from experience that "good musicians are not necessarily good teachers." The music classes are augmented by the use of recordings and the piano, and the museum course is conducted by a docent of exceptional ability.

Environment: Peabody sits right in the middle of Baltimore, a cosmopolitan city that still retains some provincial charm. The architecture of Peabody combines ornate French and English Renaissance. Baltimore has recently been revitalized and given a face lift. A decrepit harbor has been transformed into a glittering array of boutiques and restaurants. One can even cruise the harbor in a ship. The aquarium and Walter's Art Gallery, built in the style of an Italian Renaissance palazzo, are two of the big-city treats to be found in Baltimore. The old city still has homes with bright white marble stoops on cobblestone streets.

Housing: Elderhostelers sleep in modern, air-conditioned dormitories. The high-rise, elevator buildings that surround a central mall are adequate. Separate men's and women's lavatory facilities are on the same floor. The bedrooms are good size, and there's a pleasant central lounge. When revisited, the urban dormitories were found "down at the heels."

The Peabody management was so appalled by the lengthy lists

Peabody Conservatory, Baltimore (Photo: Barbara L. Silvers)

of rejected hostelers, they have instigated triple sessions. Some Elderhostelers are housed in a motel with all meals and classes held in the same facility. They go to the institute only for daily evening recitals. My repeat reviewers, ardent Peabody alumni, reported "no diminution of the musical experience."

Food: Predictable college fare is served in a student dining room. "It is ordinary college food—not gourmet." A more critical couple, with a great deal of Elderhostel experience, judged the food "poor." One couple wrote, "Baltimore's wonderful seafood gave us midwesterners restaurant fever."

Unique Attributes: Peabody Institute educates intense, dedicated students of music, and the Elderhostelers reflect this serious approach. In the spring, many high-quality recitals are given by graduating students, and Elderhostelers are encouraged to attend the concerts because the students need practice playing before an audience. In addition, concerts and master classes are frequently given by Peabody faculty. Discount tickets to the Baltimore Symphony are available.

"You are surrounded by music from early morning through bedtime. The sounds of voice and instruments pour from practice rooms constantly, delightfully." "Wall-to-wall music," enthused another panelist. "For anyone interested in music this is heaven!"

Peabody is within walking distance of the waterfront redevelopment, restaurants, two outstanding art museums, and recently gentrified areas of the city. Public transportation is convenient and has good schedules. Program directors are "helpful, good-humored, and accommodating."

Shortcomings: Peabody always receives accolades for its program. My sample would indicate that Peabody is as popular on the East Coast as the University of Judaism is on the West Coast. However, the critical couple found the food not as good as most of the Elderhostels they have attended. When revisited, "the classrooms were in a shambles. . . recording and tape players did not work." If you dislike the ambience of a city motel, I suggest supplementing your registration with a telephone call.

Going Solo: Rated 5 out of 5. Single accommodations are available. "Several singles in our group, all veteran Elderhostelers.

They seemed very comfortable and added to the group's [musical] education due to their experience."

Getting In: Peabody is a very popular destination and usually has waiting lists for the Elderhostel program, particularly in the spring when student recitals are required by the curriculum. Even with early registration, admission is not assured. Apparently the move to triple sessions has eased the length of the waiting lists. Just go for it.

Getting There: Baltimore is served by all forms of public transportation. Major air carriers, buses, and railroads all have frequent service.

Ocean City—University of Maryland, Eastern Shore

Courses of Study: Issues in Love Relationships; Hearts of Flame (literature, poetry, short story); From Court Jesters to Clowns; Eastern Shore Architecture; Chesapeake Bay Harvest; Literature and Film

Quality of Instructors: The university has three hundred major subjects. Some departments are sound, some average, and some poor.

Environment: The Carousel Hotel is located directly on the boardwalk that fronts the Atlantic Ocean. For nostalgia buffs, this is hotel genus American Seaside of the 1880s. Ocean City is primarily a summer resort; the weather during other seasons is unpredictable. Some reviewers lucked out with pleasant temperatures in February, while others found it cold and windy in November.

Housing: The Carousel is a luxury hotel with double beds, private baths, and kitchenettes. There is even maid service.

Food: "Dreadful. Breakfast was the only decent meal." Only one dinner entrée is offered, either regular or vegetarian. Lunch is a sandwich.

Unique Attributes: The hotel has an indoor pool, an indoor skating rink, luxurious sleeping quarters, and a lovely dining room that overlooks the ocean. Beachcombing or boardwalk biking or strolling can be delightful. Scenic national and state parks are nearby but only convenient for individuals with their own automobiles.

Shortcomings: The pool, sauna, and skating rink are available for a fee when they are operative. One couple who labeled Ocean City the worst of 23 Elderhostels attended were there during a week that none of the facilities were open. In addition, there were no planned extracurricular activities and no rooms provided for the hostelers to talk and lounge. Another couple voted Ocean City the worst of 11.

Going Solo: This destination is only for solitary, beachcombing types. The limited accessibility, lack of a lounge, and inadequate resident coordinator are negatives for single travelers.

Getting In: Reputedly, this is one of the movement's most popular destinations. Long waiting lists and lotteries are common. I, too, have tried unsuccessfully to register a couple of times but shan't try again until I hear a different story from my reviewers.

Getting There: An easy drive from East Coast urban areas; tricky if you want to use a combination of public transportation. One may fly or take Amtrak to Washington, then hop a Greyhound bus. The Elderhostel management is not very cooperative.

Takoma Park—Columbia Union College

Courses of Study: Revolutions and Science; Music of Black Composers; Historical Survey of Washington, D.C.; Health Psychology; It's Strictly for the Birds; How to Use a Home Computer

Quality of Instructors: The college professors at Columbia Union are excellent.

Environment: The school is situated just 7 miles from Washington, D.C., and offers a wonderful opportunity for students to get to know and see our capital firsthand. Takoma Park is really a bedroom community for Washington. This college is a church-related school. The Seventh Day Adventists prohibit any smoking or drinking of alcoholic beverages on campus.

Housing: Elderhostelers stay in quite satisfactory student dormitories. The dorms are air-conditioned, and single rooms are available.

Food: Rated good to excellent. Very tasty vegetarian, with a well-stocked salad bar, delicious casserole dishes, and a frozen yogurt machine. Great home-baked goods, too. Despite the Seventh Day Adventist belief to the contrary, coffee is served to the Elderhostelers.

Unique Attributes: This is a small college in a suburban community located right on the Washington metro line if one wishes to do any additional sightseeing on one's own. The program-conducted tours of the Smithsonian, the Capitol, the monuments, and the memorials are very interesting and enjoyable because of the harmonious group. If you visit Washington in the spring, try to include a stroll through the National Arboretum, the most comprehensive arboretum in the country and the only one to house a collection of seventy varieties of dogwood.

This is a very conscientiously run program; "The final banquet is as fancy and beautifully set up as any Elderhostel I've attended."

Shortcomings: My reviewers all mentioned the meatless menu that might be a problem for some attendees. Otherwise, no shortcomings were noted.

Getting In: The school's proximity to Washington, D.C., makes it a relatively popular destination.

Getting There: Either taxi or metro can be taken from Washington's National Airport to Takoma Park. One group of hostelers stayed overnight at a motel near Dulles International Airport before proceeding to the college. Washington can also be reached by Amtrak, interstate bus, or private car. The Union Railroad station has recently been remodeled and might be worth a visit to see the refurbished marble floors and architecture reminiscent of Roman baths.

MASSACHUSETTS

Amherst—Amherst College

Courses of Study: Crime and Detective Fiction; Literature to Film; The U.S. and Latin America; The Soviet Union as a Multiethnic State; *Don Quixote,* a Reading of Cervantes' Masterpiece; The Family, Has It a Future?

Quality of Instructors: A plus. Highly renowned academics.

Environment: Amherst is a typical New England small college town. The Lord Jeffrey Inn, just off the town square, is a favorite Hollywood rent-a-locale because of the lovely colonial furnishings and charming gardens. The town's location in the Pioneer Valley provides easy access to all the summer concerts, art exhibits, and ballet offerings at the western end of the Massachusetts Turnpike.

The 1,570 undergraduates are privileged, pressured, and academically exceptional. The Five College Interchange program permits students to take courses at Hampshire, Mount Holyoke, Smith, or the University of Massachusetts.

Food: "At the price you could get a lot worse." "We learned to love that steamed, gingery Indian pudding."

Housing: The Elderhostel dorm is spacious and well kept, but access is difficult.

Unique Attributes: This is a first-class institution, offering a first-class Elderhostel program in a charming area of Massachusetts. The athletic facilities, indoor pool, and tennis courts are more than adequate for a small college. The academic facilities, library, and classrooms are likewise. A campus center houses a theater, snack bar, post office, and game rooms. Local sightseeing could include Emily Dickinson's home in Amherst or a 12-mile drive north to Old Deerfield, a well-preserved ghost of a 300-year-old

hamlet. The few blocks of Old Deerfield's wide main thorough-
fare are lined with exquisite examples of colonial architecture.

Shortcomings: The coordinator is too young and too inexperi-
enced.

Getting In: Luck of the draw. This is a very popular program, with
a limited number of Elderhostel weeks.

Getting There: One can fly to Bradley International Airport in
Windsor Locks, south of Springfield; take a Greyhound bus to
Northampton; or ride Amtrak to Springfield. Obviously, auto-
mobile is the preferred means of transportation.

Amherst—Hampshire College

Courses of Study: The Nuclear Age; Media Analysis; Language and
the Human Mind: Noam Chomsky's New Perspective; Introduction to Semantics: The Meaning of Meaning; A Short History of
History

Quality of Instructors: Dynamic instructors whet the intellectual
curiosity of the Elderhostelers.

Environment: Hampshire College is a relatively young school
founded by a consortium of four neighboring institutions, Amherst, Smith, Mt. Holyoke, and the University of Massachusetts.
It is an academically nontraditional school that encourages
individualism.

The college has a wooded campus located in the Pioneer Valley
near Amherst and Northampton. The school is ideally situated
for enjoying the cultural attractions and special events at all five
colleges, and a free shuttle bus provides transportation between
them. Unlike its more elite neighbors, the campus at Hampshire
is not lush; in fact, it's rather plain.

Housing: The dormitories, built in apartment-style clusters, are
shabby and unappealing and have the usual shared bath facilities.
But they do have kitchens and living rooms.

Food: The cafeteria serves an excellent menu designed to please
the health-conscious school population. "If you're not into

sprouts, you might find the meals on the light side." Meat and fish as well as vegetarian entrées are served.

Unique Attributes: The school boasts excellent recreational facilities. It even has an indoor, glass-enclosed swimming pool and a sauna. Hampshire is an unorthodox small school that encourages creativity. "Hampshire," reported one pair of Elderhostelers, "usually does one serious subject in great depth; therefore, it attracts an intellectually curious, earnest group of Elderhostelers." "One brilliant instructor pursues one subject to a fault. Even the participants are better educated than at any other hostel we've attended," enthused another couple.

The Pioneer Valley is a rich scenic area along the Connecticut River with foliage that glows in both the spring and fall. Downtown Amherst is within walking distance of the campus, and Elderhostelers can enjoy the strip of ultra-chic shops, quaint cafes, and restaurants in town. They can also attend foreign films, concerts, and lectures at the other colleges in the area.

Shortcomings: The accommodations are not up to par.

Getting In: This is a very popular destination during the height of the fall foliage season. But early reservations are mandatory year-round.

Getting There: Buses and limousines carry passengers between Bradley Field and Amherst, but this destination is easily reached by automobile over high-speed turnpikes.

Haverhill—Bradford College

Courses of Study: The Supreme Court; Beethoven; Kings of England; Explorations of the Northwest Passage; The Music of Early America; TV and the American Culture

Quality of Instructors: "A friendly, warm faculty that is outstanding, excellent, and knowledgeable."

Environment: Massachusetts was the nation's leading producer of shoes and textiles in the mid-1800s, and Haverhill was once the shoe center of the state. Relics of that period can still be found in abandoned factory buildings. Bradford College, founded in 1803, lies across the Merrimack River from Haverhill, 30 miles north of Boston. The school has a very broad curriculum for its 450 students.

Housing: Elderhostelers stay in brand-new dormitories with shared bathrooms and no air-conditioning. "The beds are nailed to the floor under the windows."

Food: "Wonderful. The hostelers have their own dining room. The course ends with a farewell lobster dinner!"

Unique Attributes: Despite a week of rain, my respondents enjoyed the field trips and the indoor swimming pool. They found the trip to the reconstructed mill town of Lawrence particularly interesting.

Shortcomings: "The furniture in the Day Room is all plastic. It makes for a very hot Democratic National Convention."

Getting In: No problems reported.

Getting There: Either fly to Boston or enjoy the leisurely sociability of Amtrak to Boston, then North Shore buses to Haverhill. Automobile traffic in and around Boston is very congested.

Northfield — Northfield-Mount Hermon

Courses of Study: Shakespeare's *Othello*; One Voice Two Cultures: Autobiographical Literature; Dante's *Inferno*: Sins and Sinners; Shakespeare's *Henry IV*; Safe at Home: Baseball and the Meaning of Life; Real Crimes in Literature

Quality of Instructors: "Top drawer." "Superb." "Sometimes equaled but never surpassed." One five-year Northfield cheerleader wrote, "The skill and enthusiasm of the teachers is unrivaled in the Elderhostel movement."

Environment: The green rolling hills of this campus have a pleasing symmetry that typifies the best of New England. Two co-

Between-class socializing, Northfield-Mt. Hermon

educational boarding schools make up one large community known as the Northfield-Mt. Hermon School. The campus is a blend of old brick and more recent buildings, fit together like a lovely calendar picture, whose backdrop is a charming view of the distant mountains. From the second and third floors of the dormitories, one can see the Connecticut River winding through the valley.

Housing: Starting in the summer of 1991, Elderhostelers will be housed in a recently renovated dormitory on the Mt. Hermon campus across the river. These accommodations will in all likelihood be better than the dormitories used in the past, and I look forward to reporting the change in the next edition. I do hope the reviewer, once intrigued by the "ancient, hundred-year-old clawfoot bathtubs," will not be too disappointed.

Food: The Elderhostel program at Northfield-Mt. Hermon is privileged to have its own kitchen, staff, and dining room. The menu is fancier and more plentiful than most Elderhostels. Fresh fruit, coffee, and cold drinks are available 24 hours a day. A nice touch.

Unique Attributes: The Elderhostel staff is superbly sensitive to the needs of an Elderhostel population. They are unusually accessible and join the group at all meals and extracurricular activities. The atmosphere is one of mutual respect and appreciation between staff, teachers, and students. One admirer wrote, "This is a model to be emulated throughout the Elderhostel movement."

The school's facilities are excellent. Dormitories and classroom buildings have congenial communal rooms and porches for lounging, an outdoor pool and an Olympic-size indoor swimming pool, and golf and tennis nearby. For the most part, Northfield attracts serious students of literature and Shakespeare. The area is picturesque, and evening activities are well planned. An extracurricular boat ride and picnic supper on the Connecticut River are enjoyable. Within walking distance, there's a general store, post office, and gas station. This is beautiful rural country.

Shortcomings: The lack of air-conditioning or other cooling system in the dormitories, dining room, and almost-new, fine theater can be brutal when New England suffers an unusually hot spell.

Going Solo: Not particularly suitable. The recidivism rate about which Northfield boasts creates a batch of cliquey couples who return year after year. They arrive in automobiles, with prearranged bridge, golf, or tennis foursomes. The scene can be pretty darned clubby. This Elderhostel program even has some trappings of a private club; they mail an annual chatty newsletter to "members." I would suggest this destination only for the most self-confident, outgoing solo travelers. My files include a letter from a single, midwestern woman who, isolated by using public transportation and requesting a single room, had a painfully lonely time at Northfield.

Getting In: Northfield-Mt. Hermon only holds its Elderhostel program for three weeks each summer, so early registration is a must. The program director boasts that Northfield has the highest reenrollment rate in Elderhostel.

Getting There: Northfield-Mt. Hermon is best reached by automobile. Greenfield, Massachusetts, 15 miles away, is served by Amtrak and interstate bus lines. Eastern Airlines flies into Keene, New Hampshire, some 20 miles north.

Rowe—Rowe Conference Center

Courses of Study: Woodland Ecology; Perennial Flower Gardens; Broadway Musicals; Social and Cultural History of New England Folksongs and Balladry; Gentle Hatha Yoga; Cross-Country Skiing

Quality of Instructors: An unusual group of horticulturalists, naturalists, and specialists. All rated excellent.

Environment: The center is tucked away in the mountains within walking distance of a small New England village on the Mohawk Trail, a scenic highway that runs from central Massachusetts to the New York border. An old Indian path following the Cold River, the trail has switchbacks along sheer ravines and passes through a few tiny villages. The conference center is part of a 1,000-acre wildlife preserve. Rowe has a peaceful village green bordered with steepled churches and an old town hall. Low, stone walls mark the property lines and edge the roads. The countryside is particularly spectacular after the first frost turns the white birch leaves to gold and clothes the maple trees in scarlet.

Housing: The old New England farmhouse in which Elderhostelers are housed has adequate shared rooms and one large bath. Privacy is minimal.

Food: "Absolutely beyond belief!" Homemade breads, cookies, desserts, and artistic salads are served family-style.

Unique Attributes: Either try to arrange a fall foliage trip to join the leaf lovers or go in April when the sap begins to run in the sugar maple trees. Make it soon, before this wonderful annual harvest has been completely mechanized by gathering sap through ugly plastic tubing instead of the charming old wooden buckets.

Participants set tables, bus, wash dishes, and scrub large pots and pans. This activity, though resented by some hostelers, in a large measure promotes a real sense of family among participants. Wonderful opportunities are offered for hiking, canoeing, and photographing the countryside. The sweet fragrance of the woodlands will remain in your memory long after you've returned home.

Shortcomings: These are very strenuous programs. The distances walked are very long, and cross-country skiing requires great fortitude. It is essential that the attendees be very congenial because of the elbow-to-elbow KP duty.

Going Solo: A perfect destination except for the limited means of access. The sense of family and the nature of the courses attract a large number of singles.

Getting In: During the height of the fall foliage season, this program develops long waiting lists. Early registration is recommended.

Getting There: Rowe can only be reached conveniently by automobile. One can fly to Hartford / Springfield to the south, take an Amtrak train to Greenfield, or fly to Albany, New York, then rent a car at any of those destinations.

Waltham—Bentley College

Courses of Study: Creative Writing; Civil Law and You; Boston: Historical, Cultural, Commercial; The New England Tales of Nathaniel Hawthorne; The Joy of Computing

Quality of Instructors: "Top-notch." What with fifty colleges in a 30-mile radius of Boston, the atmosphere is academically invigorating and highly competitive.

Environment: Waltham, 9 miles from downtown Boston, is a lovely, quiet, pleasant community on the shores of the Charles River. The town, an early industrial center, was the site of the state's first paper mill. Bentley College sits on a hill several miles from any commercial activity, and offers the best of both worlds —a self-enclosed green suburban campus, with easy ties to the metropolis on the clean, subway system called the T. The tree-shaded 110-acre campus has very hilly terrain.

Housing: A plus. "Dormitories in the best condition I've ever seen," wrote an Elderhostel addict with 26 notches in his gun. These are new, air-conditioned residential buildings.

Food: Excellent Marriott food service.

Unique Attributes: Field trips to Boston, one of the country's most interesting cities; its narrow, winding streets are rich in history. Visit the "Cradle of Liberty," Paul Revere's House, Old North Church, or Faneuil Hall. On your own, you might take in the 24-acre Public Garden, the country's oldest botanical garden, rowing regattas on the Charles River, or Boston Pops free concerts given on the Common all summer. Don't miss the gracious, gaslit Beacon Hill area; it's still the city's bastion of Brahminism.

Shortcomings: Classrooms are crowded, and air-conditioners are noisy. However, I believe many New England destinations would welcome a noisy air-conditioner during a hot, humid summer. Good walking shoes are recommended for climbing Boston's charming old cobblestone streets.

Going Solo: Five out of five because the program is well planned and well executed. "Staff do everything possible to make the week pleasant," wrote a seasoned single traveler. "Highest recommendation."

Getting In: Not yet a problem. I imagine Bentley's popularity will increase after this positive evaluation.

Getting There: Logan International Airport in Boston. Greyhound bus and Amtrak offer frequent service to Boston. There is bus service from the campus to the airport or train station. If you drive to Waltham, I do not suggest using your own car for sightseeing in Boston. As a 19-year resident of Massachusetts, I can testify to the narrow, curved streets with blind corners and irrascible drivers. A rigorous ordeal for the uninitiated.

Williamstown — Williams College

Courses of Study: Philosophy of Religion; Culture of Modern Japan; Analysis of *Macbeth* and Ghosts

Quality of Instructors: Exceptional academic programs are taught by caring, cooperative professors. The atmosphere is intellectually exciting.

Environment: Williamstown, at the western end of the Mohawk Trail, is a charming college town of just 9,000 people. The town, like the college, has lovely ivy-covered brick buildings and tree-shaded sidewalks. The setting is idyllic: the Berkshire mountains are snow-covered in the winter, rich and green through the spring and summer, and a blaze of scarlet and gold in the autumn. Williams, with only 2,000 undergraduates, is a small school with a big reputation for providing quality education. It is tucked into a wooded countryside, and the school grounds, lawns, and walks are meticulously cared for.

Housing: Student dormitories with unusually spacious single rooms and shared bath facilities. Above average.

Food: Plentiful and very good.

Unique Attributes: Williamstown is the home of two fine art museums, most unusual for a small town. The Clark Art Institute has an unbelievable collection of French impressionist paintings, including 53 Renoirs; and there is the recently renovated college art museum. The Summer Repertory Theatre is famous as the place where many Hollywood and Broadway stars have gotten started in the profession.

Shortcomings: No provisions are made for any sightseeing trips.

Getting In: This is a *very* popular destination. I have tried unsuccessfully to register at Williams and have heard tales about long waiting lists and many, many attempts to win acceptance.

Getting There: My reviewers took a long, pleasant bus ride from New York City. I would suggest flying to Bradley Field at Windsor Locks, Connecticut, renting a car, and making the long, beautiful drive from Greenfield to Williamstown over the Mohawk Trail. The 67-mile road has a classic hairpin turn, switchbacks, and memorable vistas of Mt. Greylock and the Deerfield River.

MICHIGAN

Bloomfield Hills—Cranbrook Educational Community, Academy of Art

Courses of Study: Cranbrook: A World of Art and Science; Poetry and the Pursuit of Value; Astronomy, the Space Above Us

Quality of Instructors: "Outstanding." "Tremendous instructors in poetry and astronomy."

Environment: Bloomfield Hills is a fashionable suburban community 25 miles north of Detroit, the automobile manufacturing capital of the United States. There are 360 acres of spectacular landscaping, gardens, sculpture, and fountains. The buildings are architectural gems designed by the Saarinens. An air of elegance and history pervades the academy. "Outstanding."

Housing: Luxurious accommodations in a carpeted castle. No air-conditioning, but quiet fans are provided.

Food: A kitchen force of three people prepares meals exclusively for the Elderhostelers. The menu is comparable to an excellent hotel.

Unique Attributes: All of Saarinen's designs—buildings, furniture, drapes, and fixtures; the sculpture by Carl Millis and his students; the spectacular museum and church. Outstanding tours of these various components of the educational community are conducted by experts. "The attention, foresight, and devotion of Jean Smart and her associates is a marvel to behold and experience." Her attendance to detail includes "bellhop" check-in service and delivery of luggage to rooms. "Best of five Elderhostels," wrote one of my reviewers.

Shortcomings: The high-ceilinged dining room tends to be noisy. In an intense heat wave, the lack of air-conditioning might be troublesome.

Going Solo: Quite suitable. "Art buffs would love it." One of my panelists interviewed the single participants during his stay. All were pleased and satisfied with the congeniality of the group.

Getting In: At this writing, Cranbrook is not yet oversubscribed.

Getting There: Detroit is a major transportation center with frequent plane service, interstate buses, and trains. Regular van service runs from the airport or bus stations to Bloomfield. It's about a 40-minute drive.

Mt. Pleasant—Central Michigan University

Courses of Study: Faith, Fantasy, and Folktales; Women Artists of the Eighteenth Century; Amusing and Amazing Musical Anecdotes

Quality of Instructors: "If not the best of all—certainly equal to the best."

Environment: Mt. Pleasant lies in the heart of Michigan, on land that was an early hunting ground for the Chippewa Indians. Magnificent pines and hardwoods led the area to become a major lumbering center. The university has a fine, wooded campus set amid beautiful scenery.

Housing: Two bedrooms, sitting room, and bath for each two persons. Very clean and in very good repair.

Food: "Fancy dancy." "As good as any summer resort. Wide choices, nicely prepared, with a printed daily menu." "Cakes and cookies all made on the premises! And a festive farewell dinner that is remarkable. Would you believe voice and piano dinner music?"

Unique Attributes: The campus has an excellent swimming pool and very friendly students. The program has two dedicated directors and an exceptionally fine mix of extracurricular offerings. A favorite field trip takes the hostelers to the Chippewa Indian Reservation, which abuts the town of Mt. Pleasant. There's also the Chippewa Nature Center, a 900-acre park of woods, fields, ponds, and rivers. Mid-Michigan offers a wide variety of recreation opportunities: horse racing, golf at 6 tournament courses, canoeing on the Chippewa River, antiquing, as well as the largest county fair east of the Rockies.

I hope you won't need the health services, but an acquaintance described a very reassuring experience with two "wonderful" doctors at the health clinic.

Shortcomings: None. One panelist, returning to Mt. Pleasant for a second visit, wrote, "I went with some trepidation. Could it be as good as I remembered? It was *better.*"

Going Solo: One single panelist gave this destination a 5 out of 5. "The program is so full there's little time to feel alone, and there's a lovely lounge where everyone mingles. Someone is always looking for a bridge fourth or a voice to join impromptu concerts."

Getting In: No doubt it will be more difficult from now on.

Getting There: It is an effortless drive from the airport in Lansing, Michigan, to Mt. Pleasant. The town is located right off the major north / south highway in the state.

Rochester Hills—Michigan Christian College

Courses of Study: Fine Tuning Your Listening Skills; Nature Walks and Talks; You Can Make the Difference!

Quality of Instructors: "Jovial and very articulate." "Top-notch academics."

Environment: The college has a delightfully small, friendly campus around two lakes and the Clinton River. It is a coeducational Christian school that prohibits smoking anywhere on its grounds. Rochester Hills lies just a half hour drive north of Detroit; the winds from Lake Michigan make the area one of the cloudiest sections of the United States. Michigan is a state of two peninsulas separated by Lake Michigan; the upper peninsula is best known as "the shores of Gitchee Gumee." This is a vacationland of 11,000 lakes and rivers.

Housing: Alma Gatewood dormitory is built with one bathroom for each pair of double rooms.

Food: The college cafeteria, catered by Marriott, is very well managed, and a choice of two entrées is offered to diners.

Unique Attributes: The college president establishes this program's uniquely convivial atmosphere when he rolls out the welcome mat at the opening orientation meeting. This Michigan-style *willkommen* creates a special esprit among Elderhostelers. After the congenial kick-off, students mingle freely with the faculty and are in a receptive frame of mind for all the courses. The music instructor illustrates his lectures with wonderful recordings; the course on interpersonal relations is a lively exchange of ideas; and the evening on-campus programs are great.

Shortcomings: Smokers would definitely have a problem on this campus.

Getting In: My reviewers attended this particular program as a second or third choice when they were unable to get in elsewhere. Michigan Christian College proved to be an unexpected treat, "a wonderful surprise—we'd recommend it unconditionally."

Getting There: Take public transportation to Detroit and rent a car for the 24-mile drive to Rochester Hills if you wish to explore some of upper Michigan's lakes and rivers before or after the Elderhostel.

MINNESOTA

Camp Northland—Vermilion Community College

Courses of Study: A Changing Global Environment; Spring Means Wildflowers; Antique Collectibles: The Best of the Old; The Steger North Pole Expedition; Storytelling: Art, History, and Culture; Painting Along the Lakeshore

Paddling a canoe similar to those of the 1800s fur traders, Burnside Lake, Minnesota
(Photo: Bill Behrends)

Quality of Instructors: A very pleasant couple conducts the program both indoors and out. The woman enhances the courses with craft and candle-making demonstrations.

Environment: This program is given at Camp Northland, a YMCA camp on the wooded shore of Lake Burnside 18 miles north of Ely. This is remote northwoods, almost on the Minnesota / Canadian border. The camp is located 0.25 mile south of a unique region known as the Boundary Waters Canoe Area Wilderness. Ely, a village of just 3,800, is located within the Superior National Forest, a place of unbelievable natural beauty.

Housing: Elderhostelers are housed in double- and triple-occupancy, heated cabins. Toilet and shower facilities are in a centralized building. Classes and activities are conducted in a communal lodge.

Food: Plain, home-cooked food is served in a lakeside dining hall.

Unique Attributes: Because of the nature of the institution, this program has daily flag raising and lowering ceremonies as well as a prayer before each meal and at the evening campfires. This program offers a wonderful week of spiritual rebirth and renewal as well as an opportunity to enjoy sunsets, stars, and sunrises in a lovely setting. When not in class studying wildlife preservation and protection of our natural lands, Elderhostelers are free to paddle the canoes, swim in the lake, fish in the ponds, and sail. After a second visit a couple wrote, "There are so many wonderful things to do one doesn't want or need to go anywhere."

Interaction with the adjacent children's camp makes the evenings more interesting.

Shortcomings: The centralized shower and toilet facilities are some distance from the sleeping cabins, a problem for night usage.

Getting In: No problems reported.

Getting There: Private vehicles are necessary for traveling to Lake Burnside. One could fly to Duluth and rent a car or board a motor coach there. Duluth is right on the Minnesota / Wisconsin border.

Duluth—College of St. Scholastica

Courses of Study: Bible; From the Great Wall to Tiananmen Square; Chinese Health Practices; Francs, Rubles, and Crowns: A Diversity of Economic Systems; The English Sonnet; Storytales and Storytelling: The Oral Tradition; It's Your Body: Inside and Outside the Kitchen

Quality of Instructors: Excellent. "When the nun scheduled to teach us was hospitalized, we were moved to the University of Minnesota-Duluth campus for a course without missing a beat."

Environment: Duluth, a city of over 90,000, is just a bus ride away from the school. City buses conveniently stop right on the campus. Duluth is an interesting city named for a French fur trader and settled by Scandinavian and German immigrants. It is on the far western edge of Lake Superior, and it is awesome to watch oceangoing vessels sail out of the city headed for the Atlantic Ocean—some 2,400 water miles away. The college sits at the top of a hill with a wonderful view of the lake.

Housing: Elderhostelers stay in modern college dormitories with showers and baths down the hall.

Food: Plenty of good but not fancy food is served.

Unique Attributes: Very fine evening programs are offered at St. Scholastica, while academic programs are handled cooperatively with the University of Minnesota in Duluth. The Bible study course can be particularly stimulating when active participants are members of the three principal Western religions and bring diverse points of view to the discussion.

Shortcomings: An automobile is needed if one wishes to see the off-campus sights of North Shore, Gooseberry Falls, and Split Rock State Forest. Some beds have "weak" mattresses, but one reviewer suggested that attendees request bed boards or an extra firm mattress in advance. If the management can fill all such requests, the problem is not irreparable.

Getting In: Even though this college can accommodate a fair-sized group, early registrations are necessary. This one gets rave reviews.

Getting There: Duluth can be reached by all forms of public transportation. Northwest Airlines has frequently scheduled flights.

Faribault—Shattuck/St. Mary's School

Courses of Study: Woodland Adventures; German-Speaking Countries in Europe; Whatever Happened to "Rosie the Riveter"?; Word Processing: A Computer Introduction

Quality of Instructors: Vigorous and well qualified.

Environment: Faribault is located 50 miles south of the Twin Cities, Minneapolis and St. Paul, which rise out of the plains like an optical illusion. The campus of Shattuck / St. Mary's, a coeducational college preparatory school, has been cited as a historical district. The 175 acres are located on a wooded plateau overlooking the town of Faribault. Nature trails where one can see herons and occasional bald eagles traverse the campus, while giant Canada geese honk overhead.

Housing: The dormitories are English-style limestone buildings. Accommodations are very good.

Food: Excellent. The menu is more stick-to-the-ribs than haute cuisine.

Unique Attributes: The campus is located close to town—a nice walk. The golf course across the street permits free play for students of Shattuck / St. Mary's, and there are tennis courts and a nice indoor swimming pool.

Shortcomings: The lack of air-conditioning in the dormitories can be a problem in June. The climate in this part of Minnesota is more like Nebraska and Iowa, not like the lake regions. My recommendation to all Elderhostelers planning a summer sojourn in a non-air-conditioned dormitory—bring along a novel set in a cold climate. *Dr. Zhivago* comes to mind.

Going Solo: One reviewer, a single man, asked for opinions from a group of single attendees, and they agreed the site was completely acceptable.

Getting In: Not yet a problem.

Getting There: The Twin Cities are a major transportation hub with good connections to Faribault.

St. Joseph—College of St. Benedict

Courses of Study: "Who Do You Say That I Am?" Diverse Portraits of Jesus in the Gospels; Creative Writing: A Gift from the Past for the Future; The American Indian: Fact and Fiction

Quality of Instructors: "An excellent group of instructors who piqued our interest."

Environment: St. Joseph is a very small town, with a population of approximately 1,500. St. Cloud, 5 miles away, has a shopping center and good restaurants. This is the area of Minnesota immortalized by Garrison Keillor, the radio humorist, in his book, *Lake Wobegon Days*. St. Joseph may be "the town that time forgot, that the decades cannot improve." The area was settled by Norwegians and Germans, who grow wheat, corn, oats, and alfalfa. St. Benedict is a four-year Benedictine college located 70 miles northwest of the Twin Cities.

Housing: The accommodations are all modern, well kept, clean, and comfortable. Some of the dormitories and apartments are new, air-conditioned, and in excellent condition.

Food: Well-prepared meals are served in a ground-level, air-conditioned dining room that is conveniently located adjacent to the dormitories and classrooms.

Unique Attributes: The small town environment is charming, and St. Joseph is just an hour and a half away from the Twin Cities. The trip can be made by bus, although only one trip daily is scheduled each way. St. Benedict is a liberal arts school for women, St. John's University in Collegeville is the brother school for men, and St. Cloud State University is a close neighbor.

Minnesota is a pleasant surprise for people from the south, west, and east—this state has ten thousand lakes!

Shortcomings: No shortcomings reported.

Getting In: There's a waiting list every summer for this much-in-demand program. One pair of Elderhostelers wrote that they tried three times before they were accepted.

Getting There: St. Joseph can be reached by interstate bus and commuter flights on Midwest Aviation.

Winona—St. Mary's College

Courses of Study: River Journey: A Study of the Upper Mississippi; Memory: Mastering the Art of Remembering and Forgetting; The Plight of Job: Prototype of a Successful Failure

Quality of Instructors: The quality varies from well prepared and well informed to a "warm, interesting maverick whose digressions were as fascinating as his subject matter."

Environment: St. Mary's has a beautiful 350-acre campus. Downtown Winona, a picturesque river town secluded in the Hiawatha Valley, is just 2 miles away. Do you remember how Hiawatha in Longfellow's poem "crossed the mighty Mississippi" and stood on the meadow at "the Great Red Pipestone Quarry"? You can see both the quarry and the Mississippi on this adventure. Pipestone, also known as catlinite, is a soft red stone revered and used for centuries by Indians.

Housing: Elderhostelers are housed in very adequate, traditional dormitories, neither fancy nor air-conditioned.

Food: A vast variety of excellent food is served in an air-conditioned dining room. The final banquet is an elegant affair with linen cloths and napkins and silver-plated samovars.

Unique Attributes: St. Mary's is a small college under the auspices of the Brothers of the Christian Schools and has a Catholic viewpoint. It is located only 120 miles from St. Paul and Minneapolis. The romance is not all gone from the Upper Mississippi River. It is still home to modern barges hauling cargo and is the largest resting spot in North America for bald eagles, whistling swans, and falcons. Watch out! Winter comes early, can be bitter cold, and stays late in Minnesota.

The program makes good use of its location on the water, in the woods, and on the campus.

Shortcomings: The shower room can be too messy for fastidious Elderhostelers, but the problem could be solved with the use of less skimpy shower curtains. The lack of air-conditioning in the dormitories makes them uncomfortable during a summer heat wave.

Getting In: No problems reported.

Getting There: Good public transportation is available, and Winona is situated on major thruways. Rochester, Minnesota, has the nearest airport.

MISSOURI

Hannibal — Hannibal-La Grange College

Courses of Study: Mark Twain Studies

Quality of Instructors: A group of teachers who bring a fresh perspective and enthusiasm to a familiar subject.

Environment: Hannibal-La Grange is a Southern Baptist institution. Smoking and the use of alcoholic beverages on campus are prohibited. The town has been immortalized as the birthplace of Mark Twain. It sits on the shores of "Old Muddy," the brown Mississippi River.

Housing: Elderhostelers are housed in very comfortable air-conditioned buildings.

Food: The school practices Mark Twain's dictum, "Nothing helps scenery like ham and eggs."

Unique Attributes: Hannibal is a living memorial to the city's most famous son, Samuel Langhorne Clemens. It has the Mark Twain Museum, the Mark Twain Cave, Jackson's Island, and even Mark Twain Lake with a picnic grove on its shore. The famous fence is marked with a plaque and stands next to Clemens's boyhood home. A towering bronze statue of Twain looks over his beloved Mississippi from a park, and a statue of Tom Sawyer and Huck Finn honors the adventurous boys. One can almost feel the presence of Huck Finn and Injun Jim. The course covers Twain's historical fiction, social fiction, essays, humor, travel books, and short "tall" stories, as well as the better-known classics. The school has a nine-hole golf course and lovely wooded walking paths from which one can watch the streamlined river boats that have replaced the stern- and side-wheelers traveling the Mississippi.

Getting In: None of my reviewers reported any problems.

Getting There: One has the option of using almost all forms of public transportation to get to Hannibal. Fly to St. Louis for connections to Quincy, Illinois, on a commuter airline; Quincy is 20 miles from Hannibal, so one can finish this journey by bus, limo, or rented automobile.

Potosi—YMCA of the Ozarks

Courses of Study: Human Dynamics and Group Interaction; The Shutter Bug; Natural History of the Ozarks; Journal Writing with a Purpose; Golden Age of the Silver Screen

Quality of Instructors: Courses are taught by naturalists and folklorists sensitive to the importance of our history and the variety of our landscape. "Instructors are excellent and are recognized experts in their fields."

Environment: The camp is situated on the shores of Lake Sunnen, in 3,000 acres of oak and pine forest in the low Ozark mountains, only 1,800 feet above sea level. "The grounds are extensive and beautiful." This is romantic country where the buffalo roamed. Potosi is south of St. Louis, a city frequently considered the boundary between the grain belt and the west.

Housing: Elderhostelers stay in Trout Lodge, in top-notch accommodations with private baths and queen-size beds. The lodge also has a lovely view of Sunnen Lake. "Superb housing. Each room has a patio or balcony facing the lake."

Food: My reviewers gave the meals high praise. "This is a well-known resort that caters to guests expecting the best." "Handsome dining room with scrumptious food." There is a good deal of intermingling with conference guests and vacationers at mealtimes.

Unique Attributes: The classrooms, dining room, and sleeping quarters are all conveniently located in the same building. Wonderful field trips and guided nature hikes are taken to see rocky bluffs, caves, and clear, cold springs. The autumn foliage glows on the hickory, oak, and maple trees on the bluffs. Elderhostelers may hike the trails blazed by Daniel Boone. The course in Ozark history and literature helps us understand from whence we've come and thereby gives us a better sense of where we're going. The trout pond is free to guests who bring their own gear, and there are horses to ride and trails to hike.

Shortcomings: Summers in the Ozarks can be hot, humid, and uncomfortable.

Going Solo: Earned a 4 out of 5. The instructors are in residence and share most activities with the Elderhostelers, and the director and his very good desk staff are immediately responsive to the needs of all guests.

Rooms are only available for double occupancy, a plus or minus depending on your personal taste. There are nice lounges with cards, newspapers, and television, and after classes attendees are free to enjoy the resort facilities rather than having planned activities. Staff make an effort to make mealtimes congenial, and there are lots of early morning hikers and joggers. "Reticent, nonathletic solo travelers had better bring a book or some knitting."

Getting In: Need I say? Most weeks are oversubscribed. Register early.

Getting There: St. Louis is a major transportation center with excellent air, railroad, and bus service. Transportation from St. Louis to Potosi can be arranged.

NEBRASKA

Chadron — Chadron State College

Courses of Study: Heritage of Western Nebraska: Step by Step

Quality of Instructors: Professors are very skilled at integrating their lectures with the field trips. The course covers the culture, history, geology, and social development of the region.

Environment: The campus of Chadron State College sprawls through a town of 6,000 in the Pine Ridge country of northwestern Nebraska. Chadron is located one hour south of the Black Hills and Mount Rushmore. This region of Nebraska is home to modern cowboys in pickup trucks. They work the huge cattle ranches still found on the prairies. The small school is host to only 2,450 students, most of whom come from Nebraska and adjoining states.

Housing: Traditional dormitories that are fully acceptable.

Food: Very good homemade food. One picnic supper of buffalo stew!

Unique Attributes: If it is sightseeing and entertainment you seek, Chadron is the place for you. This school has been hosting Elderhostel programs for over ten years and is very responsive to the needs of their participants. My reviewers voted this destination the "best small college" of a dozen Elderhostels attended. Daily field trips by van visit Custer Park, the Bison Range of the Black Hills, Fort Robinson where Crazy Horse was jailed, the homestead of author Maria Sandoz, and the South Dakota Whitehouse of President Theodore Roosevelt.

Shortcomings: Long since ironed out. Advance mailings tell participants to bring comfortable shoes, cameras, and binoculars. Nebraska suffers great extremes of weather, very cold in the winter and very hot in the summer. It is also plagued by tornados and hailstorms.

Getting In: Not oversubscribed.

Getting There: Greyhound bus and Amtrak are recommended if you do not wish to drive. The nearest major airport is Rapid City, South Dakota.

Cherry County National Forest
near Halsey—Kearney State College

Courses of Study: Listen to the Land (a history of hearty pioneers pressing westward to establish homes); Ecology of the Sandhills; Cultural and Social Life of Homesteaders

Quality of Instructors: Excellent to superior. One much-traveled couple wrote, "Of all the Elderhostels we have attended, these Kearney State instructors are the most knowledgeable."

Environment: The 4H camp is nestled within the rolling hills of the only man-made national park in the United States. The park is one of Teddy Roosevelt's conservation plans, and all the trees were planted and the seeding done during his administration. It is cattle raising country, 50 miles west of Broken Bow and 65 miles northeast of North Platte. Nebraska is not a state frequented by tourists; even ardent travelers do not know this land. One must get off the interstate to discover the real America, to see the regional architecture, a farm combine, a barn, or a grain elevator. Sightseeing in Nebraska means hay, cattle, sand dunes, and tall prairie grass. This is America's heartland, where the spirit of the pioneers and frontiersmen still lingers.

Housing: The Elderhostelers are housed in either double cabins with each pair of rooms sharing a bath or in Eppley Lodge, a segregated dormitory. Extra washbowls are built into each bedroom. The accommodations are rustic but adequate.

Food: Good wholesome food is served in a nice dining hall.

Unique Attributes: This Elderhostel is addressed to nature lovers and photographers. My reviewers report the presentations as outstanding, so mesmerizing they felt themselves a part of the westward movement and settlement! The physical plant of this particular camp is more comfortable than most woodland retreats. There are paved walkways to all cabins and the Elderhostelers' luggage and belongings are transported from parking lot to cabins by motorized carts operated by 4Hers.

Shortcomings: My reviewers had a few minor suggestions such as better lighting on the cabin paths and a more convenient parking lot.

Getting In: This program has a maximum capacity of twenty-two attendees, so early registration is absolutely necessary.

Getting There: This is a remote area in the middle of the state, best reached by automobile. The closest airport is in North Platte, not very close. It handles commuter flights from Omaha.

NEW HAMPSHIRE

Durham — University of New Hampshire

Courses of Study: Word Processing; Personal Writing Skills; Flower Garden Maintenance and Design; The Magic of Opera; Great Trials of History; Spinning Wheels and Patchwork Quilts; African-American Music and Literature

Quality of Instructors: Recently increased attention to academics at the school has improved the faculty. Panelists' opinions—"excellent" to "good."

Environment: Durham is a pleasant, stereotypical New England college town. In fact, the university of 11,131 is the town. This school, 65 miles north of Boston, is where Elderhostel began. The location near the coast between Boston and Portland is ideal for doing a shoreline trek, and you are just an hour's drive from the White Mountains. The seaside villages are not as spectacular as the rockbound coast of Maine, but the neat mansions reflect the area's colonial and maritime past.

Housing: Double check before you enroll. The university is in the throes of a face lift as well as an uplift and currently in the midst of much construction. "Good building, but the interior was ravaged. What a mess!"

Food: Excellent quality.

Unique Attributes: Some splendid facilities—swimming pool, library, and fine conference center. The Memorial Union Building is a great hangout with a good bar and restaurant. The highlight of extracurricular activities is a two-hour boat ride on a lake.

Shortcomings: The miserable condition of dormitories, elevators, and hallways. Lots of walking is required over moderately hilly terrain.

Going Solo: This is just rated a 3 since most attendees will be couples using their own cars. Not much is offered in the way of evening activities.

Getting In: The management has lots of experience with hostelers. They seem to absorb registrants without any difficulty.

Getting There: It is best to drive your own vehicle, but there is bus service from Boston to Durham.

New London—Colby-Sawyer College

Courses of Study: The New England Poetic Tradition; No, But I've Seen the Movie; Politics of South Africa; Currier and Ives; Introduction to Opera; Creative Poetry Writing

Quality of Instructors: A splendid poet; a bright, warm, witty, and wonderful film buff; and a young man who did his level best to breathe life into a dull subject. One panelist wrote, "excellent to good."

Environment: The charming village of New London stretches out along the highway, just 2 miles from Lake Sunapee. The population swells in the summer with lake traffic, fairs, and festivals, despite its lack of a true village square. Lovely dooryard gardens front green shuttered houses where chin-high yellow and orange daylilies lean against the white clapboard walls.

The small, handsome school also fronts the highway. A cluster of lovely red brick buildings surrounds a grassy quad. Just 550 students occupy facilities with a capacity for 750; in fall 1990, the cast changed with the admittance of Colby-Sawyer's first group of male students.

Housing: The dormitory has seen better days, but nothing that some paint, plaster, and soap and water couldn't cure. The bathroom and shower facilities are barely adequate. No air-conditioning and no elevators, but husky students are on hand to wrestle Elderhostelers' luggage up the three flights of stairs.

Food: The Marriott food service is ample, nutritious, and varied. But the cafeteria arrangements share a weakness I've found at sev-

In the crow's nest, Lake Sunapee, Colby-Sawyer College

eral institutions: meals are scheduled at times convenient to the service staff, not the diners.

Unique Attributes: This is Colby-Sawyer's tenth year of hosting programs, so the college is very experienced and administrators are cordial. A new $8 million sports facility with an Olympic pool and an aerobics room is to open in 1991. The splendid library, a converted barn and silo, has won numerous architectural awards.

An activity is scheduled every evening, including a Lake Sunapee boat cruise, a Currier and Ives lecture, square dancing, and a cocktail party. The scene is pleasant for walking, but there are no diversions on campus and not much more in town—a small mall, a general store, and a couple of antique shops.

Shortcomings: The program needs an on-site resident coordinator for medical and other emergencies. The students in residence have daytime jobs elsewhere. All classes are held in the same spacious, soft-chaired room, but it lacks air circulation and acoustics.

In the cafeteria, "Elderhostelers are treated as poor relations!" They were given an ungracious "bum's rush" in and out of the hall in order to accommodate a large scientific conference. Not nice, guys! Leisurely dining is gracious and aids digestion.

Going Solo: An irate single man, a well-traveled hosteler, rated this one a 2. He wrote, "Good place to spend a quiet, restful week. Great place to read, write, or contemplate one's navel. I would not recommend it to any friends." I'd give Colby-Sawyer a 3 because there is a very nice television lounge in the dorm, but the hands-off program director leaves the singles at sea. Colby-Sawyer is primarily accessed by car, so two duplicate bridge clubs could almost fill the dorm, take over the lounge, and leave the unattached hostelers feeling like pariahs.

Getting In: This is a relatively popular destination. I advise a last-minute telephone call to the school to try to pick up a cancellation.

Getting There: A beautiful drive north on superhighways, Interstate 91 or 89. Concord, the state capital, is 35 miles away. One might fly to Concord and rent a car or hop a relaxing Vermont Transit bus in downtown Boston.

NEW JERSEY

Hoboken—Stevens Institute of Technology

Courses of Study: Sigmund Freud; The American Presidency; New York, New York: The Metropolitan Scene; Contemporary American Poetry; Crime and Punishment

Quality of Instructors: A very good faculty is supplemented with foreign-born teaching assistants.

Environment: Hoboken's main attraction is its proximity to New York City. An industrial city, it sits just across the Hudson River, a swim, ferry ride, or 15-minute train ride away. Stevens' undergraduate and graduate schools of engineering are renowned, and the campus offers unobstructed views of the New York skyline.

Housing: For an additional fee, Elderhostelers may reserve single rooms with private baths in an air-conditioned dormitory.

Food: Nourishing but not great institutional meals are served.

Unique Attributes: New York, New York, it's a wonderful town. The program is geared to the needs of hostelers who are unfamiliar with the city and offers them a course in the city's history and current scene. After classes, the group provides a relatively secure way to visit the Big Apple. "This is for able-bodied, out-of-state people who do not know New York," commented one panelist.

Shortcomings: Attendees who do not wish to learn about New York are left without any program from 1:00 p.m. until dinner. No quiet lounge, no bridge tables, "not even a scrabble set!"

Getting In: Easy.

Getting There: Also easy. Fly to Newark International Airport or take Amtrak or commuter train or Greyhound or Trailways bus directly to Hoboken.

Pennington—The Pennington School

Courses of Study: International Perspectives on Soviet Communism; The Art of Acting; American Revolution in Central New Jersey; International Folk Dance; The Arabic People and Their Islamic Religious Faith

Quality of Instructors: Good academicians.

Environment: The historic community of Pennington, New Jersey, just 10 miles north of Trenton, is physically attractive, much like nearby Princeton or the lovely towns of Bucks County, Pennsylvania. Pennington is surrounded by many famous sites of the American Revolutionary War. The private, coeducational school serves a select student body of just 330 advantaged youngsters.

Housing: "Excellent." Single rooms with private bath are available for a minimal extra charge in a new air-conditioned dormitory.

Food: The cafeteria isn't bad.

Unique Attributes: A widely traveled Elderhosteler wrote, "I've been to many hostels, but this leader was exceptional. He, his wife, and children attended to our every need." Wonderful field trips to Longwood Gardens in Delaware, the Mercer Museum, Washington's Crossing, and to Princeton to hear the Westminster Choir.

Shortcomings: Bring your own bed pillows.

Getting In: Despite the school's location among the East Coast megalopolises, the program is not yet oversubscribed.

Getting There: An easy drive from anywhere. The railroad station in Trenton is the nearest Amtrak station, but Princeton is a commuter stop on the New York to Philadelphia line. Newark Airport is a far distance away.

Wayne—William Paterson College

Courses of Study: Evolution: Fact or Fantasy?; From Gossip and Tall Tales to Tale Telling; Television Workshop: The Social Responsibility of Talk Shows; The Invisible, Imperial, and Institutional Presidency; All That Jazz; Immigrant Pursuit of the American Dream

Quality of Instructors: An impressive group of media professionals augments the teaching staff.

Environment: Wayne, a city of 50,000, is located in the heart of New Jersey's industrialized, heavily populated metropolitan zone. Once noted for its thriving textile and dyeing industries, it is now full of silent mills standing amid the residential streets and parks.

William Paterson College has 250 acres of campus for its 9,500 students, a haven of mature wooded landscape high on a hill, with a view of the Manhattan skyline. The school boasts superb modern buildings, a science complex, performing and visual arts center, a health spa, and its own radio / TV studios.

Housing: Elderhostelers are housed in dormitory rooms that are dingy and dirty but air-conditioned.

Food: The new food service is more reliable than the catering service during our last evaluation. It has been graded "pretty good" and "much improved." The Elderhostelers now sit by themselves in an air-conditioned dining room and may mingle with students if they wish.

Unique Attributes: Paterson is a school that educates the inner city youngsters from Paterson and many nearby communities. Elderhostelers are exposed to the career-oriented educational goals of the school and its unique achievements. The Elderhostel TV hands-on workshop actually produces talk shows for WPC-TV, while the same experience prepares undergraduates for jobs in the media.

The Elderhostel field trips to view urban renewal minority housing projects in town and the Paterson Waterfall are unusual experiences. The waterfall is historically significant; it is the reason Paterson was chosen by Alexander Hamilton to be the first industrial city of the fledgling U.S.A. The trip to the Statue of Liberty and the new Immigrant Museum on Ellis Island is much appreciated and is enhanced by the presence of a knowledgeable guide and the security of a group. Hostelers also enjoy plays put on by performing arts students, the use of the indoor pool and an evening of square dancing. There is a new on-site program director who stays overnight on the campus and encourages "day commuters" to join the program.

Shortcomings: This is an institution that has overcome its previous shortcomings. Give them an A for effort.

Getting In: I was told that the program can accommodate many more participants.

Getting There: Wayne lies just across the Hudson River from New York City. It is served by commuter buses with frequent runs to the New York City bus terminal. In addition, it can be reached by major or commuter railroad lines, airplane to Newark International Airport, and multilane arterial highways.

NEW MEXICO

Albuquerque/Rio Rancho Best Western Inn— New Mexico Community Foundation

Courses of Study: Centuries in the Enchanting Land—New Mexico; Traditions in Southwest Landscape Art; Natural History; New Mexican Authors; Wildlife of the Rio Grande; Artistic Traditions of the Southwest

Quality of Instructors: A group of instructors from the University of New Mexico and the College of Santa Fe teach the courses at the inn. The quality varies.

Environment: The Inn is situated in the country 10 miles from downtown Albuquerque, a city of 450,000. Albuquerque is the state's largest city, renowned for its Old Town. This historic area surrounds a plaza where some of New Mexico's best artists and artisans exhibit their work in shops and galleries, and Indians from nearby pueblos spread their wares on blankets. Nearby barrio residents still farm one-acre plots of land. Unfortunately, the rest of Albuquerque is filled with commercial highway strips of gas stations, fast food emporiums, and motels, but it does lie on a bend of the Rio Grande. The climate is high, dry, and invigorating.

Housing: Elderhostelers enjoy private motel rooms with private baths! The very pleasant first-floor accommodations are air-conditioned, too.

Food: "Poor. No choices. Very limited menus—sometimes we were only served sandwiches."

Unique Attributes: "We learned how to spell Albuquerque!" In and around the city, one can see classic gems of pueblo architecture with horizontal lines, thick adobe walls, rounded corners, and earth tones. In an effort to preserve the culture and heritage of the Hispanic settlers, the New Mexico Foundation is currently restoring 100- and 200-year-old crumbling adobe churches.

Shortcomings: Problems were noted with the food and the lack of a central lounge in which groups can gather. The inn needs a bus rather than the "Molly Trolley" for tours. Since the inn is out of town, Elderhostelers without automobiles "feel like second-class citizens."

Going Solo: Too many couples with cars, lack of public transportation, and lack of central lounge for socializing make it a no-no.

Getting In: Moderately difficult now; will become more popular because of the private bath facilities.

Getting There: Albuquerque has good transcontinental air service as well as interstate bus service and trains. Rio Rancho administrators meet Elderhostelers at the airport.

Las Cruces—New Mexico Community Foundation

Courses of Study: Fine Arts and Architecture; New Mexico Style; Storytelling: A Cultural Treasury; Historic New Mexico Architecture; Ancient Art of Egypt, Nubia, and the Sudan

Quality of Instructors: Primarily the owner of the inn and his own architectural firm. The New Mexico Community Foundation is a private, nonprofit organization dedicated to the preservation of the multicultural heritage and way of life in the small villages of the state. The courses relate to the work of the foundation.

Environment: Las Cruces, the second largest city in New Mexico, is some 45 miles north of El Paso and just 40 miles from the Mexican border. It exhibits a pleasant blend of the three dominant cultures, Indian, Spanish, and Anglo. The Organ Mountains lie to the east and the Rio Grande to the west. The Elderhostel program takes place in a lovely restored 100-year-old adobe inn, a beautiful Mexican hacienda in downtown Las Cruces.

Housing: Elderhostelers are accommodated in rather small double rooms with private baths, but no air-conditioning.

Food: "Minimal and repetitious." "Beans, rice, and pasta. Coffee served in Styrofoam, tablecloths not always fresh, and the times for meals are erratic." "Half the hostelers went out for more than one dinner and the farewell dinner never came off—too many had gone out to eat that night."

Unique Attributes: "The kitchen was clean, with beautiful appliances."

Shortcomings: Almost unlimited free time. The only afternoon trip offered is to the university museum, but no transportation is provided. Tickets are sold at $7 each for the evening events at the university. There are no local buses in Las Cruces so hostelers without wheels must rely on expensive taxis. The common room has insufficient furniture and there is no library to engage one's interest or to add to one's knowledge. The group is told on arrival "no field trips or excursions; the purpose of Elderhostel is to educate."

Going Solo: Don't. My single reviewer wrote, "The particular mix of the group was exclusive. A golf foursome brought clubs and played daily, and a card-playing group monopolized the tables after dinner every night."

Getting In: If this program was ever oversubscribed in the past, it won't be in the future.

Getting There: Greyhound and Trailways buses have service to Las Cruces, or one can fly to El Paso International Airport. Of course, a car is the transportation of choice.

Santa Fe—College of Santa Fe

Courses of Study: Ritual: Sacred and Profane; Romance in Opera from the Renaissance to the 20th Century; Survey of Pueblo History; Poetry in the Southwest; Mexico: Good Neighbors, Bad Neighbors; Southwest Indian Arts and Crafts; Puccini: The Man and His Music; Southwestern Geology

Quality of Instructors: Wisely chosen by the program director. Professors or retired professors with the droll humor, wisdom, and

College of Santa Fe, Santa Fe, New Mexico

cynicism that come with maturity. The nonacademicians in the program are highly talented and versatile.

Environment: Santa Fe is one of the most appealing, livable cities in the United States. The state capital, it sits in the foothills of the Sangre de Cristo mountains at an elevation of 7,000 feet. The climate is temperate, and tourists flock to the city all seasons of the year. Strict building codes ensure the architectural heritage, a handsome blend of Indian, Spanish, and Anglo, and building height is restricted.

The college is located right in town within walking distance of shopping and restaurants. The campus boasts a handsome library with an Elderhostel section, an excellent bookstore that sells Elderhostel T-shirts, and a splendid theater, a gift of Greer Garson.

Housing: Elderhostelers stay in college dormitories with semi-private baths. The accommodations are perfectly adequate. There's a small lounge room on each floor with a refrigerator, and coffee is available around the clock.

Food: The food service has been improved by the addition of a salad bar. Don Nolder, the very conscientious director, is making a valiant effort to improve the menu. He gets an A for effort. The unattractive, World War II quonset hut is unimproved. An assortment of fast-food emporiums and some wonderful Mexican restaurants are located just a stone's throw from the college, though the cafeteria offers huevos rancheros for breakfast and tacos for lunch.

Unique Attributes: Santa Fe is an artist and tourist mecca with a labyrinth of shops and art galleries that surround a flower-filled downtown plaza. The heart of Santa Fe since 1610, the plaza, with its shade trees and benches, is a tempting spot to rest and people watch.

Arrangements are made for a night at the world-renowned opera in the summer, but you must buy your own tickets. Some great sightseeing tours, such as the Museum of Folk Art, are included in the registration cost. Some groups attend the theater, and others make field trips to augment their classwork. The backstage tour of the Santa Fe Opera is a special bird's-eye view of the mechanics of building sets and creating costumes—a not-to-be-missed thrill for opera buffs.

The advance mailing, which includes points of interest and driving directions, is very complete. This popular program has embraced a new philosophy under the aegis of its new director. Students and faculty are friendly. Many hostelers stay on for a second week when space permits.

Shortcomings: To thoroughly enjoy the sights and sounds of Santa Fe, a car is necessary.

Going Solo: All the elements necessary for a positive solo experience are present at the College of Santa Fe: spacious single rooms if you wish, a small lounge for after-hours socializing, a solicitous director, staff in residence, and a nice mix of free time and scheduled activities. Though this program appeals to many couples, arrangements are made for the couples to share their automobiles with wheel-less hostelers.

Getting In: This is a very popular destination, but they offer Elderhostel programs 49 weeks a year, so waiting lists should not be too long. In addition, they host very large groups—as many as 100 attendees at one time. From coast to coast, Santa Fe is rated high on a list of desirable places to go.

Getting There: The nearest airport is Albuquerque, and public transportation is available from the airport to Santa Fe. An automobile is a better bet if one wishes to enjoy all of Santa Fe's special attractions. A pair of Elderhostelers from the East Coast recommend flying and renting a car in Albuquerque, or if you prefer the relaxation of the train, Lamy, just south of Santa Fe, is the railhead.

Silver City—Western New Mexico University

Courses of Study: Country School Legacy in America's One-Room Schools; Flora and Fauna of the Southwest; Western Style à Mano Paper Making; Ghost Towns and Mining Camps; Mining, Minerals, and Men: Shaping Southwest New Mexico; Birding in the Southwest

Quality of Instructors: The quality varied from imperfect to excellent, with the professor from the local college given a rating of excellent.

Environment: Silver City is in a sparsely settled area of a sparsely settled state. The town of 10,000 is a pleasant blend of past and present. The area is rich with myths and legends, stories of desperadoes, and booming gold strike towns. The town is still surrounded by working copper mines. Rural Silver City remains a place of long country vistas; the evening sky can be enjoyed without being dimmed by concentrations of street lights and office buildings.

Housing: Elderhostelers are housed in modern, comfortable, double-occupancy dorms on the campus.

Food: Traditional steamtable, no-frills menu.

Unique Attributes: The location of Silver City is this program's greatest asset—just 30 minutes from Gila Cliff Dwellings National Monument where five natural caves are situated high on the face of a cliff. The dwellings were built by Mogollon Indians between 1170 and 1350. One of the caves can actually be visited up a steep trail and steps. The Silver City Museum in a Victorian house with a square tower was the home of a prospector who struck it rich in the 1870s. Mannequins in period attire evoke the mining boom time, and it is possible to visit present-day copper mines. Field trips take hostelers past stark cliffs and shadowy mountains that are spectacular.

Shortcomings: None.

Getting In: My reviewers had no difficulty making reservations.

Getting There: Silver City is definitely off the beaten path, but it can be reached by Greyhound or Trailways bus from Las Cruces. Or fly to El Paso, Texas, and rent a car.

Taos—Las Palomas de Taos

(a nonprofit learning center)

Courses of Study: Pueblo Culture: Southwest Indian Art; Writers and Painters; Taos as an Art Center; Faces of the Southwest

Quality of Instructors: No consensus among reviewers. Opinions ranged from "well-educated in the subject matter" to "enthusiastic" to "disappointing."

Environment: Taos lies in a hollow whose natural beauty, magical sunlight, and red-colored canyons are like an artist's palette. The town is small and quaint and bustles with too many tourists shopping the umpteen stores and galleries that ring the Plaza. Mabel Dodge Luhan was the colorful mistress of a Taos grand salon in the '20s and '30s. She gathered writers like Willa Cather and artists like Georgia O'Keeffe and John Marin to establish a uniquely American art form, its inspiration arising from our own natives, the American Indians. Luhan created an oasis of culture in the Southwest.

Housing: A small group of Elderhostelers can be accommodated in Mabel Dodge Luhan's hacienda called the Big House. The mansion has one "gorgeous room that sleeps five and several other elegant twin-bedded rooms." It has been designated a

At Mabel Dodge Luhan's hacienda, Taos, New Mexico

"historical place in the arts." Most of the rooms have magnificent views of the mountains and fireplaces framed in hand-painted Talavera tile. Staying in the hacienda is an experience to be shared and felt. A new annex adjacent to the hacienda has been opened for Elderhostelers. It is architecturally so perfect, one would believe it was part of the original property.

Food: Very good regional food is beautifully served in the mansion dining room. An American Indian cook prepares southwestern specialties and teaches her culinary skills to interested Elderhostelers. I've heard that this privilege is only earned by a "lucky few."

Unique Attributes: Taos is a paradise for art lovers, particularly for lovers of southwestern art. Local artists are regularly invited as guests of the program. The homelike atmosphere and small number in the group establish a delightful spirit of congeniality. "At the end of five days we felt like old friends in a familiar place." The group interacts from an early morning exercise class through to the evening's activities, which may be as simple as an exhibition of Indian dances. Classes are spread through the day—one morning, one afternoon, and one evening. The gardens and grounds of the hacienda have lots of inviting little sitting areas. A fine reading list is mailed to participants prior to the event.

The Elderhostel hosts are very accommodating. They escort the group to museums and to festivals and dances at the almost 1,000-year-old Taos Indian Pueblo. "It's the next thing to being in Mexico," gushed one very experienced pair of hostelers.

Shortcomings: The housing problems have been solved, leaving the 7,000-foot altitude as Taos' only possible discomfort for some Elderhostelers.

Going Solo: Accessibility would be the only difficulty for a single traveler. Otherwise, the convivial ambience is ideal.

Getting In: This is a very popular program and has limited space. It is absolutely necessary to enroll early. One woman wrote that of ten Elderhostels, Taos is her favorite. She returned a second time to determine if Taos is more beautiful in the winter or summer. "It's a draw," she said.

Getting There: Taos is accessible by major airlines to Albuquerque, then bus to Taos. The commuter airline Mesa Air also makes the run between Albuquerque and Taos.

If you are driving to Taos, give yourself enough time to take the spectacularly scenic "high road." You'll see active pueblos, pueblo ruins, and mountain settlements as the road twists and turns through a national forest. All the photos in the world can't do justice to this drive. By the regular highway, the drive is a 130-mile run.

NEW YORK

Alfred—Alfred University

Courses of Study: Beowolf: Roots of Modern Life in Ancient Past; The American Labor Movement; Aqua Exercise; China: Tiananmen Square; Fit for Life; Electron Microscopy for the Layman

Quality of Instructors: Scholars rated "wonderful to outstanding!"

Environment: Alfred is a small village in the Finger Lakes region of New York State. The area is characterized by gracious living, vineyards, and freshwater pastimes. The environment is rural and pastoral, with innumerable lakes and streams and apple orchards. Queen Anne's lace blooms along the roadsides, farmers sell apples off the tailgates of their trucks, and the trees have a last flashy fling each fall before the bleakness of winter arrives.

Alfred was the first coed university in the state of New York. The school, a small, self-contained college tucked away in the woods, is home to just 2,500 students.

Housing: Elderhostelers stay in traditional dormitories that are more than adequate.

Food: Meals are served cafeteria-style in the school dining room. They are well presented, and there are many choices at every meal.

Unique Attributes: The Finger Lakes were created a million years ago when ice masses formed long narrow lakes in deep gorges. The area is topographically unique and boosters boast about its 1,000 waterfalls.

Very good evening entertainment is scheduled for the Elderhostelers. Programs include chamber music concerts, carillon concerts, and village band performances in town. The 47-bell Davis Memorial Carillon, used for demonstrations and concerts, is the pride and joy of Alfred College. It contains the oldest carillon bells in the Western Hemisphere. Although a small school, Alfred has excellent facilities: a computer center, an observatory with five telescopes, seven tennis courts, and an Olympic-size pool. The student body produces fine theatrical and dance programs, and popular entertainers and rock stars visit the campus, too.

The Elderhostel staff, directress, and assistants received rave reviews. "Considerate, helpful, courteous, and caring" were some of the compliments I heard. "A delightful experience—an A in every area." A much-traveled Elderhosteler listed this as her favorite destination after attending Elderhostels all over the United States and abroad.

Shortcomings: No weaknesses reported, although I would caution attendees to be prepared with "bug dope" for the six-week black fly infestation in early spring.

Getting In: No difficulties reported, but after these kind reviews I'd advise early registration.

Getting There: Most area visitors tour by automobile using the New York Thruway. Greyhound bus has service to the Finger Lakes area, and there is a small airport at Elmira / Corning.

Batavia—Genesee Community College

Courses of Study: Golf Instruction; American Folk Music; Henry David Thoreau; Abraham / Isaac Story in Art and Literature; From Design to Product; Peoples of the Genesee Region

Quality of Instructors: Excellent. Intellectually stimulating.

Environment: Batavia is a rural community of 18,000 in upstate New York, midway between Rochester and Buffalo. Students consider themselves relatively isolated and make the run to the appealing old city of Rochester or the blue-collar city of Buffalo for social activities. For urbanites, one of the pleasures of the northern reaches is to stroll campus paths after dark to enjoy the night sky ablaze with stars. This pleasure is long gone from our cities and is now endangered in our suburbs as well.

Housing: Elderhostelers enjoy very nice, clean, two-bedroom suites with bath, kitchenette, and living room.

Food: "So good there's even a coffee pot on at 7:00 a.m. in the residence hall."

Unique Attributes: "A staff of student aides anticipated our every need, and their careful, considerate attention made our stay enjoyable." Evening get-togethers and field trips are well planned and executed. One might combine the Elderhostel with a drive to Niagara Falls, one hour away by four-lane expressway, a trip to Toronto, or some vacationing in the Finger Lakes area. Sixty-five miles southwest of Buffalo is the lakeside village of Chatauqua where a full schedule of lectures, opera, and musical performances is held every July and August.

Shortcomings: Hilly terrain, and some step climbing required. Enrollees had better be more than just ambulatory. Beware of the winged tyrants, the diabolical deerflies that swarm in the Adirondacks.

Going Solo: Though this site is primarily accessible by automobile, my panelists gave the program a 4. "Everyone is friendly and sociable," they said. The on-site hostess and scheduled evening events may overcome the danger of "cliquey couples."

Getting In: No difficulties reported.

Getting There: Fly to Buffalo or Rochester and rent a car if you do not wish to drive the entire way.

Keuka Lake—Keuka College

Courses of Study: Hier war Konig Georg III. von England Kurfurst; Gymnastik und Bewegungsspiele; Stimmen aus dem Osten

Quality of Instructors: Good to excellent, a stimulating faculty.

Environment: Keuka College has a picturesque 173-acre campus on the western shore of Lake Keuka. This lovely freshwater lake is used extensively for fishing and canoeing. Views from the college campus include sailboats, sunsets, and fishing skiffs. This campus offers a fine place for frazzled city dwellers to find some tranquillity and to breathe in the damp woodsy air. The school has a coeducational enrollment of only 500 students.

Housing: Elderhostelers sleep in typical dormitory rooms with one communal bathroom on each floor. "But these are cleaner than most," wrote one couple after their second visit to Keuka College. Bedrooms are all second- and third-floor rooms without benefit of an elevator.

Food: The cafeteria provides more than adequate, good food.

Unique Attributes: Sprechen sie Deutsch? This program is conducted in the German language.

Elderhostelers can swim in clean, blue, Lake Keuka just a short walk from the dormitory. I've heard the lake is so transparent one can identify the species of fish in the water. South of the lake lies the town of Elmira, where Mark Twain spent twenty summers. He wrote *The Adventures of Huckleberry Finn* here. Twain referred to Elmira as "the Garden of Eden." The area is renowned for its vineyards and large wineries. In 1829, the Reverend William Bostwick planted a few grapevines near the shore of Lake Keuka. The grapes flourished in the local topsoil and found the weather conditions ideal, so that by the late 1880s, a large winery was built in the area.

Shortcomings: Several attendees had difficulty doing the physical fitness routines in the non-air-conditioned gymnasium.

Getting In: The programs do not seem to be oversubscribed.

Getting There: Most people enjoy touring the Lakes Region by automobile, although Greyhound bus is available. If one wishes to fly, the nearest airport is in Elmira / Corning, and Saranac Lake has an airport served by Piedmont Commuter Airlines.

New York City—Fordham University

Courses of Study: New York's Art: The Frick Collection; W. A. Mozart: Musical Genius; A Literary Look at Immigration; Art in America; American Concert Music in the Twentieth Century; On and Off Broadway: Plays Today

Quality of Instructors: All presentations are interesting. "One excellent, one young and enthusiastic, and one knowledgeable but elitist."

Environment: Very urban. The Rose Hill campus of Fordham is located in the borough of the Bronx, between the Botanical Gardens and the Zoo. The streets are people-packed, especially in the summer when the heat in the high-rise apartment houses forces families outdoors. Tourism in the city also peaks in the summertime. The campus is 90 acres of old buildings and grass courtyards, with an enrollment of 13,000 students.

Housing: Great new dormitory. Each room has a private bath.

Food: An agreeable array with lots of choice. "But the huge cafeteria can be confusing."

Unique Attributes: The proximity to Manhattan is a major draw for this program. Courses fully utilize the city's attributes: one can visit the Metropolitan Museum or the Frick Museum, tour immigrant neighborhoods, or attend a Mostly Mozart concert with a knowledgeable instructor and in the security of a group. Summer brings lots of alfresco music onto the streets. If you wish to tour on your own, downtown is accessible by subway, train, or bus. Crane your neck to look up at the dramatic heights of skyscrapers. See the glitter and the glitz, and feel the excitement. Or perhaps come face to face with the depressing realities of an urban city.

Shortcomings: Lack of air-conditioning in the new dormitory can be troublesome. The city's stretches of concrete tend to retain heat much longer than the grassy leas of the suburbs.

Getting In: Not yet a problem.

Getting There: If you fly, remember La Guardia airport is much closer to the city than Kennedy is. Taxis from the airport into the city are very expensive, so try to use a bus from Kennedy or the subway from La Guardia.

Oswego—State University of New York at Oswego

Courses of Study: Gorbachev's USSR: Glasnost and Perestroika; A Panorama of American Popular Music; Aqua-Robics; Why Take a Picture of a Dirt Pile?; Tennis Anyone?; Is There Anyone Out There?

Quality of Instructors: A broad array of mind-enlarging courses, taught by excellent professors.

Environment: The campus of SUNY at Oswego is a modern tree-lined complex that stretches along the southern shore of Lake Ontario. It is a 700-acre residential campus; the school's enrollment is about 6,000 students. The area has been immortalized in the adventures of the frontiersman, Leather Stocking, in James Fenimore Cooper's *Pathfinder*. Oswego is a beautiful medium size city of 20,000 people on Lake Ontario, 40 miles northwest of Syracuse. A National Historic District, it is surrounded by green, round-topped hills. In season, the restocked lake is thick with trawlers fishing for chinook and coho salmon.

Housing: Elderhostelers are housed in very comfortable dormitories.

Food: The food is good, plentiful, and nicely presented, and the end-of-school week is celebrated with a lavish banquet. "Good salads."

Unique Attributes: The lakefront location is special. One couple, veteran travelers to Oswego, voted this their number one favorite destination. "Would recommend it highly." The state university seems to have superb facilities for both recreation and education: the music program is enhanced with live performances, there is a dinner theatre on the premises, and all the side trips are interesting and well organized. An Oswego "must see" is Tioga Gardens, a solar-domed conservatory that houses a fabulous herb garden and lily ponds.

Shortcomings: None reported. Some courses, such as aqua-robics and tennis, attract an athletic crowd rather than an intellectual one.

Going Solo: My reviewers, all couples, were uncertain about how to reply to my question. I know this school has an avid following of couples who return as often as possible. As outlined in the introduction, they are not always eager to spread a welcome mat for the single travelers. The atmosphere may be clubby.

Getting In: No difficulties now, but perhaps after this rave review, the demand may increase and early registration will be required.

Getting There: Oswego is best reached by automobile over interstate highways but also can be approached by feeder airlines, bus, or train.

Paul Smith—Paul Smith College

Courses of Study: Heart-Smart Cuisine; You Are What You Drink —A Water Quality Sampler; Conifer Identification for the Layman

Quality of Instructors: An environmentally sensitive group of specialists: nutritionist, botanist, and hydrologist.

Environment: The 50-acre campus sits on the shore of lovely St. Regis Lake, surrounded by wilderness mountain streams and trails, not far from Lake Placid. This area of the Adirondacks is known for wild scenery and tumbling streams. Paul Smith is a small coed school whose students major in forestry or hotel and restaurant management.

Housing: The accommodations are very pleasant; Elderhostelers stay in private rooms with private baths.

Food: Since restaurant management is a major, one might expect gourmet cuisine.

Unique Attributes: The Adirondacks are by an 1894 statute a "Forever Wild" wilderness, yet they are an easy drive from the major cities of the Northeast. The mountains are most beautiful in the spring when the trees are budding or in the fall when the hills are washed with orange and amber hues. The lake, with miles of shoreline, offers excellent facilities for swimming, canoeing, and fishing, while the woods provide some of the country's best well-marked hiking trails. The village of Lake Placid has an ersatz Swiss main street, good summer theater, concerts, and films.

The "Heart-Smart" class includes cooking demonstrations with hostelers sampling food and sharing recipes. One session of the water quality course is conducted on the lake, and the "Conifers" course takes students walking in the woods and the bogs. "Something planned for every evening, and the whole program is well managed." This college typifies a program that has been vastly improved since it was visited a few years ago.

Shortcomings: Elderhostelers have no central lounge facilities for socializing, but the large living room in the dormitory seems to serve the purpose.

Going Solo: "When the number of couples exceeds the number of singles 3 to 1, the singles may feel unwelcome." Particularly when most of the couples are alumni of the program. Fifteen couples with six singles is the sort of ratio many singles wish to avoid. But the courses are not "heavy," and the program should draw a congenial, frolicsome group.

Getting In: Just mail in your application. Not oversubscribed.

Getting There: Attractive auto routes are available to the area. Interstate bus, feeder airline, and train are also possible because Lake Placid is popular as both a summer and a winter resort.

Potsdam—Clarkson University

Courses of Study: Uneasy Neighbors: The Mohawks of Northern New York; Unraveling the Controversies of the Vietnam War; The Forces of Physics; Eclectic Experiences with Music; Mass Media in the Drama of Contemporary Life; Video Production

Quality of Instructors: Excellent instructors. "Absolutely tops."

Environment: Clarkson has a beautiful rambling campus and attractive modern buildings for its 3,825 students. The school is reputed to have a challenging curriculum, especially in engineering and science. This area of the St. Lawrence Valley is truly remote, hidden away in the wilds of upstate New York. The nearest large city is Montreal, Quebec, 100 miles away. Artists and writers have immortalized the glories of the Adirondacks, the wildflowers, and sweet-scented balsam trees. The village of Potsdam is a small paper-manufacturing town of just 11,000 people. In addition to being the home of two universities, Clarkson and SUNY, it is the marketplace for all the neighboring towns and hamlets.

Housing: Excellent. Elderhostelers are housed in low brick buildings where the rooms have private baths. Clarkson wins an A plus for cleanliness.

Food: The meals are very good and plentiful. A pleasant outdoor picnic and barbecue enhance the program.

Unique Attributes: Campus athletic facilities are excellent. The indoor swimming pool and tennis courts are available all day— no limitations on Elderhostel hours. Buildings are conveniently situated and the campus is fairly level for easy walking. Elderhostel staff are considerate and hospitable and help to make this a favorite destination. A refrigerator in the dormitory lounge is convenient for safekeeping of medications.

Nearby Lake Placid is a well-known winter and summer resort. The area, a tourist mecca, abounds with flea markets, antique fairs, and craft shows in the spring, summer, and fall. From Potsdam, one has a view of New York State's highest peak, a mere 5,344 feet.

Shortcomings: Do not forget the insect repellent for the six-week irksome black fly season that ends in late June.

Getting In: "Real tough. We were wait-listed until we received a telephone acceptance."

Getting There: Most people go by car along the Adirondack Northway, but there are some commuter flights to the Lake Placid area from Montreal. Some public bus service is available.

NORTH CAROLINA

Asheville—University of North Carolina at Asheville

Courses of Study: The Evolution of the Presidency; Writers in the Blue Ridge; Asheville and the Land of the Sky; Pivotal Elections in American History

Quality of Instructors: Knowledgeable university professors pique the students' interest. Rated "very good."

Environment: The University of North Carolina at Asheville is a small liberal arts college nestled between the Smoky Mountains and the Blue Ridge Parkway. The school combines the intimacy and the friendliness characteristic of the South; and the charming town surrounding the campus epitomizes the grace and mores we associate with old-fashioned America.

Asheville—gateway to the Parkway, a Cherokee Indian Reservation, and a national park—has become a favorite tourist center. Its comfortable size (population 60,600), mountain location, and cool summer evenings draw many summer visitors.

Housing: Elderhostelers stay in high-rise dormitories with semi-private rooms, four people sharing a bathroom. The buildings have elevators and air-conditioning; lovely views of the mountains can be seen from the upper levels.

Food: Good North Carolina specialties—ham, grits, and buttered biscuits—are served.

Unique Attributes: One set of reviewers gave this program an A plus. Visits to Thomas Wolfe's home and the cemetery, an evening at a theater, extracurricular activities, and picnics are all well planned and executed. Some classes include interesting demonstrations of mountain music. Elderhostelers are kept busy, and the management is on call at all times.

Smoky Mountain National Park straddles the border of Tennessee and North Carolina. This 522,000-acre tract is the most visited of all our national parks. Mountain laurel as tall as trees blooms from May through July. Bus tours can be taken from Asheville to the park. The city also has a botanic garden in which one can view spectacular, tree-size azaleas and rhododendrons. If you are in search of a touristy diversion, you might visit the Biltmore House and Gardens, the 250-room mansion that was the elaborate home of George Vanderbilt. This famous estate was designed to replicate a French château.

Shortcomings: "None—everything's perfect," wrote one pair of well-traveled Elderhostelers.

Getting In: This is a much-applauded program. Early reservations are an absolute necessity.

Getting There: Asheville can be reached by public bus, private car, or major air carrier to its own very busy airport. If one wishes to tour Smoky Mountain National Park, a car is recommended.

Boone—Appalachian State University

Courses of Study: Geography in the News; Material Culture of the Southern Appalachian; Nonverbal Communications; Judaism in the South; Inside China Today; Appalachian Folklore

Quality of Instructors: Full professors of the university teach the Elderhostel courses. "In all my college work I never had better—give them an A plus," wrote one well-traveled and well-educated hosteler. The course selection and content also received an A plus rating from an Elderhostel fan.

Environment: This wonderful and most cordial 255-acre campus, which has an enrollment of 9,907 students, is part of the University of North Carolina system. The town of Boone lies in the Blue Ridge Mountains amid gently rolling hills. It is a resort community situated 3,300 feet above sea level. "I recommend Appalachian State as a perfect introduction to Elderhosteling," wrote another Boone booster.

Housing: Elderhostelers stay in an elevator-equipped residence hall that is convenient to dining and classes. Even the parking is nearby.

Food: Elderhostelers dine in the school cafeteria with a particularly friendly group of students and are invited to eat as much as they wish. Bountiful quantities for those with hearty appetites.

Unique Attributes: The town of Boone offers scenic vistas of the Blue Ridge Parkway where azaleas and dogwood turn the roadsides pink in the spring. School-sponsored field trips are well conducted and well designed for acquainting Elderhostelers with the lovely countryside. The entire place—school, classrooms, dining hall, and outdoor classrooms—abounds with a feeling of hospitality and congeniality. Proud, rugged people live on this rugged land where the skills of handcrafting are still admired. A drive into the country will reveal spinning wheels, musical instruments, cane chair seats, and fabrics—all handmade.

Shortcomings: "Nonexistent," wrote my Boone booster.

Getting In: Expect to be wait-listed here. Immediate acceptance is chancy.

Getting There: Boone can be reached by interstate bus and plane to Winston-Salem, but an automobile would be advantageous in the mountainous part of North Carolina.

Chapel Hill—University of North Carolina

Courses of Study: All That Jazz (3 courses—History and Illustrations, Performance Techniques Laboratory, Performance Mediums); From Print to Electronic Media; Magnolias, Mockingbirds, and Moonshine; What is a Person?; Cultural Ecology of Disease; Bach and Before

Quality of Instructors: "Super excellent, give them five stars," wrote one music-loving couple.

Environment: Chapel Hill is a town of contrasts. Its special Southern quality—colonial gardens and tree-shaded streets fragrant with magnolias and wisteria—retains some vestiges of plantation psychology but is balanced by the school's atmosphere, unexpectedly enlightened and cosmopolitan.

The university, one of the leading public universities in the country, is rightfully proud of its green, lush, attractive campus. All this charm contrasts sharply with the Chapel Hill-Raleigh-Durham research triangle of contemporary high technology.

Housing: Elderhostelers stay in high-rise, air-conditioned dormitories, two people to a room, with one bathroom shared by every pair of bedrooms. Dining, swimming, and parking are all located conveniently nearby.

Food: The cuisine offered in the college cafeteria is excellent. "Too much, too good," groaned one couple I met at another Elderhostel. "They stretched our self-control to the limit."

Unique Attributes: If you wish to revisit the twenties and thirties on a musical stroll down memory lane, the jazz course is designed for you. You'll survey ragtime, blues, instrumental jazz, big bands, bebop, modal, free, and fusion. You'll hear some greats and play along, too! The "All That Jazz" program combines three courses presented through lectures, demonstrations, video, and records. Soften a reed for your old sax or licorice stick, loosen the valves on your brass trumpet, pack them tenderly and bring them along, so you can sit in with the jam session. "The teaching is superb. Jim Kecht has wonderful communications skills and can demonstrate his lectures with his trumpet, which he plays like Louie Armstrong!"

The university president is supportive of the Elderhostel program. The Student Union shows free films, and the town of Chapel Hill is a delight. Astronomy fans, don't miss the Morehead Planetarium.

Shortcomings: "When the weather is pleasant, the half-mile walk from dorms to classrooms is wonderful, but in the dog days of summer it can feel like you are climbing Mt. Everest."

Getting In: Classes are always full, so early registration is essential. "Many students are second-time and third-time repeaters."

Getting There: Splendid bus, train, and airplane service is available to Chapel Hill. American Airlines has recently established a hub at Raleigh-Durham International Airport.

Highlands—The Mountain Highlands Camp and Conference Center

Courses of Study: Appalachian Stories and Legends; Natural History of the Blue Ridge Mountains; Walk with a Mountain Woman; Restoring Natural Ecosystems; Appalachian Folksongs and Ballads; Newspapers in a Changing Society; Astronomy

Quality of Instructors: "Wonderful," said one attendee. They "bring a fresh focus to familiar subjects."

Environment: The camp, a year-round Unitarian-Universalist retreat, is situated on top of a 4,000-foot mountain. Despite the location, the grounds are comfortable and cozy, and the walking is easy. In the fall, the Smoky Mountains are a blaze of color, and the weather is perfect. Highlands, 60 miles southwest of Asheville, is one of the resort towns in the Smokies.

Housing: There are two types of accommodations: a lodge with dormitory rooms that sleep four and rustic but comfortable cabins. The cabins have front porches from which there are spectacular views of the Smokies.

Food: Three times a day, Elderhostelers are served food that is too good. "The best of any hostel," wrote one much-traveled correspondent. Traditional black-eyed peas are often on the menu.

Unique Attributes: The friendly people and cordial atmosphere have induced one of my correspondents to return to "The Mountain" five times. The performance of the local storyteller and folk singer is a favorite. Appalachia is the home of defiant, industrious, independent people with a musical tradition of guitars, fiddles, banjos, dulcimers, and bluegrass bands. The people have a great love of place and strong regionalism.

Vans are available in Asheville for trips on the Blue Ridge Parkway, winding through mountains carpeted with evergreens that get bluer and bluer as they recede into the distance. The Great Smokies are famous for having more than 100 varieties of trees, and rumor has it that one can hardly drive through without seeing one or more bears.

Shortcomings: Raingear and insect repellent are suggested for trips into the Smoky Mountains in the summer.

Getting In: After this enthusiastic review, you may have to gamble on a lottery to get enrolled in this program.

Getting There: Although private automobile is the preferred method of transportation, one can get to Highlands on an interstate bus. Asheville, 60 miles away, is the nearest airport.

Mars Hill—Mars Hill College

Courses of Study (Intensive Studies): Trails to Treasures: Hiking the Heart of the Southern Appalachians; Looking Homeward with Thomas Wolfe; A Week in the World of a Professional Repertory Company

Quality of Instructors: "Well informed and experienced—fun to be with."

Environment: Mars Hill is located just 18 miles north of Asheville, nestled between the Blue Ridge and Smoky mountains. Unlike its neighbor, whose streets swarm with tourists, Mars Hill is a quiet, small, country town with one little set of stores—florist, druggist, and so forth. "Definitely off the beaten path." The campus is a charming mix of old stone and red brick buildings, "many new and gorgeous."

Housing: Very comfortable. Beautiful new two-story buildings. One connecting bath for every two bedrooms.

Food: "You wouldn't go hungry—there's always a salad buffet and peanut butter." "A passable cafeteria."

Unique Attributes: "The beautiful country." The intensive hiking program takes you deep into the breathtakingly beautiful Southern Highlands where wildflowers grow in the savannas and the trees and vines shut out the sun. Participants have required pre-course readings and are asked to keep a log.

Look Homeward, Angel enthusiasts (aren't we all?) can spend a week rereading Thomas Wolfe's best fiction and visiting the author's boyhood haunts. An advance bibliography is mailed to class participants.

The repertory theater course offers an insider's view of professional playmaking for Elderhostelers who love the smell of greasepaint. Daily seminars are supplemented with visits to rehearsals and performances.

Shortcomings: "Not much to do at night. No one encouraged any group participation, and we were a distance from Asheville." Lack of a resident program director is always a weakness.

Going Solo: "About a 4. To travel alone one must be an 'up' person no matter where you go. There's a pleasant lounge for socializing, and this course attracts many 'old-time' Elderhostelers. I'm a bridge player so I usually do well."

Getting In: Many returnees. Mars Hill has an avid following, so book early.

Getting There: If using public transportation to Asheville, one may rent a car or hire a cab for the 18-mile ride.

Murphy—John C. Campbell Folk School

Courses of Study: Intensive Studies of Appalachian Crafts through the Folk School Experience, i.e., Basketry; Woodcarving; Enameling: Jewelry; Spinning. Also a program of Appalachian Music and Dance

Carding wool at John C. Campbell Folk School, Murphy, North Carolina
(Photo: Mae Woods Bell)

Quality of Instructors: Above average, caring, expert craftsmen.

Environment: The 365-acre campus of the Folk School is located 7 miles from the village of Murphy in the lovely Blue Ridge Mountains. This is the western tip of North Carolina in the Nantahala National Forest bordering Tennessee. Nantahala is a Cherokee Indian word that means "land of the noonday sun." It is said the valleys are so narrow and so deep that they receive direct rays of the sun only at noon.

The school is internationally recognized for its role in promoting and preserving Old World crafts. "I've found it to be a habit-forming institution," wrote a frequent participant at the Folk School.

Housing: Varies—there are a few modern buildings and other rustic ones with "lots of character."

Food: "Too much—too good." Hospitable tables for 6 or 8, and hostelers clear their own tables.

Unique Attributes: "A staff that can't do enough for Elderhostelers." "For early risers they have lots to hear, see, and do! Coffee is set out in the great room, often by a roaring fire." Great evening get-togethers for folk dancing or group songfests. "This is probably one of the most hospitable Elderhostels in America." "And the view—wow!" The Blue Ridge Mountains rise in an unbroken sweep to an altitude of 6,000 feet.

Shortcomings: May not be a great destination for anyone with cardiac problems or on crutches. The terrain is rough and one walks up steep paths to classes. But for the vigorous and resolute, this may be an enticement.

Going Solo: "Only a zombie would not make friends here. The innumerable opportunities to mix, the care taken by the staff, and the informal atmosphere are conducive to friendship."

Getting In: Book early! "This place gets more requests than it can handle—and justifiably so," wrote another Campbell School fan.

Getting There: By car is best. If you wish to fly, it is necessary to make arrangements with the management in advance.

Waynesville—Western Carolina University

Courses of Study: Appalachian Literature: Reflections on a Lifestyle in Transition; The King of Instruments: The Pipe Organ; Sing the Songs of Scotland; Update on Latin America; Carnival Music Around the World; Master of Mystery

Quality of Instructors: The university professors and the graduate student assistants received compliments for their excellence.

Environment: This is an off-campus program conducted in a sylvan setting at the Waynesville Country Club. Waynesville is near Asheville, in the most scenic area of the state, between the Blue Ridge Parkway and the Great Smokies. The Blue Ridge Parkway, despite its name, is not a wide macadam thruway—it is a charming, winding road that meanders through the mountains, affording travelers wooded vistas in all seasons of the year. Take a leisurely drive in the spring to see the hills carpeted with pink azaleas and white dogwood.

Housing: The accommodations for this program are unusually luxurious. Attendees stay in rooms with private bath facilities at the country club.

Food: Meals are "waitress served." My reviewers found the quality and variety very good.

Unique Attributes: The beautiful, mountainous location is very special. Elderhostel staff are helpful and courteous and classes are conducted in a setting of natural beauty at a country club that is situated midway between the university campus and Asheville. The club has a lovely 27-hole golf course with rolling green fairways. This destination is a favorite among our more sybaritic hostelers. The physical plant and atmosphere appeal to individuals who prefer being waited on.

Shortcomings: No weaknesses reported.

Going Solo: Only if you are a golfer willing to try for a pickup foursome, but you might find yourself excluded by a lot of prearranged games. A solo female might register for a week when a flock of very friendly "golf widows" are in residence.

Getting In: The program may be a sleeper. Much to my surprise, no one reported long waiting lists.

Getting There: Waynesville can be reached by motor coach or plane to Asheville.

Wilmington — University of North Carolina

Courses of Study: Humans and the Marine Environment; The Dynamics of Wellness; The American Foreign Policy of the Bush Administration; The Writings of Luke in the New Testament; American Political Issues for the 1990s

Quality of Instructors: An excellent, thought-provoking faculty.

Environment: Wilmington, a city of 44,000, is the chief port of the state; not a candle and curio seaport but a working harbor. Tobacco thrives in the rolling land of the North Carolina coastal plain.

The University of North Carolina is the oldest state university in the country and reputed to be a member of "the public Ivy League." This branch at Wilmington only serves 6,553 students.

Housing: In a pleasant, comfortable air-conditioned hotel near the campus.

Food: "So-so, but the dining room is clean and cheerful." Meals and classes are in the same hotel.

Unique Attributes: This is a very interesting historic area. One can visit a Revolutionary War battlefield at Moore's Creek Bridge where the Whigs defeated the Tories in 1776, former plantations converted to lovely public gardens with ancient oaks and magnolias, or restored plantations whose manor houses are completely refurbished. The course includes a field trip to the Atlantic Ocean, just 6 miles away, and a tour of Old Wilmington.

Shortcomings: None reported. However, if you enjoy the ambience of a college campus, fraternizing with students, using the library and other facilities, this program is not for you, since classes, housing, and meals are all off-campus.

Getting In: This site is popular among the hostelers who prefer air-conditioned hotel accommodations.

Getting There: American Airlines has established a hub at the Raleigh-Durham airport, so there should be frequent connecting flights to New Hanover County airport in Wilmington. Piedmont Airlines and Greyhound bus also serve the area.

OHIO

Athens—Ohio University

Courses of Study: Television Criticism; TV / Video Production; Television and You; Baseball: Historic and Modern Perspectives; The Great American Ancestor Hunt

Quality of Instructors: A fine crew of teachers who animate the mind.

Environment: The school, located in a typical small university town in the rolling hills of southeastern Ohio, is very proud of its tree-lined brick walkways and its location overlooking the Hocking River. Athens, though just a small community, comes alive at night with student partying. The surrounding area is rich farmland, woodland, and state parks.

Housing: Elderhostelers report the housing as adequate. The university dormitories have recently been renovated.

Food: The bill of fare is abundant and delicious. Quantities are ample enough to satisfy appetites stimulated by exercise, mental or physical.

Unique Attributes: This is a very athletic campus; the 9-hole golf course and aquatic center are right on the premises. There is an old swimming hole two miles away, and in winter there is a lot of snow, great for downhill and cross-country skiing. The theater, dance, and art departments of the university sponsor events and exhibits and invite guest performers to the campus. Nearby is Hocking Hills State Park, an extrordinary park with cliffs of a geologic wonder called black sandstone. Look for rock shelters and small waterfalls and hiking trails that wander through the hemlocks and birch trees.

Shortcomings: No weaknesses reported.

Getting In: This site has developed a following of people who enjoy the athletic facilities.

Getting There: Athens can be reached by private car over turnpikes, by interstate bus, or by regularly scheduled airlines to the Athens airport.

Dayton—University of Dayton

Courses of Study: Aviation Heritage (lectures, group activities, and tours)

Quality of Instructors: "Good." They had better be better than good. This is one of those situations where the students may have more experience in the field than the instructors.

Environment: This university of 10,980 students is located in the outskirts of Dayton, a metropolitan city of more than a million. The quiet campus is away from the traffic and bustle of downtown Dayton, yet close enough for Elderhostelers to get there by public transportation. The former St. Mary's College was founded by the Marianists and is still a Roman Catholic institution.

Housing: The dormitories are single-sex buildings.

Food: "Fine." The aviation zealots are not fussy about food.

Unique Attributes: "This program, together with the Air Force Museum nearby, is a real treat for aviation enthusiasts—especially if they have been connected to the Air Force." Retired members of the Air Corps, both male and female, and flying wannabes immerse themselves in memorabilia and aviation history starting with the Wright Brothers. The course is scheduled to enable attendees to stay over for the Dayton International Air Show.

Shortcomings: If the program has any weaknesses, there isn't a chance they'd be reported.

Going Solo: This destination is a bastion of male solo travelers. They "love the camaraderie" and thoroughly enjoy the experience.

Getting In: Not yet oversubscribed.

Getting There: A van runs from the Dayton airport to the college campus.

OKLAHOMA

Guthrie—Logan County Historical Society

Courses of Study: A Stolen Capital; Interior Design of the Victorian Period; Researching the History of a Building

Quality of Instructors: Members of the Historical Society who treat their subjects with great affection. One instructor is so steeped in his subject, he "dresses in the fashion of the times, wearing a different costume each day."

Environment: The city of Guthrie is located in the middle of the state on the Cimarron River north of Oklahoma City. Harrison House, the headquarters of this program, is in the center of the Guthrie Historic District. Guthrie is also the home of the Territorial Museum, which depicts life in the territory at the turn of the century.

Housing: "Plush." Hostelers sleep in Victorian elegance in authentically furnished rooms with private baths.

Food: Elderhostelers breakfast in a charming turn-of-the-century parlor but are given tickets to eat other meals at local cafes. The choice is wide and the food very good.

Unique Attributes: This bed and breakfast setting is a far cry from the usual uncarpeted college dormitory. Oklahoma, a state noted for its Indians and oil wells, is not a much visited tourist destination. Will Rogers, the famous Oklahoma cowboy-humorist once said, "There ought to be a law against anybody going to Europe until they had seen the things we have in this country." You might start by visiting the Will Rogers Memorial Museum at Claremore. In front of the museum is a statue of the legendary Rogers on his horse, Soapsuds.

Shortcomings: No group arrangements for lunch or dinner. The attendees have little contact with one another.

Getting In: No problem with an early reservation.

Getting There: Fly to Oklahoma City on most major airlines and rent a car or take a bus to Guthrie. It's an easy drive on major thruways.

Stillwater—Oklahoma State University

Courses of Study: Storytelling Traditions and Techniques (an intensive studies program); Mexico and the U.S.: Distant Neighbors; American Robber Barons and Reformers; The Great Good Place of the Essential Hangout

Quality of Instructors: Nationally known storytellers and excellent professors from the university.

Environment: Stillwater is a rural community of 35,000, and despite the college nightlife, it is far from being a lively municipality. It is in the north-central area of the state, where grain elevators and steel derricks rise up right out of the flat plains. In addition to the exploration for minerals, natural gas, oil, and coal, these rich grazing ranges are populated with white-faced Herefords.

OSU was founded in 1890 as a school for agriculture and applied sciences, and agriculture is still one of the most popular areas of study. The school is reputed to have one of the most beautiful campuses in the state, with a mix of high-rise and traditional residence halls.

Housing: Hostelers stay in the Student Union Hotel, part of the student union complex that is centered on the campus. Nicely appointed rooms with private baths.

Food: "Too much, too good, and too available." A very convenient arrangement—meals are served and all classes taught in the student union building.

Unique Attributes: The intensive study program attracts some of the country's best storytellers to attend and perform for the Elderhostelers. Hostelers tell their stories to a receptive and appreciative audience and learn tricks and techniques. "This is a great program," wrote an alumnus of almost 30 hostels. If you drive to Stillwater, there are numerous rodeos throughout the state in June, and in July, the Will Rogers Rodeo is held in Claremore, northeast of Tulsa.

Shortcomings: None.

Getting In: Enroll early.

Getting There: One may fly to either Tulsa or Oklahoma City, then hop a bus or drive to Stillwater.

Tahlequah—Northeastern State University

Courses of Study: Native American Tribes of Northeastern Oklahoma: Trail of Tears to Modern Nations; Recording Your Experiences; Native Arts and Crafts

Quality of Instructors: Classes are taught by experts in each Indian craft.

Environment: Tahlequah was the capital of the Cherokee nation, and the city still retains the spirit of its historical heritage. A town of 14,200, Tahlequah lies in northeastern Oklahoma in the scenic hills of the Ozarks, an area noted for steep hills and swift mountain streams. For 50 years during the 1800s, Oklahoma was known as Indian Territory, and the state is still home to many Indians.

This state-supported university was founded as an institution of higher learning for the Cherokee. The school is a small, friendly institution, home to 8,707 graduate and undergraduate students.

Housing: "Dormitory rooms are better than most." All air-conditioned.

Food: Not a fancy cafeteria, but the food is dandy.

Unique Attributes: Lectures are conducted by chiefs of various Indian tribes—Cherokee, Creek, Kiowa, Miami, and Shawnee. This course is a thorough indoctrination into the traditions, heritage, and histories of the nine tribes of the northeastern corner of Oklahoma. In hands-on demonstrations, Elderhostelers make pottery by the Indian method, using buffalo chips to make the hot fire. Interesting field trips include the famous drama, Trail of Tears, and a tour of the Indian village, Tsa-La-Gi, where the Cherokee maintain an ancient way of life.

Shortcomings: None.

Getting In: The great plains states of our country are largely overlooked by residents of the east and west coasts. Not an overly popular destination.

Getting There: If you fly to Tulsa, the college will meet you with a van. Bus transportation is available, and the highways are excellent.

OREGON

Ashland—Southern Oregon State College

Courses of Study: China: The Mysteries Unfold; T'ai Chi: The Ancient Exercise; Life and Times of Will Shakespeare; Last Call! A Week at the Theater; Costuming the Shows; Cheers! Here's to Wine

Quality of Instructors: The instructors received rave reviews: "outstanding," "fantastic," and "superb." Many instructors for Shakespeare courses are selected from among festival personnel, and the other specialists show great affection for their subjects.

Environment: Southern Oregon State College has been hosting Elderhostelers since 1980 and has developed an avid fan club. All of the evaluation questionnaires returned to me were dotted with exclamation points and superlatives. Ashland is a "gorgeous college town." It has lovely turn-of-the-century homes, and the playhouse is an excellent replica of London's Old Fortune Theatre, an outdoor Elizabethan stage.

The atmosphere of the college is friendly. There is no institutional feeling and Elderhostelers are encouraged to stay for two weeks. "The atmosphere is conducive to making lifelong friends."

Housing: The dormitories are immaculate and comfortable, "better than average." Some stair climbing is necessary.

Food: One not-so-enthusiastic couple rated the meals "very good most of the time." Everyone else gave the cafeteria fare a grade of excellent or splendid. A special area of the dining room is reserved for use of the Elderhostelers, an arrangement that is much appreciated by the single travelers. Elderhostelers share clean-up responsibilities.

Unique Attributes: "The play's the thing." Ashland is the home of the famous Shakespeare Festival that runs annually from July to Labor Day. "We saw Shakespearean theater performances as fine as Stratford!" wrote one couple from the East Coast.

Ashland's Elderhostel program offers an opportunity to see top-flight theater performed (tickets reserved but cost extra). In addition to Shakespeare, modern plays and carefully selected classics are performed. Costumed madrigalists sing and dance to Renaissance music. One reviewer has attended Ashland seven times in three years. He wrote, "I return because of theater and the instructor who teaches Beatles and folk music."

The quality and organization of the total program is superb. Staff are attentive 24 hours a day. The campus is within walking distance of town where one can shop, visit the parks, and play tennis. Expert river pilots are available for souls brave enough to try white water rafting. Ashland has a very healthful climate. It is close to the mountains and to Medford, the fruit capital of Oregon.

Shortcomings: The following is indicative of the response of most reviewers. "We've attended three Elderhostels at Southern Oregon State and cannot find any weaknesses." A few attendees mentioned the stair climbing, and two reviewers were disappointed in the cafeteria clean-up system.

Going Solo: "Highest rating of suitability. Theater attendance is in groups, no safety problems in town or on campus, and friendliness of college, theater, and townspeople can't be beat."

Getting In: Getting accepted at Ashland is very difficult because this is one of the country's most popular destinations. Early registrations are recommended even though the national registration department is probably forced to use a lottery system for filling these classes. One reviewer wrote, "After three visits I would gladly go there again and again." A hot tip from my alumnus who has made seven trips to Ashland: "Long waiting lists for summer classes—spring and fall are generally easy."

Getting There: Transportation by private automobile is easy because Ashland is located 350 miles north of San Francisco, not at all off the beaten path. If they arrive in Medford by plane or bus, Elderhostelers are usually met by college vans. This is not only convenient but also establishes a cordial feeling. I have been advised that because of the undependability of plane arrival times at the Medford airport, the Elderhostel director is now suggesting that attendees try to share a taxi or limo from the airport to the college. The airport is frequently shrouded in fog, which can make landing something of an uncertain adventure.

Forest Grove— Pacific University

Courses of Study: Photography in the Pacific Northwest; Images of Light; Women in Literature; Cults in America: Why Do They Survive?; Who Gets What and Why?; Contemporary Poetry in the USA

Quality of Instructors: Varies. "Excellent, good, and fair," according to my panelists.

Environment: Forest Grove, a quiet town of 11,500 people, is just a half hour from Portland and one hour from the scenic Oregon coast. The campus is small and tree-lined and has a flat topography that lends itself to easy walking.

Housing: Elderhostelers stay in a brand-new three-story dormitory. No elevators; but good parking nearby.

Food: Typical college cafeteria fare but sometimes not up to par. Portions are skimpy, and "the food is cold at breakfast."

Unique Attributes: Here's a first! The School of Optometry offers free examinations to Elderhostelers. In addition, this program contains all the components necessary for a successful Elderhostel experience. A host and hostess are in residence at the dormitory, available for assistance and sightseeing information at all times. The program coordinator is efficient and eager. The college arranges interesting trips to the nearby wineries, and public bus service to Portland is available, so an automobile is not a necessity. The classroom building is air-conditioned and has good acoustics and an elevator.

Shortcomings: Food service needs improvement. Hostelers are assigned very early meal hours because the cafeteria is shared with other groups, and quantities are scant at times.

Going Solo: My reviewers did not rate this destination, but it is obvious that single travelers should fare very well here. Only hearty eaters should steer clear of Pacific University until an effort is made to improve the menu and eating arrangements.

Getting In: Good chance.

Getting There: If you fly to Portland, the college van will meet you, but an automobile is helpful for taking a coastal trip. Amtrak has a bustling station in Portland; the Coast Starlight Route follows the coast from Los Angeles to Seattle, but first-class space on these trains is sold out months in advance of the peak travel seasons.

Monmouth—Western Oregon State College

Courses of Study: Folk Architecture in the Willamette Valley; The Music of Broadway; Memories of Past and Present; American Congressional Elections; The Nature of Controversy

Quality of Instructors: A multifaceted group. "Everyone held our attention and stirred our imagination."

Environment: Monmouth is a medium-size university town cradled midway between the driftwood-littered Oregon coast and the Cascade Mountains. The school is located in the pastoral Willamette Valley, an agricultural and sheep grazing area of the state. The campus boasts of having the tallest Christmas tree in the world.

Housing: Elderhostelers enjoy the luxury of private apartments in a modern dormitory building. Each apartment consists of a sitting room / study with picture windows and desks, a separate bedroom, a closet, and a private bathroom. Some apartments, however, are on the third floor of a walk-up building.

Food: The food served in the cafeteria is said to be very bad. "Barely edible," was the disdainful comment of one pair of roommates.

Unique Attributes: Western Oregon State College runs a perfectly organized program. The woman in charge is right on top of her task from the first evening orientation program until the party on the final night. The materials distributed at check-in are informative, clear, and helpful.

The Nature of Controversy course is a week-long exploration of the subject through a variety of academic disciplines. Students examine the role controversy plays in social, political, aesthetic, and scientific development.

Elderhostel evening programs are very entertaining; there's a box supper on the lawn, a folk dancing display, a slide show, and a concert. A small museum on the campus contains a unique and fascinating collection of Eskimo artifacts. One gentleman, a former northeastern urbanite, observed, "The natives pronounce the name of their state as Orry-gun, Orry-g'n, or Organ. Never Aura-gahn, the way we outlanders do."

Shortcomings: The poor quality of meals in the cafeteria seems to be this program's only weakness.

Getting In: No registration problems were reported to me.

Getting There: The automobile drive to Monmouth is over lovely winding roads. Salem, Oregon, a short distance from Monmouth, can be reached by plane, train, or bus.

Sandy—Alton Collins Retreat Center

Courses of Study: Oregon History; Human Sexuality; Strum for Fun: Ukulele for Beginners; Comparative Religions; Conversational Spanish; Cascadian Forest Flora

Quality of Instructors: All of the teachers, scholars, and naturalists were rated as excellent.

Environment: Alton Collins is a new adult education center in the Oregon rain forest. It is set in the snow-covered Cascade Mountains amid mountain hemlock and silver fir trees. Elderhostelers can stroll over lava beds created by thousands of years of eruptions and hike over trails gutted with cracks and crevasses.

Housing: The sleeping accommodations are superior. Elderhostelers are housed in carpeted, double-occupancy bedrooms with private bathrooms.

Food: The meals at Alton Collins are graded as superior. "Home-type gourmet" meals are served family-style at large round tables that encourage congeniality.

Unique Attributes: The accommodations and woodland surroundings are splendid. The camp is encircled by hiking trails through Oregon's tall timber of red cedar and maple. One program's highlight is a field trip to majestic Mt. Hood, the dormant 11,245-foot volcano with its glacier-clad slopes. Elderhostelers gain a profound understanding of the word "scenic"—"We didn't go sightseeing, we lived it."

The people of Oregon are like their state—open, friendly, and outdoors oriented. No overcrowding or smog in this state. Plan to go in June if you wish to visit Portland's highly regarded Rose Festival. Portland also boasts a five-and-a-half-acre Japanese garden that's open year-round. Sandy lies just 35 miles southeast of Portland.

Shortcomings: One needs an automobile to thoroughly enjoy the experience.

Getting In: This seems to be a rather popular program. Some of my reviewers wrote about waiting on lists for acceptance. Early registrations are recommended.

Getting There: Portland can be reached by interstate bus, airplane, and train, although a leisurely drive up the Oregon coast is recommended as the most pleasant method of transportation.

PENNSYLVANIA

Shippensburg—Shippensburg University

Courses of Study: Gorbachev, Glasnost, and All That: The Reality Behind the Image; The Big Band Singers; Art: An Intriguing Servant to Humanity; Biology, Study of Genes and DNA; Backstage at Musicals; Mystery, Detection, and Solutions

Quality of Instructors: "All excellent, innovative, and informative, and each presentation is well prepared."

Environment: The college hamlet of Shippensburg is located 40 miles southwest of the state capital, Harrisburg. The town is in the midst of the fertile Cumberland valley, an area of well-kept Pennsylvania Dutch dairy and field crop farms. Lots of mushrooms are grown here, too. Rolling green hills give way to broad fields with farmhouses and barns that are decorated with colorful folk symbols, known as "hex" signs. Amish farmers still travel these roads in black horse-drawn buggies.

The campus of state-supported Shippensburg consists of 200 acres over which are spread some old gray Pennsylvania fieldstone buildings amid some modern high-rise glass fronted structures. No alcohol is allowed on campus.

Housing: "Houskeeping is very good." Apartments with private bathrooms please the fussbudgets among us.

Food: "Very good choice and a very good salad bar." Menu includes Pennsylvania Dutch specialties, such as scrapple for breakfast and pickled eggs.

Unique Attributes: "The entire program is exactly what the original Elderhostel organizers envisioned. Everything from courses to extracurricular activities is just perfect." My panelists completed their eulogy by saying, "Shippensburg is the best of the 23 Elderhostels we've attended!" The entire school is involved with the Elderhostelers—students as well as professors and even the faculty who are not part of the program.

The town of Hershey is very near Harrisburg and is well worth a side trip. When the wind is right, the rich chocolate odor permeates the air miles away. Shippensburg is also not much more than a stone's throw from Gettysburg National Military Park, certainly worth a visit if you didn't spend a day at the site of the famous Civil War battle with your high school senior class.

Shortcomings: Obviously, none.

Going Solo: Rated a 5 out of 5. My reviewers wrote, "But no destination is good for the shrinking violet."

Getting In: To date, no difficulty. I'd suggest registering early in the future.

Getting There: Automobile is your best bet, but Harrisburg has an Amtrak station and an international airport. Greyhound has good bus service in this part of Pennsylvania.

SOUTH DAKOTA

Yankton—Mount Marty College

Courses of Study: We Got There on the Train: Railroads in the Lives of Americans; We Heard It on the Radio: History and Development of Midwest Radio

Quality of Instructors: Very good. The instructors cast old ideas in a new light.

Environment: Yankton is a city in the southeast corner of South Dakota on the Nebraska border overlooking Lewis and Clark Lake. South Dakota is famous for windswept prairies and extremes of unpleasant weather—dust storms in the summer and heavy snow in the winter. Mount Marty is a small Catholic coed college with an enrollment of 620 students. It is a Benedictine institution with a nice rolling campus.

Housing: Elderhostelers stay in very clean, neat, two-person dormitory rooms. The air-conditioned bedrooms have their own washbasins, and the toilet and tub bathrooms each serve a pair of bedrooms.

Food: The meals are satisfactory.

Unique Attributes: The Benedictine Sisters who direct the Elderhostel program work very hard to make the attendees' stay pleasant and comfortable. The well-planned extracurricular field trips include a delightful midsummer Swedish Festival and an Indian mission. The evening entertainment includes a great demonstration by a folk- and square-dance group, all of whom are over age sixty-five. South Dakota has many wonderful sightseeing attractions—the barren canyons of the Badlands, prehistoric fossils, the ancient Black Hills and gold mining claims, and Mount Rushmore Memorial.

Shortcomings: Some individuals might be nettled by the lack of shower facilities.

Getting In: My reviewers were registered on their first try.

Getting There: Fly to Omaha and rent a car for the drive to Yankton. The airports at Sioux Falls, South Dakota, and Sioux City, Iowa, are closer to Yankton and equally convenient for touring South Dakota before or after the week of school.

TENNESSEE

Montgomery Bell State Park— Austin Peay State University

Courses of Study: Will Gorbachev Dominate Russian History?; Southern Playwrights and Tennessee Williams; Montgomery Bell—Tennessee's Greatest Ironmaster; Changed? The U.S. Constitution; Wildlife of Middle Tennessee; American Folk Art

Quality of Instructors: "Superlative." Foresters and ornithologists augment the staff as required.

Environment: Montgomery Bell is a beautiful state park overlooking Acorn Lake in mid-Tennessee, some 45 miles away from the university. The lake is ringed with dogwood and maples. Even those who are not bird fanciers will probably pick up a bit of ornithology along the way.

Housing: Elderhostelers stay in a motel-style inn. "Great privacy and good meeting rooms—real southern hospitality."

Food: "Plain, wholesome meals are served. Good quality and ample quantity." Unpretentious.

Unique Attributes: "Exceptional faculty, spectacular fall scenery, and outstanding field trips." My reviewers recommend spring and fall for this destination, when one won't encounter the heat and humidity of the Tennessee summer sun. A comfortable bus is used for the field trip to Nashville to see the full-scale reproduction of the Parthenon in Centennial Park and the beautiful flowers at the Cheekwood estate. If you are a country music or bluegrass fan, you might add a visit to Music Row in Nashville where the studios and record companies are concentrated. Or try to get a ticket for the Grand Ole Opry, though sellouts are common for their shows.

Going Solo: "No contraindications as to suitability for single travelers."

Shortcomings: None.

Getting In: A piece of cake.

Getting There: Nashville has a thriving airport and a bustling bus terminal, then a rental car is necessary for the rest of the journey.

Paris Landing State Park— Austin Peay State University

Courses of Study: Gunboats, Snow, and the Turn of a Battle: Fort Donelson and the Civil War; Fairy Tales, Wild Women, and Wise Old Men; Jazz, Jazz, and All That Jazz; Pioneers, Their Children and Their Children's Children; 300 Million Years Ago; Tennessee: The Constitution and the Presidency

Quality of Instructors: The very good professors from Austin Peay are assisted by local experts as required.

Environment: Paris Landing is a state-owned park located in the Land Between the Lakes Recreation Area, which includes two beautiful lakes and a wilderness area. A bird refuge and the National Military Park and Cemetery at Fort Donelson are also part of this recreation complex set among green rolling hills. TVA dams form the most completely controlled river system in the world.

Housing: Elderhostelers are housed in a deluxe Hilton Inn owned and operated by the state of Tennessee. The modern hotel, whose rooms have private baths, overlooks the majestic Tennessee River.

Food: Superb meals are served buffet-style. "Expect "down home" food in Tennessee.

Unique Attributes: The deluxe accommodations (not always found in Elderhostels) received many compliments. This program includes many particularly interesting field trips. The van takes Elderhostelers to the famous Civil War battlefield at Fort Donelson where General Simon Buckner surrendered to Ulysses S. Grant. Relics of the battle—sabers, muskets, trenches, and gun batteries —mark the North's first major victory in 1862. Elderhostelers also visit the Homestead, a model 1850 farm complete with live animals, spinning wheels, and weaving looms.

Birders have an opportunity to identify many varieties of cardinals and spot wild turkeys and mockingbirds in the bird sanctuary.

Shortcomings: The university and park are 45 miles apart. Although Elderhostel administrators and teachers join the group for dinner at Paris Landing, several much-traveled Elderhostelers believe the distance has a negative impact on the program. There's a lack of after-hours camaraderie with the faculty, and the use of other university facilities is precluded.

Getting In: The hotel is able to accommodate fairly large groups and has not been troubled with long waiting lists to date.

Getting There: Clarksville, Tennessee, can be reached by regularly scheduled flights, and there is public bus service to the park. If you wish to thoroughly explore the countryside before or after the program, my reviewers suggest traveling by private automobile.

TEXAS

Austin—St. Edwards University

Courses of Study: Religions of the World; Enjoyment of Music; Planning Ahead to Get the Most out of Life

Quality of Instructors: Top-notch professors who are effective communicators.

Environment: St. Edwards enjoys a great college environment in Austin, the state capital and site of the largest university campus in the state, the University of Texas. The land rolls gently, and the horizon is far-reaching. Austin sits in the middle of the state and is a booming high-tech city, but it retains an old-fashioned walkable downtown. The Capitol itself is a red granite version of the Capitol in Washington, D.C., with a lone star at the apex of the Texas dome. Cattle still graze on the outskirts of Austin.

Housing: Elderhostelers stay in comfortable, handsome dormitory rooms with semiprivate bath and toilet facilities. The rooms are air-conditioned, and singles are available.

Food: The university cafeteria provides delicious, filling meals— "classic college fare," I was told.

Unique Attributes: The Elderhostel director, Sister Madeline Sophie Weber, tends tirelessly to every need of the attendees. Texas oil money has made the University of Texas a prosperous institution and Austin a fast-growing metropolitan city. In response to huge student demands, Austin has film festivals, opera, traveling theater, and excellent museums. There are literary events, good bookstores, record stores, and funky cafes—all patronized by the students. There is also an avant-garde music scene, both jazz and country.

Shortcomings: Texas can be hotter than the hinges of hell in the summer, but fortunately all the buildings at St. Edwards are air-conditioned.

Getting In: St. Edwards University has been able to accommodate Elderhostel registration requests as received.

Getting There: Austin is a metropolitan city that has frequent service by major air carriers, buses, and trains.

UTAH

Cedar City—Southern Utah State College

Courses of Study: Geology of Southern Utah's Color Country; A Review of Four Decades of Nuclear Testing; Archaeology of Southwest Utah; The Literary Essence of Shakespeare; Radio in the Golden Years; Utah Shakespearean Festival

Quality of Instructors: "The teachers at Southern Utah are competent in their fields, witty, and have an easy, likable manner."

Environment: "The environment is exquisite." The school has a charming little campus set in the heart of town. "It's one of the cleanest, most wholesome places I've ever been." This is a pretty area of Utah, not all dust-dry creekbeds and sagebrush as one might expect. Cedar City, at 5,800 feet elevation, is located midway between Salt Lake City and Las Vegas, Nevada.

Housing: Elderhostelers stay in tiny but adequate rooms in an old-fashioned dormitory with communal bath and toilet facilities. The air-conditioned building used for July and August programs is a three-flight walk-up. In September, Elderhostelers are housed in a commercial facility.

Food: A small, nice cafeteria in the student center serves food that is "the best of many Elderhostels."

Unique Attributes: Cedar City is the home of the renowned Utah Shakespeare Festival. Student productions of Shakespeare are presented in the evening in an outdoor theater designed to replicate the Globe in England. There is also an indoor theater for use in inclement weather. "A beautifully costumed, well-rehearsed cast performs on handsomely designed sets," wrote the reviewer. Each evening performance is preceded by a morning seminar and an evening precurtain lecture on the current production. Tickets for three performances are included in the Elderhostel registration fee.

The Elderhostel program also includes a day trip to two splendid national parks. Participants visit the monoliths of Zion National Park—natural arches, mesas, and buttes striated in red and pink—and the great stone pinnacles and horseshoe-shaped amphitheaters of Bryce Canyon.

Shortcomings: The weather in southern Utah can be very wet in August. Apparently the indoor theater is used frequently then. Another panelist reported that in his opinion the students performed with "mediocre proficiency." This was a drawback but not serious enough to keep him from reenrolling at this destination.

Getting In: In spite of all the accolades, the Cedar City Shakespeare Festival is not as well known as the Oregon Festival. My reviewers experienced no difficulty in registering for the program.

Getting There: Cedar City can be reached by interstate bus or by a commuter airline from Phoenix, Arizona.

Provo—Brigham Young University

Courses of Study: Beginning Genealogy Workshop; Composing Your Personal History; Genealogy Library Workshop; Western History and the Mormons; Painting a Landscape in Oil; Masterpieces of Music and Literature

Quality of Instructors: The Mormon professors are very serious about education and have a somber approach to marriage, child-rearing, and family. All teachers are very proficient.

Environment: Brigham Young University is owned and operated by the Church of Jesus Christ of Latter Day Saints, whose tenets create a pleasant but very conservative atmosphere. The university has a code of honor, a dress code that prohibits the wearing of shorts, and a prohibition against caffeine and alcohol. Even the students' hair length is regulated; the boys may not wear pony tails. The absence of student cafes makes Provo very quiet at night, but the cleanliness and well-tended landscape of the town and campus make for a very pleasant quality of life. Brigham Young has an attractive suburban campus that spreads along the shores of freshwater Utah Lake.

Housing: The dormitories, like the rest of the campus, are spotlessly clean. There are central television rooms and swimming pools right in the sex-segregated dormitories.

Food: The meals are wonderful—lots of homemade breads and delectable homemade ice cream. At Brigham Young the groaning board really groans. The invention of caffeine-free cola was met with great eagerness at Brigham Young.

Unique Attributes: The largest library on the subject of genealogy is the Mormon Library in Salt Lake City. Although Provo doesn't swing at night like many university towns, the school has its own symphony, an active drama department, fine cinema, and a jazz group. All sporting events are well attended. Because of the Mormon belief in education, Utah boasts a uniquely high percentage of high school and college graduates. Every Elderhostel day opens with an interdenominational prayer—"a nice touch, not offensive to anyone," said one of my panelists. The automobile drive to Provo takes one over steep switchbacks, past cobalt blue lakes, stone arches, and natural bridges.

Shortcomings: None. The Elderhostel program at Brigham Young is top-notch in every respect.

Getting In: I would have expected to hear complaints about long waiting lists for this destination, but no such reports were forwarded to me.

Getting There: Provo has good interstate bus service and can be reached by connecting airplane flights from Salt Lake City.

VERMONT

Poultney—Green Mountain College

Courses of Study: All the World's a Stage; Beginning Bird Identification; Ancient Heroines Updated; Robert Frost, Vermont's Poet Laureate; Body Recall; Remember the Ladies: American Women of Letters

Quality of Instructors: Reports ranged from very good to gifted and outstanding.

Environment: Poultney is a quaint New England town located on the New York-Vermont border, 20 miles southwest of Rutland. It's in the midst of some major ski areas—Killington, Stratton, and Bromley. The mountainous countryside is beautiful in all seasons, green and lush in the summer, ablaze in brilliant color in the fall, and a still blanket of whiteness in the winter.

Green Mountain College has a 155-acre campus. Its modern facilities include an art center with studios, a television and audiovisual lab, and a physical education complex of swimming pool and dance studios. Green Mountain is a very small coed school of 350 students with buildings in classic New England college style.

Housing: This small school has six residence halls. Elderhostelers stay in twin-bedded dormitory rooms with communal bath facilities. There are alternate floors for men and women, and single rooms are available.

Food: The menu is ample and the quality of food served is satisfactory. My reviewers complimented the cafeteria staff for their very nice variety of salads, and they developed a fondness for that special Vermont deep-orange cheddar cheese.

Unique Attributes: The quality of courses offered at the Green Mountain College program received accolades from my panelists. Particular note was made of the teacher who brought the Frost poetry course to life and the wildflower walks in local fields and meadows. This program can put you in touch with nature, people, and ideas. The extracurricular activities are very good; they include a picnic and swim at a nearby state park and lake and an outdoor barbecue on campus. In Rutland, the Norman Rockwell Museum, with 2,000 pieces of Rockwell memorabilia, is worth visiting. One couple recommended a stop at the Calvin Coolidge home and museum.

Shortcomings: None noted.

Getting In: My panelists were accepted on the first try.

Getting There: Poultney is situated on excellent interstate highways and has an Amtrak railroad station. Rutland is the nearest airport.

VIRGINIA

Ferrum—Ferrum College

Courses of Study: Blue Ridge Folklife; Traditional Music of the Blue Ridge; Craft Traditions of the Blue Ridge

Quality of Instructors: Excellent instructors, who know and love their subject, are assisted by local traditional craftspersons and musicians.

Environment: The college is located in a rural setting on the eastern slopes of the Blue Ridge Mountains, 35 miles south of Roanoke. The campus adjoins a restored nineteenth-century farm and is close to the Blue Ridge Parkway, the most scenic drive of the South.

Housing: Double or single dormitory rooms are available with separate communal toilet and shower rooms.

Food: "There's a great salad bar, but too much fried and rich food." The cafeteria is standard steamtable specializing in southern-style cooking.

Unique Attributes: Wonderful hands-on craft courses in the Blue Ridge tradition—basketry, blacksmithing, and open hearth cooking. There are field visits to homes of local craftspeople and evening concerts of traditional music performed by local musicians. "A most unusual experience. We were totally immersed in a unique way of life. The staff made every effort to be helpful."

Shortcomings: The men's bath and shower is inconveniently located one flight up. A well-lit sitting area is needed for evening socializing. Rooms are clean but shabby.

Going Solo: Not for a single single. Most attendees arrive by automobile, which generally means a predominance of couples in attendance, couples who use their cars for sightseeing during free time. My reviewers observed a group of singles who drove together and "seemed to have a good time."

Getting In: No difficulty.

Getting There: The staff will meet participants who arrive in Roanoke by plane or Greyhound bus. Amtrak has a bus that connects with its "Cardinal Route" at Clifton Forge, Virginia. Most participants drive their own cars.

Staunton—Mary Baldwin College

Courses of Study: Shenandoah: The Great Valley of Virginia; The World of Beethoven: The Man and His Music; Presidents Jefferson, Madison, Monroe, and Wilson

Quality of Instructors: The professors are exceptional. Very good, skillful communicators.

Environment: The college has a beautiful campus of cream and white buildings spread on a hillside overlooking historic Shenandoah Valley. Staunton is a city of 25,000 people whose southern life-style is more leisurely and more hospitable than their neighbors to the north. The predominant architectural style of Staunton is a European classic design that uses local materials of red brick and painted wood. Virginia has a countrified grandeur, and its residents seem to have pride in and a deep sense of our country's valuable heritage.

Housing: The dormitories are pleasant, very clean, and well equipped. They are comfortable without air-conditioning because they are well shaded; elevators make the upper floors easily accessible.

Food: One Elderhosteler, with a low threshold of culinary resistance, complained that the meals at Mary Baldwin are too enticing. "Nothing ordinary about this college fare," she said. "Lots of fruits and salads, all beautifully served," wrote another panelist.

Unique Attributes: Staunton is ideally located for visiting historic shrines and for enjoying a national park. It is near Charlottesville, the Harding birthplace, and Monticello, the home of

Thomas Jefferson. Woodrow Wilson's birthplace is at the edge of the campus. One historic old church, visited during the program, has twelve Tiffany windows. The countryside is dotted with memorials to great men and great Civil War battles. The Skyline Drive runs along the top of mountain ridges of Shenandoah National Park. One Elderhosteler commented that her visit to the roots of democracy "strengthened her awareness of the ideas and forces that promoted freedom in the past."

Shortcomings: The campus is very hilly and has many steps, difficult going for people whose walking ability is limited. Mirrors are used to mark the many blind corners. The opportunities for sightseeing are wonderful, but that means taking your own car to the campus.

Going Solo: "Give it a 5. The experience is so great I hate to think of anyone staying away." "A number of single persons in attendance and they seemed well assimilated."

Getting In: Because of Staunton's proximity to the East Coast megalopolises, there are long waiting lists for some programs.

Getting There: If one has the time and energy for a heavy dose of American history, an automobile is the preferred method of getting to Mary Baldwin. If not, Staunton can be reached by Trailways or Greyhound bus, Amtrak, or Piedmont Airlines. The college van will meet air arrivals.

WASHINGTON

Ellensburg—Central Washington University

Courses of Study: Computer Skills; The Physiology and Psychology of Exercise; Cross-Country Skiing; Sign Language from Chimpanzees to Children; Forensic Anthropology; Indian Art and Mythology

Quality of Instructors: The teaching staff is excellent.

Environment: Central Washington University is a coed, state-supported institution of 6,300 undergraduates. The spacious, beautiful campus is spread along the Yakima River and surrounded by mountains. Kittitas Valley is a high green valley nestled between mountains and desert. The area is dotted with alpine lakes and apple orchards, the winters are white and cold, and the air is free of pollution. Central Washington is filled with stands of Douglas fir, ancient forests that are valuable as lumber and also with an intangible value as wilderness areas. Washington is aptly named the Evergreen State.

Housing: Accommodations are in a conference center that has both single and double rooms.

Food: The university cafeteria is better than most. Elderhostelers enjoy lots of fresh berries and local apples used in a variety of recipes.

Unique Attributes: The Elderhostel program administration gets a rating of five stars. The director is a young woman with a master's degree in recreation, and, according to my reviewers, she must have earned all As in her courses. The boat trip, field trips, and evening activities are planned and executed in an exemplary fashion. All field trips are included in the cost of tuition. Many programs are of 2-week duration with a mid-Saturday excursion to a local museum, winery, or art gallery.

Shortcomings: None, unless one has difficulty with the extensive amount of walking required.

Getting In: My reviewers said that Ellensburg is their favorite of 14 Elderhostels attended. If it isn't popular yet, I'll wager it soon will be.

Getting There: The nearest airport is Spokane, but I've heard that the drive over Snoqualmie Pass is especially beautiful and well worth the effort.

Packwood—Lower Columbia College

Courses of Study: Mount Rainier: Past and Present; Mount St. Helens: An Experience with the Volcano

Quality of Instructors: A very good husband and wife team; he is a physical education teacher and she is a botany instructor. Members of the Forest Service staff add lectures, demonstrations, and field trips to the classwork of the college faculty.

Environment: Packwood is a small lumbering town 75 miles north of Portland, Oregon, in the Cascade mountain foothills of Mount Rainier. It is a superbly scenic area. Alpine flowers push through late snow in the meadows beneath jagged peaks and waterfalls. The town is located just a few miles from the entrance to the half-million acres of the national park.

Housing: Elderhostelers stay in the Royal Inn Motel in Packwood. No singles are available, but all rooms have private baths. The motel amenities include an indoor pool, cable TV, and telephones.

Food: Poor. Breakfast and dinner are served in a local restaurant with a fixed menu and no choices. Some meals are unappetizing and meager. Lunches are served picnic style—sandwiches and fruit are to be eaten in picnic areas of the park. "On the last night, a very good outdoor salmon bake was hosted by the instructors at their nearby home."

Unique Attributes: Experienced hikers only are invited to either of these programs. One program is a week of daily hikes and explorations of the magnificence of 14,410-foot Mount Rainier. The mountain, which seems to hover over Seattle, still has gassy fumes spewing out of its volcanic cone. Wildflowers edge the glaciers, and dense forests of cedars and fir cover the south slope. The newest program is designed to increase understanding of the eruption of Mount St. Helens and its impact on the environment. Rugged participants hike into the devastated areas.

Shortcomings: My reviewers were unhappy with the accommodations. The bedrooms are very small and lack drawer space for the storage of clothing. The proprietors provided milk cartons for storage, but attendees must primarily live out of their suitcases. Bring your foul weather gear.

Getting In: No problems reported. My reviewers were accepted on the first try.

Getting There: Packwood can be reached by bus, plane, or train. One can fly to San Francisco or Portland and rent a car for an interesting drive with stops at Columbia River Gorge, Crater Lake, and Lake Tahoe.

Seattle—Seattle University

Courses of Study: The Symphony; The Real and Ideal in Ancient Athens; The Self-Portrait; Wonder and Wisdom: An Introduction to Philosophy; Art of Gardening; An American Welfare State?

Quality of Instructors: Extremely well qualified, good-humored professors with pleasant personalities.

Environment: The university has an urban campus right in the heart of Seattle, but the atmosphere is so conducive to scholarly pursuits that the city does not intrude on the Elderhostel program. Seattle enjoys a mild maritime climate, albeit cloudy and sometimes rainy. The climate during the summer is perfect—it stays light until 10:00 p.m. There is a manageable downtown district, replete with bookstores, art galleries, and jazz clubs, and the arboretum boasts 600 kinds of camellias. It is a prosperous city, a condition that had its beginnings in the Klondike Gold Rush of the 1890s. Some historic artifacts of the period can be found in the city's museums. Seattle University is a Jesuit school on a clean, beautiful, 41-acre campus that is within walking distance of Puget Sound waterfront.

Housing: Elderhostelers are usually housed in a large modern dormitory, alternating floors with college students and people enrolled in other programs. The bathroom facilities seem inadequate when the dormitories are fully occupied.

Food: Excellent food is served in abundance in the school cafeteria. Once again I heard the same old lament—"too much, too good." While in Seattle you'll be served lots of small, crisp, locally grown apples, reminiscent of the fruit of your childhood, as well as plenty of fresh fish.

Unique Attributes: The dormitory is in a lovely building that also has a very large lobby with comfortable social group seating. Each floor has a small television and "nibble" room with coffee, tea, and cookies available at all hours. The dining room is also in the same building. The school is conveniently located, within walking distance of beautiful shopping arcades and right on a public bus route to the downtown area. The city has a passion for parks; in spring the blooming Japanese cherry trees rival those in Washington, D.C. There's also a famous farmers' market with fishmongers and flower stalls. Elderhostel staff are attentive and well prepared, and the program is well balanced. One couple attended a session when the campus was deserted except for the Elderhostelers. They found the experience pleasant.

Shortcomings: Some reviewers believed the bathroom facilities inadequate for the number of people in the program. "Otherwise everything's perfect."

Getting In: Now that Seattle has been honored by several polls that selected it as one of the country's most livable cities, I imagine waiting lists for this destination will lengthen.

Getting There: Seattle is a major city easily reached by all forms of public transportation.

WISCONSIN

Ashland—Northland College

Courses of Study: Early Days Around the Bay; Understanding and Overcoming Upset Feelings; Ecology of the North Woods

Quality of Instructors: A dynamic group of professors of wildlife management and environmental studies.

Environment: Ashland is located on Chequamegon Bay, a bustling port on Lake Superior, and the campus is just one mile away. Chequamegon Bay, according to legend, is the "Shining Big Sea Water" of Longfellow's epic poem, "Hiawatha." Wisconsin is a favorite vacationland; its glistening lakes and streams, hundreds of waterfalls, hardwood forests, and cool summer weather are great attractions. This area is part of the Mississippi flyway; flocks of birds migrating in the spring and fall fly over herds of Guernseys grazing in the meadows.

Housing: Elderhostelers are housed in usual college dormitories.

Food: Satisfactory. No *Guide Michelin* stars.

Unique Attributes: Northland is a small school founded to bring higher education to isolated logging camps and farm communities. It is affiliated with the United Church of Christ. Elderhostelers enjoy swimming in the refreshing waters of Lake Superior and watching the fishermen deep-water trolling. On campus in an earth-sheltered, solar-heated building is the Sigurd Olson Environmental Institute. "A good mix of recreation and studies," wrote one reviewer. Elderhostelers take field trips into woods and swamps and to historic Madeline Island. The 23 glacier-created Apostle Islands are clustered in the cold waters of Lake Superior. Madeline Island, with lovely soft sand beaches on the sheltered side, is one of them. Bring your binoculars along with your inquiring mind.

Shortcomings: Summer is short and the winters vigorous in Wisconsin.

Getting In: I am not aware of any registration difficulties at this destination.

Getting There: Ashland is serviced by the Duluth, Minnesota / Superior, Wisconsin airport.

Eagle River—Trees for Tomorrow
Natural Resources Education Center

Courses of Study: Trees: A Resource for Tomorrow; Wading into Wildlife; Natural History of the Northwoods; Autumn in the Northwoods: An Ecological Study

Quality of Instructors: All are working specialists who demonstrate their particular skills.

Environment: This 40-acre education center is hidden away in the backwoods of northern Wisconsin. It is situated on the Eagle River chain of lakes, deep in a grove of pine trees adjacent to Yellow Birch Lake where "tree leafers" can touch, smell, and feel the wonders of autumn. Eagle River is situated east of the dense Chequamegon National Forest, a woodland dotted with sparkling lakes.

Housing: In bunk beds in a not new but cozy lodge. The women's shower facilities are new.

Food: Very good home-cooked meals are served in a quaint dining hall overlooking the lake. "A great fresh fish boil is held outdoors."

Unique Attributes: Evening lectures are augmented with daily field trips to a floating bog, a cranberry bog, and forest management stations. Participants learn about forest fire control and tree identification. Instructors with reverence for the trees proselytize Elderhostelers from all over the United States as they take participants tromping in the woods. Strongly committed conservationists preach reforestation, fire control, and preserving nature's ecological balance. My reviewer belongs to an Elderhostel Club that meets monthly and shares experiences. Eagle River was recommended as a unique destination. "It really is," my friend said.

Shortcomings: One must be in very good physical condition, so this program's for active hostelers only. There are many bus trips and hikes in the woods.

Going Solo: Highly recommended for robust singles. The rustic accommodations attract a casual, congenial crowd.

Getting In: This one requires perseverance, but it is well worth it. The Center can accommodate only 45 hostelers at one time.

Getting There: If you fly to Rhinelander, Wisconsin, staff will meet your plane. Most attendees drive.

Green Lake—American Baptist Assembly

Courses of Study: Developing a Feel for Art; Stewardship of Our Planet; Swimnastics; Creative Writing; Bible Study

Quality of Instructors: "Excellent. One instructor, who I have heard frequently, could read the telephone book and charm the class."

Environment: The motto of the American Baptist Assembly is "For a Closer Walk With God." This 1,000-acre forest and prairie is the national training and conference center for American Baptists. The grounds are beautiful and extensive, a real vacation paradise nestled beside Green Lake. The lake, 40 miles southwest of Oshkosh, is the deepest of Wisconsin's 8,000 lakes. Loons and other waterfowl can be found breeding there.

Housing: Hostelers stay in double rooms with private baths in the Roger Williams Inn, a handsome year-round hotel on the lakefront. The inn is listed in the AAA hotel guide. Its commodious lobby houses a very fine collection of gemstones, much of which will eventually go to the Smithsonian.

Food: Excellent resort food is served in the hotel's Veranda Dining Room, which has lovely views of the lake.

Unique Attributes: The recreational opportunities are superb. Lawsonia Links is one of the finest golf courses in the United States. There are a competition-size swimming pool, boats on the lake, nature trails for hiking, and an arts and crafts building equipped for lapidary, stained glass, and ceramic classes. There's a library, and a gift shop and bookstore for the shoppers. In addition, the warm, friendly staff considers all Elderhostelers a part of the "family."

Shortcomings: None, unless you consider the "no liquor" regulation a drawback.

Going Solo: "You'll never walk alone," my single reviewer wrote, after her third visit to Green Lake. "A definite 5 on all counts. A spirit of fellowship is fostered and carried out in all activities."

Getting In: Early application is a must. However, this is my advice for all popular programs.

Getting There: Easily accessible by car, bus, train, or plane. Staff charge a modest fee for pickups at depots and airport, which must be prearranged.

Milwaukee—Mount Mary College

Courses of Study: The Zoo and Beyond: Animals, the Land and Life

Quality of Instructors: "Both kites and ideas fly at Mt. Mary." The school is directed by the Sisters of Notre Dame, an order proud of its tradition of teaching excellence. An anthropologist, a geographer, and a biologist lecture in the zoo program.

Environment: Mount Mary is an urban campus right on the Menominee River Parkway in a residential area of Milwaukee, 5 minutes from a shopping mall and 15 minutes from downtown. A Catholic school for women, its Tudor Gothic buildings are all located on a level campus in close proximity to one another. The city of Milwaukee is the center of German-American culture in the United States and is also the beer capital of the country. Beer gardens, beer steins, and lederhosen give the city its special local color. "Gemütlichkeit" best describes the city's convivial atmosphere. Milwaukee covers 96 square miles on the western shore of Lake Michigan, and its harbor is the chief port on the Great Lakes. The opening of the St. Lawrence Seaway made Milwaukee a major seaport with docks and piers and large oceangoing vessels.

Housing: Dormitories have double or single rooms with one bathroom to serve each pair.

Food: Elderhostelers are offered three meals a day in the usual college cafeteria steamtable style.

Unique Attributes: The college and the world-famous Milwaukee Zoo are near neighbors, and together they designed this in-depth program, the equivalent of three Elderhostel courses. Three days of zoo safaris and behind-the-scenes visits are interspersed with class lectures. At this zoo animals stare at visitors across natural moats, not through the bars of steel cages. In addition, the college location permits easy access to downtown Milwaukee by public transportation—"if you can find the time," my reviewer wrote. Milwaukee has many diversions—legitimate theater, symphony concerts, a ballet company, and beautiful churches. It also boasts a lakefront art museum. One can "do" the city on a sight-seeing Gray Line bus. This is a particularly comfortable destination for hostelers who do not travel by private automobile. The college promotes physical fitness with a fitness center, four tennis courts, jogging and bike paths, and cross-country ski trails for winter use.

Shortcomings: No weaknesses reported.

Getting In: Mount Mary has an avid fan club, but they have not reported any registration difficulties.

Getting There: Milwaukee is a major transportation center. One can get there by wheels or wings.

Platteville—University of Wisconsin

Courses of Study: The Search for Life in the Universe; The Significance of Music as a Salutary Factor in America's Wars; *Love's Labor Lost*; Experience Shakespeare Backstage; *Othello*; Astronomy

Quality of Instructors: Among the very best. The University of Wisconsin is noted for its galaxy of professors.

Environment: Platteville, a rural community of 10,000, is in the lovely rolling hills of southwestern Wisconsin, about 25 miles from Dubuque, Iowa. It was a prairie boomtown that cropped up when miners, eager to try their luck, arrived in 1825. The new buildings of the University of Wisconsin's small branch campus are on the edge of town. The grounds are well manicured and shaded with lovely trees.

Housing: Dormitory rooms in Pickard Hall are not air-conditioned.

Food: The cafeteria serves a great variety and lots of wonderful ice cream! In our nation's dairyland, they couldn't do otherwise.

Unique Attributes: A complimentary ticket for one performance of the Shakespeare Festival is included with program registration. But the trip and prime rib dinner on a Mississippi River stern-wheeler has an additional charge. Much to see and do. Platteville has a summer music festival, there is a Chicago Bears training camp, and Frank Lloyd Wright's home is in Spring Green, Wisconsin. The director and staff give the Elderhostel group their undivided attention, and faculty and community people join many hostel functions. Very friendly ambience.

Shortcomings: If you drive to this destination, bring a fan! There were some complaints about a short church service held before the cookout at the student religious center.

Going Solo: Because most participants drive to this destination, a single single might find himself or herself surrounded by clannish couples. I suggest driving with an acquaintance or requesting a roommate if using public transportation.

Getting In: Not as difficult as some schools because Platteville can accommodate a rather large group.

Getting There: Fly to Dubuque, Iowa, and rent a car or climb aboard a Greyhound bus.

Sheboygan — Lakeland College

Courses of Study: Opera for Opera Haters; Engineering Life at What Price?; Wordsworth and the Age of Romanticism; The Lure and Lore of Scotland; The Fascinating Changing English Language

Quality of Instructors: Excellent. They demonstrate a genuine concern for students and subject matter.

Environment: Small Lakeland College, with its 1,200 students, has rural tranquillity and a bucolic atmosphere. The campus lies an hour's drive north of Milwaukee and 10 miles north of Sheboygan. The school is near both lakes and forests — Lake Michigan, Elkhart Lake, and the Kettle Moraine State Forest. Sheboygan is a popular fishing port on the western shore of Lake Michigan.

Housing: In modern residence halls that are convenient to both the classrooms and dining hall.

Food: Typical college fare is offered. One Elderhosteler, a woman weary of her domestic duties, wrote, "As long as I'm not cooking, it's all good." Sheboygan celebrates an annual event known as "Bratwurst Day," so I wouldn't be surprised if the "wurst" in Sheboygan must be the best!

Unique Attributes: Milwaukee is the center of German-American culture in the United States, and some of this spills over into Sheboygan and Lakeland College. While dairy cattle graze on the Wisconsin plains, the factories are busy pressing cheese and breweries are busy concocting beer. The state is a sportsman's paradise: sparkling lakes are full of muskellunge, pike, and bass for the fisherman, while hunters chase the deer and the really intrepid go iceboating on Lake Michigan. Nearby Kohler Village has lovely landscaped gardens and the Kohler Arts Center mounts exhibitions, dance recitals, and concerts. Sheboygan, like much of Wisconsin, has beer gardens that vibrate with music and fun after the sun goes down.

Shortcomings: My reviewers complained about the poor recreational facilities at the college. "No swimming pool—walking our only choice."

Getting In: At this time, the Lakeland College program is not troubled with waiting lists.

Getting There: Milwaukee is served by most major air carriers and interstate railroad lines. Sheboygan is on interstate bus routes.

Tomahawk—University of Wisconsin, Stevens Point/Treehaven

Courses of Study: Two-Week Intensive Programs in Field Study of Our Northern Birds; Nature Photography; Sketching or Creative Writing

Quality of Instructors: An excellent group of ornithologists, regional experts in the other fields, and full professors from the university.

Environment: Treehaven is a tranquil, wooded, thousand-acre site full of birds, trout streams, and beaver ponds. It is a fully winterized natural resource educational facility of the Stevens Point branch of the University of Wisconsin, not far from Tomahawk and Rhinelander.

Housing: Good, carpeted, dormitory style with shared baths. Singles are available; and women are on one floor and men on another. "Dorms are coed from 11:00 p.m. to 5:00 a.m.—it worked fine."

Food: Good and plentiful buffet-style. Nice cookouts and picnics on field trips.

Unique Attributes: Eager bird-watchers get their kettles boiling on voluntary 6:00 a.m. bird walks. Staff are very adept at hearing, identifying, and locating birds and conduct field trips to nearby areas stalking different species. Indoor classes are combined with outdoor excursions, and guest speakers present evening programs. This is a fulfilling adventure that keeps one in touch with nature and people. Remember your binoculars. The two-week courses permit in-depth study with considerable one-on-one instruction.

Shortcomings: None.

Getting In: No problem; my reviewer was admitted on the first try.

Getting There: "Treehaven is an easy drive over nice highways through beautiful country." Northwest and United airlines fly to Rhinelander, and staff make arrangements to meet your plane.

Whitewater—University of Wisconsin at Whitewater

Courses of Study: India; A Society in Transition; Writing Your Life Story; The American Judicial Heritage

Quality of Instructors: A particularly competent and caring group of instructors do some mind jogging.

Environment: Whitewater is in southern Wisconsin between the two largest cities, Milwaukee and Madison. The university campus sits on the edge of Kettle Moraine State Forest, 18,000 acres of rough wooded country. The buildings are spread over gentle green hills near lakes teeming with game fish, while many varieties of violets, the state flower, can be found in the woods. Whitewater is one of the two-year branch institutions of the University of Wisconsin.

Housing: Elderhostelers sleep in student dormitories with communal bath facilities.

Food: The meals served at the Whitewater program are judged to be rather too institutional. The classic college fare needs some imaginative touches to earn higher grades from the Elderhostelers.

Unique Attributes: Because of its geographic isolation, a very pleasant sense of camaraderie exists at Whitewater. Another factor that encourages the friendly atmosphere is the informal dialogue that transpires when the professors dine with Elderhostelers. One of the program highlights is an early evening cruise on Lake Geneva, a resort area famous for its palatial shoreline estates. Both Madison and Milwaukee have beer gardens that vibrate with music and fun after the sun goes down.

Shortcomings: The physical facilities are not as comfortable as many Elderhostel destinations. The dining room is some distance from the dormitory and up a flight of steps. This can be a royal pain. The lack of air-conditioning in the dormitories can be troublesome in the summer.

Getting In: I am not aware of any registration difficulties at this destination.

Getting There: Madison is the nearest major travel center, and it has excellent service by air, interstate bus, or train.

WYOMING

UCross—UCross Foundation

Courses of Study: Ranching in the Rockies: The History and Practice of Ranching. This course covers: The Cattle Barons, Ranch History, Contemporary Ranching, Llama and Fish Ranching, and the Arts and Ranching

Quality of Instructors: All are experienced in their respective fields, show excellent slides, and answer questions thoughtfully.

Environment: "Home on the range." The UCross ranch is located near Buffalo, Wyoming, close to the base of the Big Horn Mountains. The mountains, forested with pine and aspen, rise from valleys to 13,165 feet. The ranch is a restored historic facility and provides accommodations and meals for Elderhostelers. It is also open to paying guests year-round. Classes are held at another foundation facility, a conference center. Buffalo is a typical western town; its main street is lined with saloons and stores that sell fishing lures and hunting rifles.

Housing: Single rooms with private bath accommodations are in a nearby annex. Rooms are heated and have balconies. Couples are offered very comfortable rooms with private baths in the main lodge.

Food: Continental breakfast; sandwich, salad, and dessert luncheon; and a choice of entrées at dinner each evening. Milk, coffee, or juice always available. Plenty of fresh vegetables and fresh fruit. Everything well prepared by a German chef and nicely served in a handsome dining room in the main lodge.

Unique Attributes: Many. The foundation owns several facilities, the ranch and, 4 miles away, an art barn and studios and housing for artists in residence. Three vans transport the group to the barn for slide shows, outings, and daily field trips. Great trips are offered to a sheep ranch, a fish hatchery, and a cattle branding and looking for elk at the Paradise Ranch in the Big Horns. Drivers are staff people who live in and know the area. Long days start at 8:00 a.m., so everyone is ready to turn in by 10:00 p.m. There's a good variety of evening entertainment: slide talks by a pair of local artists; a presentation of Indian artifacts, beadwork, and ornamentation by an Indian artist; entertainment by the ranch staff; and a farewell night dance with seniors from a club in Sheridan.

Shortcomings: The ranch is somewhat isolated from "civilization" and not easily reached. "Nearest supermarket is 20 miles away." A distinct advantage from my point of view, but you may disagree.

Going Solo: My single reviewer gives this destination a 5. "The keen enthusiasm is infectious and everyone tends to be a lively participant. I now correspond regularly with some hostelers I met in Wyoming." This destination has many attributes for the solo traveler; it is self-contained, a private car is not needed during the week, singles are housed away from the couples, evening entertainment is offered, and the dining arrangements are gracious.

Getting In: The ranch is rather new at Elderhosteling so it is not yet at the top of the charts.

Getting There: The airport in Sheridan, Wyoming, is serviced from Denver by a local carrier. If you wish to drive, the roads are good, but the distances are deceptive—many miles long.

INTERNATIONAL PROGRAMS

Elderhostel conducts many of its international programs in conjunction with a "partner," a travel organization such as Saga, the Experiment in International Living, or IST, International Study Tours. Despite this arrangement, Elderhostel remains an educational program, and participants are expected to attend classes and lectures much as they do at host institutions in the United States. The courses given abroad are not for credit and there is no assigned homework, but the emphasis is on study, not on sightseeing.

Group travel arrangements are made for most destinations. The price of Elderhostel international programs usually includes round-trip airfare on regularly scheduled airlines; all within-country travel; full room and board; course-related excursions and admission fees; and limited accident, illness, and baggage insurance.

The Elderhostel programs in Israel, Brazil, Egypt, France, and Greece are under the auspices of IST, an organization established in Massachusetts in 1981 which offers two- and three-week programs in twenty major universities and academic institutions on four continents.

Saga Holidays, Inc., is an English company with 35 years of experience in serving the vacation needs of British pensioners over sixty years old. Saga programs have an educational focus and feature classes in England, Scotland, Wales, and the Republic of Ireland.

The Experiment in International Living is a worldwide not-for-profit federation that has been offering homestay vacations for students since 1932. Organized to improve international understanding on a personal level, their services now include United Nations projects and homestay programs for seniors in fifty nations. In 1988, programs jointly sponsored by Elderhostel / Experiment in International Living were held in France, India, Switzerland, West Germany, Mexico, and Japan.

Elderhostel programs in China (American Huajia Study) are organized in cooperation with CAEE, a nonprofit organization based at the College of Staten Island of the City University of New York in conjunction with Chinese universities. CAEE has been offering university and professional exchange programs with China since 1979. Although Elderhostelers are treated as distinguished guests, the three-week study programs, through lectures, on-site visits, and informal dialogues with instructors, students, and Chinese families, permit participants to observe China as friends and students, not just as visitors.

Some programs in Scandinavia and a half dozen northern European countries are conducted under the auspices of Scandinavian Seminars, Inc., an organization that has been providing opportunities for American college students to spend a year of living and learning in Scandinavia since 1949. The Elderhostelers spend three weeks of travel and study, with daily lectures in English.

Elderhostel programs in Japan are organized by Elderhostel and InterElder, a nonprofit Japanese organization that provides educational programs and services for older adults in Japan. InterElder Japan has arranged a varied program with experienced lecturers covering the Japanese economy, educational system, history, and the arts.

All international opportunities are more thoroughly described in the official Elderhostel catalog than are domestic destinations. Therefore, I have included here a mere sampling of some selected sites to give a sense of hosteling around the world, an experience as original and impossible to categorize as are the domestic programs.

My evaluators agreed that we would not rate any international programs for their suitability for singles. We thought that Elder-hostelers venturesome enough to register alone for a two- to four-week overseas experience would probably be well traveled and self-sufficient. The very nature of the arrangements encourages group cohesiveness, and the opportunities to forge friendships are there if one wishes to pursue them. It is the rare international program that encourages enrollees to do much solo shopping or sightseeing.

Elderhostel publishes a special Canadian catalog of international programs giving Canadian departure cities and prices in Canadian dollars. Registration forms for United States and Canada programs (deposits in Canadian dollars) must be mailed to Elderhostel Canada in Ontario.

BERMUDA

St. George—Bermuda Biological Station

Courses of Study: Atlantic Coral Reefs; Bermuda's Historical and Architectural Heritage; Introduction to Marine and Environmental Science; Island Life—The Flora and Fauna of Bermuda; Bermuda's Delicate Balance—People and the Environment

Quality of Instructors: The program is taught by an accomplished group of technicians and marine scientists deeply concerned about the modern evils of air and water pollution. The island has a particularly fragile environment, and sewage in the Atlantic Ocean is now poisoning its beautiful sand beaches.

Environment: The biological station sits on the water's edge in a tropical park not far from St. George. The Bermuda chain of islands, a British Crown Colony, lies in the North Atlantic east of the Carolinas. St. George is one of the seven largest of the bridge-linked islands. Bermuda is a very popular resort for United States citizens. Refugees from the cold, as well as artists and writers, seek the quiet warmth of the island sun, the clean air, and sounds of birdsong. The windswept islands offer a retreat into the past. Uniformed constables, carriages, bicycles, and the clatter of horses hooves are reminiscent of the nineteenth-century English countryside.

Housing: The sleeping accommodations for the program can vary. Hostelers may find themselves in the main hotel building, in cottages, or in apartments, but the bedrooms in all accommodations are unheated. The common areas at the station are heated when necessary by space heaters.

Food: The bill of fare is nutritious and delicious. A traditional English afternoon teatime is observed.

Quality of Instructors: The Elderhostel program is scheduled from Monday afternoon through breakfast the following Sunday. My reviewers wrote, "I attended a one-week Elderhostel that should have been stretched to two, so much was packed into each day." "Very strenuous program," was the comment of another panelist. Bermuda's uniqueness is its smallness and isolation, its pink sand beaches, and its devotion to English traditions. Narrow lanes and alleys, bowered in pink oleanders, are enclosed by high stuccoed walls edged with pastel-colored morning glories. The early homes were built of hurricane-resistant, whitewashed stone, and the architectural style remains unchanged. Clean, simple, comfortless, limestone block houses dot the landscape. Many of the old sounds and smells are still there, but the introduction of the automobile and traffic jams has destroyed some of the island's quaint loveliness. Fort St. Catherine is a nearby tourist attraction that dates from the early 1600s. Tourism brings problems, but it also brings excellent shopping opportunities. English goods—leather, knitwear, and fine china—are available in both tiny and spacious gift shops.

Shortcomings: The winter weather in Bermuda is unpredictable and often windy. The rest of the year it is mild, much like the Carolinas. Some of my panelists found the Elderhostel program director too young and not too understanding.

Getting In: According to the Elderhostel catalog, all international programs receive more registration requests than there are spaces to be filled. I would expect early reservations are required for Bermuda, particularly during the height of the tourist season.

Getting There: Bermuda is only a short flight from most of our East Coast cities. A cruise ship, steamer, or freighter would be a pleasant alternative means of travel.

BRAZIL

Rio de Janeiro (week 1 of 3-week program)— University of Fluminense (Universidade Federal Fluminense)

Courses of Study: Rio's Art, Culture, and Society

Quality of Instructors: This program takes Elderhostelers to three different cities and three different academic institutions; therefore, it is not surprising to find varying degrees of skill and ability among the professors and lecturers.

Environment: Brazil encompasses almost one-half of the South American continent. The vegetation is tropical, subtropical, and equatorial, and the architecture a highly decorative baroque mix imported from Portugal and Spain. The churches are lavishly decorated with gold, diamonds, emeralds, and elaborate wood carvings. Rio de Janeiro may well be the most written about city in the world. It is frequently described as a wild carnival, a city stretched along the beach throbbing with the sensual African-inspired beat of the samba. The urban elite seems totally unaware of the misery in the favelas, the shacks that litter the mountainsides just outside of town.

Housing: Elderhostelers stay in modest hotels that have twin-bedded rooms and private bathroom facilities. The hotel for the Rio week is air-conditioned and is located in Niteroi, a city just across the bridge. The location is lovely, right on the bay, commanding a gorgeous view of Rio both day and night.

Food: The meals served are excellent in all three cities. Brazilian food is a gastronomical experience: the national dish, *feijoada*, is a thick black bean stew garnished with manioc, an edible root, and pigs' ears and tails. Brazilian beer, called *chopp*, is renowned, and *cachaca*, the knock-your-socks-off traditional, alcoholic beverage is guaranteed to clear the sinuses.

Unique Attributes: Brazil is a country of vast ethnic and regional diversity, and Elderhostelers from North America have an opportunity to meet native Brazilians in three very different locations. All the field trips are stimulating and well designed and a wealth of extra activities are offered as part of the Brazilian experience. Rio is a very cosmopolitan city of ten million. Elderhostelers enjoy concerts and entertainment from around the world. One summer, a traveling troupe of young Russian singers and dancers were performing in Rio during the Elderhostelers' stay.

Copacabana Beach is the focal point of life in Rio. It is a stage where babies dig in the sand while joggers, surfers, and swimmers dodge the ever-present soccer and volleyball games. Businessmen in shirts and ties conduct business on the beach, while lines of barefooted samba dancers snake through the not-very-clean sand.

Shortcomings: Rio is dangerous; crime is a huge problem, but the location of Niteroi some distance from the big city tends to lessen the stressful elements for the Elderhostel group. Tourists must learn not to wear or carry valuables.

Getting In: Be smart and book early, and don't forget to list alternate dates and destinations.

Getting There: The Brazilian program includes round-trip flight arrangements from Miami, Los Angeles, or New York City. Elderhostel participants must pay all additional costs of airfare from gateway cities in the states and the cost of any extended touring in the host country.

São Paulo (week 2 of 3)— University of São Paulo (Pontificia Universidade Católica De São Paulo)

Courses of Study: Economy and Industry in São Paulo

Quality of Instructors: Most of the instructors received a score of very good.

Environment: São Paulo is a city of some fifteen million people. It is one of the most beautiful, densely populated metropolises in the world. It boasts superb museums, skyscrapers, cathedrals, and exotic restaurants. The urban elite, like their compatriots in Rio, are oblivious to the misery of the *favelas*, the slums of the poor that hug the mountainsides just outside of town. At the University of São Paulo, the largest of Brazil's twelve Catholic universities, Elderhostelers learn about the delicate educational and political problems facing the current democratic government.

Housing: The air-conditioned São Paulo Hotel is fine "but not in a neighborhood comfortable for walking at night."

Unique Attributes: São Paulo is a cosmopolitan melting pot resembling New York City in many ways. The towering skyscrapers that light up at night are reminiscent of Manhattan, as is the first-class array of museums, zoo, art exhibits, and international restaurants. São Paulo's climate is cooler and windier than that of Rio. Remember, the seasons below the Equator are the reverse of seasons in North America.

Shortcomings: "The automobile traffic in São Paulo is unbelievable," wrote a pair of New York City residents. "Travel to the university was time consuming and hectic." It sounds worse than trying to fight your way crosstown in New York City at rush hour.

Getting There: Brazil is huge, the fifth largest nation in the world, and has an excellent internal air system. Travel between Rio and São Paulo is fast and frequent; shuttle planes leave every half hour.

Ouro Prêto (week 3 of 3)—
Institute of Arts and Culture of the University of Ouro Prêto
(Universidade Federal de Ouro Prêto)

Courses of Study: Ouro Prêto, Jewel of Baroque Civilization and Cradle of the Brazilian Republic

Quality of Instructors: A few of the instructors in Brazil are not fluent in English and a few are not very comfortable relating to the group of senior North American participants.

Environment: Ouro Prêto is an inland mining city in Minas Gerais. It is a gem of the colonial period restored to its elaborate elegance since its designation as a National Patrimony in 1933. The beauty of the city is breathtaking. It is scattered over a series of steep hills with wonderful views of the rich valleys below.

Housing: The accommodations in Ouro Prêto are very good except for the steep, winding cobblestone hills that must be climbed. The mountainside location of the hotel makes air-conditioning unnecessary.

Unique Attributes: Ouro Prêto is one of this vast country's most picturesque areas. True to its name (Black Gold) it is the mining center for gold and many semiprecious stones. Touring Ouro Prêto offers one an opportunity to admire the rich cultural heritage of the country exhibited in eleven baroque churches, the work of the famous deformed and crippled sculptor, Aleijadinho. Born in Ouro Prêto, he became Brazil's greatest artist.

Shortcomings: Breathtaking seems to be an appropriate word. My panelists found the steep hills "breath-shortening as well as breathtaking."

Getting There: The group flies from São Paulo to Belo Horizonte, the nearest inland city with an airport. They then board buses for a spectacular 2½-hour bus trip from Belo Horizonte to Ouro Prêto over a newly paved road.

Ouro Prêto, Brazil (Photo: Barbara L. Silvers)

Rio de Janeiro (week I of 3-week program)— Faculdades Integradas Estacio de Sa

Courses of Study: Historical Rio de Janeiro

Quality of Instructors: There are four professors from the university, which is said to have outstanding courses in Brazilian history. My reviewers rated the group as excellent down to just fair.

Environment: Unlike the other Brazilian program reviewed above, in this program, both the college and the hotel are located centrally in Rio de Janeiro. The program takes place in Ipanema, a fashionable area of Rio, a city of 10 million. Ipanema is adjacent to the lively, crowded center of life in Rio, Copacabana Beach, where salesmen wander among the bathers selling umbrellas, fresh oranges, kites, and ice cream.

Housing: Comfortable accommodations in the air-conditioned Mar Ipanema Hotel on the main shopping street of Ipanema, near the beach.

Food: "Wonderful breakfast buffet, lunch buffet on campus, and dinners varied, mostly very good." Americans do not always relate well to Brazilian food. They love the abundance of fresh fruits and sweet desserts, but the well-cooked meat, rice, and beans are a new gastronomic experience.

Unique Attributes: The course integrates the lectures with field examples of the subjects discussed. The history covers colonial, imperial, republican, and industrialized Rio; the history of samba and the meaning of Carnival; and carioca architecture, painting, and sculpture. The college is located a pleasant bus ride from the hotel, past a lake and the famous Corcovado mountain. Hostelers enjoy interacting with students on the campus. A walk from hotel to campus includes 97 steps. Some hardy hikers made the journey.

An optional trip to Brasilia is offered (extra cost) on the first Saturday. Though a long day, most attendees experience this leap into the twenty-first century. The capital of Brazil, with its bright, white marble buildings is a wonderland of modernity. It is unfortunate that the group just flies in and out because Brasilia is most striking at night.

Shortcomings: The scheduling is too tight. The trip to Brasilia is too hurried.

Getting In: The program is not overbooked.

Getting There: All major international airlines fly to Rio de Janeiro. One reviewer used Varig from New York and raved about the gourmet food and service.

Bahia—Universidade Católica do Salvador/ Bahia (week 2 of 3-week program)

Courses of Study: Bahia—Brazil's Past and Future

Quality of Instructors: "Best of the trip. Two were fantastic."

Environment: Salvador is in the state of Bahia on Brazil's north-eastern coast. This picturesque city with cobblestone streets and red-tiled roofs was founded by the Portuguese, although the African heritage seems to predominate in this multiracial society. Breezes blow over the beaches of blinding white sand.

UCSAL is one of the largest Catholic universities in Brazil, serving 12,000 students. The campus is just a short walk from the hotel, and it is adjacent to one of Salvador's many ornate churches.

Housing: The Hotel Bahia do Sol is "very nice and well located." Some rooms offer a view of the bay.

Food: All three meals are served at the hotel, some buffet style, and always with a very good selection. The specialty of Bahian cooking is fish or shrimp cooked in coconut milk.

Unique Attributes: Salvador is an interesting mix of both old and new. There is less feeling of danger than prevails in Rio. Bahia is the home and soul of *candomblé*, the magical religious ceremonies and voodoo practiced by descendants of the early African slaves.

Shortcomings: The tight scheduling leaves no free time to shop or explore the city.

Getting There: The Elderhostelers take a 2-hour group flight from Rio on Varig.

Buenos Aires—Universidad del Salvador (alternate week 3 of 3-week program)

Courses of Study: Country of Diversity

Quality of Instructors: A group of well-informed women, but they are "hard to follow because they have a poor grasp of English."

Environment: Buenos Aires has an infectious spirit and 10 to 12 million inhabitants. It is a city of grand boulevards and ornate buildings, and in true cosmopolitan style, the streets are still crowded at midnight. Most of the city has been rebuilt—the only old buildings stand in the Plaza de Mayo, a central plaza bordered by a fort, an armory, the city hall, and a cathedral. Dressed up people can be found in the restaurants, theaters, boutiques, and hotels that border the plaza. The city has no river, just a muddy estuary. The University of Salvador campus is an office building just three blocks from the hotel occupied by the Elderhostelers.

Housing: The "modest" Hotel Carlton was only "fair." Single rooms are available on request.

Food: The continental breakfast seems skimpy after the sumptuous Brazilian morning spread. Lunch is served in an Italian restaurant and dinners for the most part are "poor." Hostelers have just one evening out to savor the famous Argentinian beefsteak.

Unique Attributes: The course is supplemented with field trips to a church, several museums, the National Gallery, and an interesting city tour. One reviewer found the field trips "dull." The art museum employees were on strike so it couldn't be visited, and one historic house with artifacts was "not very interesting."

The aspect of the trip most enjoyed were conversations with the Argentinian students of English who attended the Elderhostel lectures. They were "charming, interesting, and spoke excellent English."

Shortcomings: The field trips are not very scintillating. Though well warned and cautioned about the big city dangers of pickpockets and other ruffians, one Elderhosteler ignored the admonitions with unpleasant consequences. As on the previous two weeks, the scheduling is very tight, too many "late to bed and early to rise" days.

Porto Alegre (alternate week 3 of Rio de Janeiro, Salvador/Bahia, and Buenos Aires)—UNISINOS

Courses of Study: In Porto Alegre, the course title is Colonization and Immigration. (For information regarding the program in Rio and in Bahia, see above.)

Quality of Instructors: The Jesuit priests, some of whom are educated in the United States, are excellent.

Environment: Porto Alegre is the state capital of São Leopoldo, Rio Grande do Sul, the southernmost state in Brazil. This is the home of the gauchos, the Brazilian cowboys, and it has horses, bonfires, and square dancing much like the American West. A native of Rio Grande do Sul is also called a gaucho. But Porto Alegre is a bustling metropolis, a major deep-water shipping port, although the open sea is over 150 miles distant. The sea is reached by crossing over the Lagoa dos Patos, the largest freshwater lagoon in South America.

Housing: Rooms are comfortable and air-conditioned, although air-conditioning was hardly needed in May. Remember the seasons are reversed in Brazil, and in the mountains of the south, winters are not mild.

Food: I received more rave reviews for the Brazilian breakfast: sliced fresh papaya and pineapple, thinly sliced cheese and ham, platters of fresh baked sweet breads, lots of yogurt, and strong Brazilian coffee.

Unique Attributes: My panelists were most fascinated by the diversity of the country as sampled in this particular tour that visits one northern, one central, and one southern city. The varying ethnic mixtures, Germans and northern Italians in São Leopoldo, early African influence and the present-day Japanese presence in Bahia, and the Portuguese who settled much of the country and left their language.

Porto Alegre is an interesting city, built on two levels; the upper town contains the oldest sections, and the commercial district and waterfront are on the lower level. A visit to the nearby rangeland offers hostelers the sight of vast herds of cattle and the gauchos of the pampas in high pleated boots with silver stirrups and red neckerchiefs.

Shortcomings: Some travelers found the Portuguese language completely unfamiliar. Americans are more accustomed to visiting France, Spain, and Italy, where their way is eased by their varying skills in more familiar Romance languages.

Getting In: Registrations for the Brazilian programs have not been completely filled.

Getting There: Departure from three gateway cities, Miami, New York, or Los Angeles, is permitted on this program, and in some cases, airfare allows a one-month or three-month stay. "Ciao."

CANADA

NEW BRUNSWICK

St. Andrews-by-the-Sea—Shiretown Inn

Courses of Study: Salt Marsh Ecology; How Stradivarius Made a Violin; Weir Fishery to Factory; The Last Chord; Thar She Blows; Eat to Live? Or Live to Eat?

Quality of Instructors: Very erratic. "From excellent to never happened!" Guest lecturers from local museums, a community college, and the Marine Research Station are called in.

Environment: The Shiretown Inn is located in historic St. Andrews-by-the-Sea, across Passamaquoddy Bay from the state of Maine. St. Andrews is a quaint, quiet little waterfront resort town known for its crafts, particularly heavy woolen sweaters. The area was settled by Loyalists emigrating from the United States in the 1780s. Sportsmen find New Brunswick rivers, lakes, and beaches an angler's paradise. Much of our silver salmon and landlocked salmon comes from New Brunswick.

Housing: Very good. "Comfortable roomy quarters with pleasant views." Rooms are well appointed with private baths. When the Inn is full, Elderhostelers are housed in a nearby bed and breakfast.

Food: Reviewers wrote, "Food is insufficient and of poor quality."

Unique Attributes: Watching the rise and fall of the 24- to 30-foot Bay of Passamaquoddy tides twice daily. If you drive to St. Andrews, I would suggest driving up to Moncton to see Reversing Falls at the mouth of the St. James River. The great tides of the Bay of Fundy are so strong they push the water backward over the falls. The village of St. Andrews is pleasant for walking and beachcombing and for watching local boatbuilders and violin makers demonstrate their crafts. The nearby Marine Station is open to the public.

Shortcomings: "The program is run by the owner of the Shiretown Inn who cannot possibly coordinate the Elderhostel program and run her establishment." "Not enough to do for a five-day stay."

Getting In: No difficulty.

Getting There: Fly to Bangor, Maine, or St. John, New Brunswick, and rent a car, although an automobile is not necessary during the week of the program. If a leisurely trip by rail strikes your fancy, Amtrak connects in Montreal, Windsor, Ontario, and Seattle with VIA, Canada's passenger train network. There is also the ferry *The Bluenose* from Bar Harbor, Maine, to Yarmouth, Nova Scotia. This, too, requires a rental car for the drive to New Brunswick. "You have to get to this one on your own. It is not hard. It is just over the border from Calais, Maine."

NOVA SCOTIA

Mahone Bay—Oak Island Inn

Courses of Study: Mystery of Oak Island; Lunenburg—Our Heritage; Techniques of Marine Artist, Graham Baker

Quality of Instructors: Local people and professionals from the Fisheries Museum of the Atlantic in Lunenburg. "Very good and very interesting."

Environment: Nova Scotia (New Scotland) was founded by Scots escaping oppression and poverty in their homeland. Much of the province is bleak and foggy, a vista that encourages all the myths about pirates and hidden treasures. Little old towns and villages dot the south shore facing the Atlantic. The shoreline of Nova Scotia is frequently shrouded by pea-soup fog. I vividly remember a week when my husband and I were imprisoned by fog in Sydney, Nova Scotia, waiting for a flight to the island of St. Pierre. We finally gave up and boarded an overnight ferry for the crossing.

The natives and local tradespeople are friendly and forthcoming, a proud rural people of very mixed heritage. The province was settled by French, Scottish, Irish, and New Englanders. Fishing and shipbuilding have always been major forces in the economy; the native shipbuilders built fine schooners. Nova Scotia weather is usually quite pleasant. The influence of the sea makes it cooler in the summer and warmer in the winter than one would expect that far north. The fine scenery and fascinating history make the province a favorite tourist destination, particularly the coastal drive known as the Cabot Trail. Oak Island Inn is situated on the bay, only 45 miles from Halifax.

Housing: Elderhostelers stay in nice rooms in the inn, which also has a heated swimming pool, sauna, and jacuzzi.

Food: "Lousy, but only for the Elderhostelers. It is skimpy and not very good." A different menu is served to the hotel guests. One goes to Cape Breton for the natural beauty, not for the cuisine, but since fishing is a major industry, eating fish should be a major pleasure.

Unique Attributes: The inn is located across a small body of water from famous Oak Island. Among the many Oak Island myths is one that Captain Kidd buried a stash there. My Elderhostel reviewers were not permitted on the island because the world-famous treasure hunt had been renewed. The Mahone Bay treasure hunt is a search that has lasted some 193 years and has cost many lives and millions of dollars. As part of the program, Elderhostelers spent an interesting day on an island farm that has been restored to its original state. However, no transportation was furnished. Hostelers with cars invited other attendees to join them.

Shortcomings: The Oak Island Inn is a regular tourist hostelry. "The young lady in charge of the Elderhostel program has no idea what she should be doing. We were on our own for most activities. I would not go back to the inn, although I might return to Nova Scotia."

Getting In: If this program had waiting and standby lists in the past, I doubt that it will continue to have them.

Getting There: Taxi trip from Halifax airport is expensive. The Scottish cabbie who drove my panelists on their return to the airport tried to make amends by taking them on a complimentary sightseeing side trip. The Canadian passenger railroad VIA does have a station in Halifax. If you elect the *Bluenose II* ferry to Halifax, make reservations as far in advance as possible. This is a very popular crossing.

Sydney—Fortress of Louisbourg

Courses of Study: The Fortress of Louisbourg Then and Now; The Research and Archaeology of Louisbourg; The Interpretation of Louisbourg: Fishery and Food

Quality of Instructors: "Couldn't be better." One park service employee who is also a program coordinator is "superb."

Environment: "Eighteenth-century fortress life—we lived it and loved it." The reconstructed French fortress and naval base are located 35 kilometers southeast of Sydney on Cape Breton Island. Cape Breton has 4,625 miles of coastline to be explored, and the waters of the north shore of the island are suprisingly warm. Guides in period costumes interpret the park as it was in 1744. It is a "beautiful coastal site—wild, cold, and windy. Only for the hardy hosteler."

Housing: Off-site at bed and breakfast inns. "Just okay."

Food: "Excellent. Well-prepared restaurant fare in the evening, fine eighteenth-century lunch, and home-cooked breakfast at the B&B." "Good creamy fish chowder is a favorite lunch."

Unique Attributes: A wonderful hands-on experience. "We forged iron, worked copper, cut stones, cooked on an open fireplace, made lace, and assembled muskets." "Every person we encountered was knowledgeable, helpful, and interested, without exception." "This program offers a special opportunity to live with Canadians and to share their politics, problems, and outlook."

Shortcomings: The bed and breakfast does not offer much in the way of privacy. Five to eight people share a bath. "However, this shortcoming is more than made up for by the warmth and generosity of the landlady."

Getting In: None.

Getting There: Planes do fly to Sydney, but anyone who loves the seacoast should drive the incomparable Cabot Trail. For rail service or ferry from Bar Harbor, see Getting There information under New Brunswick.

ONTARIO

Kingston — Queen's University

Courses of Study: Shakespeare; Contemporary Zoology; The Nobel Le Moynes and Historic Sites of Kingston; The Stock Market; Medicine and Sherlock Holmes; George Orwell and the Modern Essay

Quality of Instructors: Excellent young professors, most of whom teach at the university the rest of the year. Queen's is one of Canada's finest universities.

Environment: Queen's, one of the oldest schools in Canada, has a quiet campus of old limestone buildings in Kingston, on the shore of Lake Ontario. Boat excursions and a free ferry to an island in the harbor are available on the lake, which also boasts some of the best sailing winds in the world.

Though small, downtown Kingston has good shopping, pubs,

and entertainment, and one may use excellent public transportation to get there from the campus. With an enrollment of 10,325, Queen's has a rich Scottish heritage that influences many of the school's traditions.

Housing: Accommodations are excellent. Mostly single rooms with washrooms, showers, and bathrooms in a central core that offers complete privacy. The residence is well kept.

Food: "Very good, with lots of variety. Gourmet food is served at the elaborate farewell banquet." Even persnickety eaters should fare well here.

Unique Attributes: The faculty and staff are cordial and the program exemplary. Summer weather is very pleasant, with warm days and cool nights. One may watch sailboat regattas on Lake Ontario, commercial and passenger vessels entering the St. Lawrence Seaway, freighters navigating the Rideau Canal, or pleasure craft circling the Thousand Islands. My reviewers also suggest visiting some of the popular summer resorts dotting the 1,700 rocky islands that lie in a 40-mile stretch of the St. Lawrence.

Shortcomings: None! My evaluator was on her second visit, but many other hostelers have been to Queen's five times.

Getting In: Not yet a problem.

Getting There: Access is easy. Montreal is 3 hours to the east and Toronto 2½ hours to the west. But one can reach Kingston by car over the Trans-Canada Highway, by plane, Canadian Pacific Railroad, or ferry.

Lake Simcoe—Kempenfelt Centre/ Georgian College

Courses of Study: Les multiples facettes du folklore canadien; Bien manger pour se sentir mieux; Les francophones de l'Ontario (This program is presented entirely in French; for bilingual Elderhostelers only)

Quality of Instructors: Two of the three instructors were very good, but the third teacher spoke Canadian French rather than Parisian French.

Environment: The Kempenfelt Centre is an attractive convention center stretched along the south shore of Lake Simcoe. Nearby are two popular Canadian resorts, Barrie and Orillia. Although Ontario was originally settled by the French, now only 10 percent of the population is French. Elderhostelers were invited to swim in the lake, but the summer weather was uncooperative. Noisy Canada geese honk and circle the lake with great frequency.

Housing: This program can accommodate a very large number of Elderhostelers in various residential facilities. When my reviewer was there, the school hosted two groups, one bilingual and one English-speaking. The main building is quite modern, but my evaluator was housed in a two-story, walk-up lodge that is pleasant and comfortable. Bathroom facilities are shared, but single rooms are available upon request.

Food: "Unbelievable," gushed my reviewer. "Real French chefs prepare superb desserts." The Elderhostel program filled the dining room for meals served in semi-cafeteria style; some waitress assistance is provided.

Unique Attributes: My reviewer rated this program her favorite of the six she attended. "Very impressed—I'd go back again," she said. The physical plant is very comfortable, with good classrooms and central lounges for socializing, and very worthwhile side trips are planned. The president of Georgian College establishes the cordial atmosphere of bonhomie by welcoming the Elderhostelers at the orientation session.

My reviewer liked the center's proximity to Toronto. One can follow the Elderhostel program with a pleasant week of sightseeing in that clean, shiny city of well-designed skyscrapers. It can be toured comfortably on its good subway, bus, or streetcar systems. Toronto has excellent museums, galleries, and dinner theater.

Shortcomings: None reported.

Getting In: This bilingual program does not seem to be oversubscribed.

Getting There: All major Canadian airlines fly in and out of Toronto International Airport, and all Canadian passenger lines have a station in Toronto. Elderhostelers taxi from the airport or railroad station to the Centre. This program does not require the use of a private automobile.

Niagara—Mount Carmel Spiritual Centre

Courses of Study: A Review of Church History (The Second Millenium); Personality Development; Introduction to Handwriting Analysis; Lands of the Bible; Stress Management and Life-Styles; Storytelling

Quality of Instructors: Two wonderful priests teach the classes and encourage after-class discussion and the exchange of ideas. "Outstanding."

Environment: The peaceful Mount Carmel Spiritual Centre is located in Niagara, Ontario, on 30 wooded acres just two blocks from the falls. A former seminary, the great old buildings are now used as a retreat by members of the Catholic clergy. The church, with its most unusual hand-carved wooden statues, is on the National Register and is visited daily by many tourists. My reviewer said, "All my life I've wanted to visit Niagara Falls. I could not have picked a better way to do it. The falls and the peaceful gardens of the retreat were just wonderful."

Housing: Lovely and exceptional. "Big picture windows in the old building gave us views of the Canadian Falls and the river." An elevator takes hostelers to their second-floor rooms.

Food: Home-cooked food served cafeteria-style in a high-ceilinged dining hall. "The windows are draped!"

Unique Attributes: A most ecumenical-educational week. Classes are concluded by 3:00 p.m. each day to enable hostelers to stroll the grounds and gardens or walk to the falls. Brave souls ride the cable cars across. Not many group activities are scheduled, but there is a pleasant boat ride on the river and a wine and cheese evening hosted by one of the five nearby wineries. Mount Carmel has a following of Elderhostelers who make an annual excursion to the center, and my reviewer said this is her favorite of 25 Elderhostels attended.

Shortcomings: Definitely none.

Getting In: It is best to register early.

Getting There: Take an airplane to Buffalo, New York, and a connecting bus to Niagara, or Amtrak's Florida-Washington-New York City line to Niagara Falls.

Ottawa—Carleton University

Courses of Study: Vincent van Gogh's Quest for Harmony; Sigmund Freud and Twentieth-Century Thought; Fun with Buildings

Quality of Instructors: Full professors are good to excellent. "Effective communicators."

Environment: The 20,500-student Carleton University is located in Ottawa, the capital of Canada. It is a safe, clean, beautiful city. The quiet campus on the Rideau Canal is set off by itself. A network of tunnels links all campus buildings—a bonus in Ottawa's snowy winters. Ottawa is the coldest national capital in the world. The canal, when frozen, is the world's longest ice-skating rink—four miles of ice right in the city center. The canal, which bisects the city, is lined with paths for walking, cycling, or jogging.

Housing: Splendid. Three one-person bedroom suites share one bathroom and a little sitting room. The suites can be closed off from the corridor ensuring quiet.

Food: My reviewers were disappointed to find plain Canadian rather than delicate French cuisine in this bilingual city.

Unique Attributes: As a capital city, Ottawa offers many urban attractions in addition to a firsthand view of national policymaking through tours of the Parliament buildings. The new granite and glass National Gallery sits at a spectacular site at the confluence of the canal and the Ottawa River. One panelist wrote,

"The museum is an architectural gem." A pleasant city, it can be viewed from a sightseeing boat in the canal, or one can sample some music, theater, or ballet. Across the bridge in Hull, Quebec, the new Canadian Museum of Civilization houses a splendid exhibit of totem poles. Visitors also cross this bridge in search of French cuisine.

Shortcomings: If you are seeking some fancy dining, you will have to seek it on your own. Ottawa is a winter wonderland in February, but all of that ice-carving and skiing requires below freezing temperatures.

Getting In: No problem.

Getting There: All major Canadian airlines travel in and out of Ottawa, as do most motor coach lines. "The Canadian," Rail Canada's premier transcontinental train, stops in Ottawa on its 2,887-mile run from Vancouver to Montreal.

Sudbury—Cambrian College

Courses of Study: Rocks, Rocks, Rocks; Nickel and Diming It!; Fur Harvest in Ontario; Northeastern Ontario Forest Industry

Quality of Instructors: The teachers are an excellent group of serious-minded specialists.

Environment: Cambrian College is located in Sudbury, the "Nickel Capital of the World," some 250 miles north of the bustling city of Toronto. The college campus is conveniently close to a world-class science center, and students are encouraged to make use of the facility.

Ontario was settled in the eighteenth century by the British and Scotch, while Quebec was settled by the French. Examples of this English heritage are visible throughout the province. North of Sudbury are cold, wild lakes, forests, and logging camps, while to the south one finds the industrial and agricultural areas.

Housing: The dormitories of the Regent Street campus have only single rooms with communal washrooms. My reviewers rated them "good." Communal washrooms and kitchens on each floor.

Food: Meals for the Elderhostelers are served in the hospital cafeteria. "Not five star but good enough."

Unique Attributes: My reviewers found this program "one of the most fascinating, unusual, and interesting Elderhostels attended." A local transit bus stops right in front of the residence hall if one wishes to try the shopping and restaurants of Sudbury, and the field trips are well planned and well executed. Field trips to the nickel caldrons in Sudbury offer students an opportunity to watch the hot slag spew forth like erupting volcanoes. During the heydays of the 1940s, Sudbury's mines poured out 92 percent of the free world's nickel. Mines of zinc, silver, and copper are found in nearby Kidd Creek, and Eliot Lake is a rich source of uranium. This week is designed for hostelers interested in metals and minerals. One can explore in-depth the interdependency of the Canadian and American economies and be sensitized to the problems created by nuclear power and acid rain.

Shortcomings: "None worth noting," my reviewer wrote.

Getting In: No difficulties were encountered by my panelists.

Getting There: Air Canada jetliners have frequent service to Sudbury. In addition, the Canadian Pacific Railroad has pullman service and daily trains from Montreal or Toronto. Sudbury sits at a crossroad of the Trans-Canada Highway.

QUEBEC

Montreal—Concordia University, Loyola Campus

Courses of Study: Montreal, The World in a City; The Environment and You—The Power of One; Beyond Bingo; Jazz, Jazz, Jazz; Watercolour: An Exciting Art Medium; T'ai Chi: A Joining of Body and Mind

Quality of Instructors: Varies. "An excellent historian with much political and economic background; a sincere but so-so individual; and a very good physical education instructor with an upbeat approach to the importance of play."

Environment: The Loyola campus is situated in an attractive suburb of Montreal, the quiet Notre Dame de Grace area. Good neighborhood facilities are within walking distance and a convenient, clean, cheap metro system is available to metropolitan Montreal. A vibrant, safe city, Montreal throbs with industry. Very cosmopolitan and very French, the Old City's narrow, cobbled streets are filled with historic sites, restored residences, and Roman Catholic cathedrals.

Housing: Typical twin-bedded college dormitories with communal bathrooms. "Cleaner than most."

Food: "Elderhostelers have their own dining room, quite elegant with tablecloths, real china, and so forth." Food is quite good and the selection adequate. Provisions are even made to accommodate vegetarians. "Yummy desserts."

Unique Attributes: "La joie de vivre." Staff and professors always dine with the hostelers. Volunteer escorts accompany manageable sized groups of hostelers on outings into the city. The schedule includes two morning courses and one evening course, so all evenings are occupied.

Montreal vibrates with street fairs and festivals in the summer, and ice-skating, snowshoeing, and skiing in the winter. The second-largest French-speaking city in the world, it boasts hundreds of Continental restaurants, bistros, cafes, and patisseries.

Shortcomings: Bathrooms are located some distance from the sleeping quarters.

Getting In: The Quebec big city programs seem to be attended primarily by Americans, but the programs do not seem to be oversubscribed.

Getting There: My panelists drove from Quebec City to Montreal, but they could have reached Montreal on Amtrak up the East Coast or Amtrak to Detroit connecting with VIA.

Quebec City—YWCA of Quebec City

Courses of Study: Literature of Quebec; The Quebec Region; Cultural and Physical Geography

Quality of Instructors: "Two excellent instructors, one dramatic and scholarly and one enthusiastic. Made a dull course very lively."

Environment: The YWCA is located in a pleasant residential neighborhood next to a public park in Quebec City. Many stores and services are nearby, and the Y is well situated for using public transportation to downtown and to historic Old Quebec. The oldest and largest province in Canada, Quebec was the first French possession in North America. Quebec City is less cosmopolitan and smaller than Montreal and has retained its French heritage in language, education, and religion. Even the architecture is French.

Housing: The Y is a modern facility that accommodates Elderhostelers in pleasant twin-bedded rooms with a sink / vanette in each room. The building is very clean, and there is maid service daily. A sufficiency of communal bathrooms prevent the facilities from ever being crowded.

Food: Adequate food is served in the cafeteria. "Very plain, with no second helpings allowed."

Unique Attributes: Old Quebec is lovely, clean, and crime-free. The narrow cobblestone streets and old buildings resemble a French town of the 1700s, and the turrets of the Château Frontenac, the well-known hotel built in the style of a château, hover over the city. Quebec, the only walled city in North America, contains many interesting public buildings, churches, and monuments. It is a city of many boutiques and art galleries. The hostelers are escorted everywhere by two charming, helpful college women. On their own, some hostelers try sightseeing in the much photographed horse-drawn taxis, called caleches. Most evenings are well planned. Fitness rooms and a good swimming pool are available on the premises.

Shortcomings: "The food could be better, but you wouldn't gain weight or get sick from it!" Quebec hosts a wonderful, snowy, winter carnival every February, but beware of temperatures that are almost always below feezing.

Getting In: None of my evaluators found this program registered up to capacity.

Getting There: Many U.S. East Coast citizens enjoy the drive to Quebec City, or one can fly to Montreal and drive the 160 miles between the two cities. All forms of public transportation connect Quebec City with the United States and the other Canadian provinces.

CHINA

Shijiazhuang (first half of 3-week program)— Hebei Teachers University

Courses of Study: History; Arts; Literature; Ancient and Modern China

Quality of Instructors: Superior. The teaching profession is highly respected in China.

Environment: Shijiazhuang, the capital of Hebei Province, is a city not yet spoiled by tourism. My major reviewer of the China program was a member of the very first Elderhostel group to walk through the "Open Door." Her daily journal is so fascinating I have quoted many excerpts here. At the conclusion of the three weeks, she wrote, "I'll return glowing in reminiscences of the wonderful, hospitable people; of the overwhelming sense of history; of the fantastic national monuments, the palaces, the ancient flat brick houses and—side by side—massive new apartment buildings and hotels going up so fast, it's scary; of the cam-

Elderhosteler in front of Hebei Medical College, Hebei Province, People's Republic of China

paigns to curb family size, use refrigerators, stop spitting, combat noise pollution, and plant trees. With no campaign at all, the Chinese are kind to kids and grandparents."

Housing: "The best they have. Don't expect it to meet U.S. standards." Although the group was scheduled to be accommodated at the Hebei Guest House in double-occupancy rooms with private baths, they were displaced by a trade fair and had to stay in a second- or third-class hotel. "Despite the brand-new red carpet (red symbolizes good luck) laid in our honor, the bathrooms were barely adequate, bedrooms so-so, and the food not up to the standard we had met elsewhere," she wrote.

Food: "Chop suey fans stay home. You'll eat noodles and noodles and noodles. You must request rice." The Chinese diet can pose problems for the uninitiated because of the heavy use of salt and cooking oil. Peking duck is served so often it loses its reputation as a gourmet treat.

Unique Attributes: Before taking the three-hour train ride to Shijiazhuang, the group stays overnight in Beijing and visits the Forbidden City. The train itself is an experience, an excellent, air-conditioned coach especially reserved for the Elderhostel group. Trains are the major means of transportation in China, and the coaches are unbelievably crowded.

Excerpts from my reviewer's journal: "We hadn't known the full meaning of hospitality until we arrived in China. That evening we were honored guests of the Hebei Provincial Government at an extremely elaborate banquet. . .TV camera crews and ceremonial tea service and more red carpets. . .round tables hosted by members of the Hebei Provincial Education Commission. . .they sang to us. . .a goodly number of toasts were drunk that evening."

One day at the Hebei Medical College includes demonstrations of acupuncture, manual massage, cupping, and moxibustion, followed by lectures on Chinese herbal medicine.

"A bus trip to a nunnery passes through the heavily populated countryside over narrow roads teeming with bicyclists, donkey-drawn carts, and heavy transport trucks. . .the city streets teem with pedestrians and street sweeping persons."

Getting In: The Elderhostel program in China seems able to accommodate a rather large group. Two buses were used to transport the participants in the program reviewed here.

Getting There: Elderhostelers embarking from the West Coast fly on JAL to Tokyo. They overnight in Tokyo with the group arriving from New York, then fly to Beijing and take the train to Shijiazhuang. Beijing is visited twice between study sites on this excursion.

Chengde (second half of 3-week program)— Chengde Teachers College

Courses of Study: Daily evening lessons in the Chinese language and prebreakfast classes in ta'i chi (the ancient Chinese graceful method of exercise) are offered as optional opportunities throughout the program. In Chengde, excellent daily lectures continue on ancient Chinese history, urban and rural life, and manners and customs.

Quality of Instructors: Courteous, concerned, caring, and intelligent.

Environment: This is a far cry from a Hilton / Hong Kong "shop til you drop" excursion in China. Chengde is located in beautiful mountainous country in the north. It is most famous as the location of the Imperial Summer Resort of the Manchu dynasty. Encircled by a 6-mile wall, it includes preserved pagodas, pavilions, remarkable landscaped gardens, and peaceful lake areas. Chengde is famous for its Buddhist and Tibetan temples.

Housing: "The best quarters of all." A five-story walk-up guest house, but Elderhostelers are assigned to first- and second-floor rooms. Small two-bed rooms with clean private bath. "Frugal but comfortable." The Chengde College Guest House has a pleasant reading room on the ground floor. "Bed pillows are filled with millet rather than the feathers and foam we are accustomed to."

Food: "And then there is tea, tea, tea!" A box lunch is provided on the train, and the dining room adjacent to the dormitory is very

Elderhosteler returns to China to teach English, Shijiazhuang Railroad Station

clean with quite elegant food service and vases of silk flowers. At the closing banquet, Elderhostelers painted a banner for their hosts for the requisite gift exchange. "The dishes prepared for this farewell banquet are works of art—butterflies, mountains, a peacock."

Unique Attributes: "We were greeted on our arrival in Chengde with a brass band and strings of exploding fireworks. . . students clapping and Elderhostelers moved to tears by the warmth of the welcome." Elderhostelers are treated to the Chengde Folk Orchestra and Anhui Opera.

Excerpts from my reviewer's journal: "an evening reminiscent of long-ago soirees at the University of Chicago. . . invited by a group of retired and active scholars. . . sharing delicate little porcelain cups of wine, tea, grapes, cakes, and snowflake pears in a cheerful bed-sitting room in a faculty apartment. . . a gentle exchange of views with the help of an interpreter. . . hosts eager to learn our customs and ways." "An Elderhostel in China is an unforgettable experience. I'm at a loss for words," wrote my reviewer, who later found the words and put them in a series of short stories.

Shortcomings: Do not expect Western standards of sanitation and plumbing in China. This is a country catapulted into the twentieth century without passing through some intermediary stages of development. The Elderhostel catalog emphatically and wisely cautions prospective travelers in frail health not to enroll in this program. My reviewer was extremely fatigued by the schedule, but this did not prevent her from returning to China the following year to spend six months teaching English, an invitation received while attending the Elderhostel.

Getting In: CAEE has been facilitating scholarly and professional exchanges between the People's Republic of China and the United States for some time. As one of the most respected exchange programs, Elderhostelers are afforded a unique view of China, a serious, cross-cultural inquiry. All partcipants receive careful and extensive preparation, and programs are only offered when the political climate is appropriate.

Getting There: The train en route to Chengde passes right through a gap in the Great Wall. "We looked up and up and there it was!" All internal travel is made by rail and bus. The native hosts make all the arrangements.

COSTA RICA

Universidad para La Paz
(University for Peace)

A two-week program: San José, to Las Espuelas, to Finca Los Inocentes; to Selva Verde Lodge; returning to the hotel in San José

Courses of Study: Naturalists Study Program

Quality of Instructors: This natural history program takes place in a series of field sites. There is no classroom work, but a native Costa Rican guide, a graduate biologist from the University of Vera Cruz, Mexico, provides all the field trip explanations.

Environment: The small Central American country of Costa Rica is famous for its scenic beauty, cultural and natural diversity, and spectacular national parks and nature reserves. The group briefly visits the "ugly" city of San José, then proceeds to extraordinary locations: a dry savanna, a humid rain forest, a seashore, and the flora and fauna of a cloud forest. Although the whole country only encompasses 19,600 square miles, the terrain varies from towering mountains to swampy coastal plains, and the climate is equally diverse. The coastal lands are hot year-round, mountainous regions are cool, and the Caribbean side averages 300 rainy days per year.

Housing: At the National Park, Finca Los Inocentes, hostelers stay in a "beautiful" old farm settlement house. "But water is inadequate for the shared bath facilities of 10 to a bath." At Las Espuelas, in the province of Liberia, accommodations are in "modern, almost luxurious comfort." The very comfortable Selva Verde Lodge in Port Viejo is "the best of all."

Food: "Always good and plentiful except for occasional on-the-road stops at native restaurants where water was scarce so sanitation was doubtful." Abundant coffee, bananas, and thin yellow-skinned guava.

Unique Attributes: One of my reviewers is a writer who, enthused and inspired by her first trip to Central America, wrote, "The trip yielded one children's story, three short essays, and a quartet of short fiction." She described many unique experiences—"meeting with Rodrigo Carazo, ex-president, friend of Jimmy Carter, at Carazo's home; watching giant leatherback turtles laying their eggs on a Pacific beach at midnight; all-day hikes through rain forests; and observing a local fiesta and breathtaking scenery." The people are "extraordinary—friendly, natural, and open, and there is very little (if any) abject poverty." From the balcony of the lodge in Selva Verde one may observe parrots, jacamars, and other exotic birds or nocturnal animals such as anteaters, peccaries, and armadillos.

Shortcomings: (1) No lecturer to relieve eager, able guide of his heavy responsibility of leading expeditions and doing all the explaining of natural features, particularly since English is not his first language. (2) Only baths to be had at Los Inocentes were in the swimming pool. Water is a problem in northern Costa Rica. (3) The group is supposed to all be on the same plane into San José, but no representative is on hand to introduce hostelers to one another. (4) The equatorial sun is brutal. Heavy sunscreen is a necessity.

The catalog wisely suggests that only "fit and vigorous" Elderhostelers should enroll in this program.

Getting In: Tough. Very popular program, especially in February.

Getting There: Miami, Florida, is the gateway city for the Costa Rican programs. Attendees are bused to the hotel for the first overnight in "noisy" San José.

ENGLAND

Cheltenham (I week of a 3-week program)— College of St. Paul and St. Mary

Courses of Study: The Changing Cotswolds; Gloucester and the Forest of Dean; Townscape and Landscape in Transition; Shakespeare's Theatre

Quality of Instructors: "On a scale of 1 to 10, at least a 20! Instructors are superbly informed, enthusiastic, and witty, too."

Environment: The Cotswolds offer some of England's finest greenery and scenery with a storybook appearance. Villages were established in the fertile valleys during the time of the Saxons, and Cheltenham is one of those villages. The town is the proud pos-

Lunching in the Cotswolds (Photo: Mae Woods Bell)

sessor of one of the most famous spas in England and has many gems of Regency architecture. It is an opulent city with an air of privilege. The St. Paul and St. Mary campus is so lovely one doesn't have to venture into town. The campus covers 30 landscaped acres originally laid out as a botanical garden.

Housing: Old-style dormitories that are comfortable. No lift, but the building is only three stories high. "Rooms are large and have lots of light."

Food: Not great. Evaluations ranged from good to fair. One panelist learned to like the classic English breakfast of eggs and potatoes.

Unique Attributes: "Cheltenham lies in the middle of the gorgeous Cotswolds. . .the campus has a small but nice botanical garden. . .near a pub where the daring can play the traditional game of skittles," and the less daring can stroll the lovely parks and residential area. There are lots of excellent field trips—to Bath, Gloucester Cathedral, Roman iron mines, and Stratford-upon-Avon to see a performance in the Royal Shakespeare Theatre. "Trips are well and thoroughly planned to correlate with the instruction." "It is possible to learn much more than from a commercial travel arrangement." "The Shakespeare course is a big hit!"

Shortcomings: "For those who want luxury, the showers and toilets are some distance from the rooms—not unreasonably so for my taste."

Getting In: "I've always managed to get in on my first try," said a woman who enjoys an annual Elderhostel in Great Britain. "St. Paul and St. Mary is tops," she said.

Getting There: Air travel from New York is part of the package. "BOAC is great."

Durham—University of Durham/ Collingwood College

Courses of Study: Exploring the Prehistoric North; Gardens in England

Quality of Instructors: Lectures are given in the library, a nice, scholarly atmosphere conducive to learning. "Outstanding faculty."

Environment: This region of northeastern England touches the Scottish border and is opposite southern Scandinavia. Durham and Northumberland counties form the core of the ancient kingdom of Northumbria—its history is more dramatic and turbulent than any other region of England. The city of Durham exhibits various influences and marks left by successive periods of English history. It is surprisingly well preserved. There are scars left from battles of pagans and Christians, roads built by Roman legions, wounds from the plunder of Vikings and Danes, and cathedrals and castles built by Norman barons.

Housing: Collingwood Hall of Residence is just 10 minutes from the center of town and has beautiful views of the neighboring countryside. "Very modern—but tricky. Collingwood College has several flights of dangerous, steep, barren steps. Stairs are very hard to maneuver." The building is situated on a hill with a high main entrance.

Rugged cliffs of Devon (Photo: Mae Woods Bell)

Food: Typical English cuisine is served, for example, roast beef with Yorkshire pudding—all family-style.

Unique Attributes: A walk on Hadrian's Wall is the highlight of the three-week Elderhostel for some English history scholars. Visiting the roots of England's history and heritage can promote a greater understanding of the myriad forces that shaped the country's growth. The craggy coastline of Durham has been immortalized in the King Arthur legends—where knights jousted on horseback, then feasted at the Round Table.

"The science labs and botanical gardens are mind-boggling—and the Oriental Museum impressive." "The campus coordinator is a real gem." The campus pub is open enough hours to make the congenial Elderhostel group even more congenial.

Shortcomings: Don't forget your trenchcoat; northeastern England can be cold and wet. "Collingwood College has several flights of dangerous, steep, barren steps. The main entrance is high because it is situated on a hill. But I'd go back if I could be assured of a more accessible room."

Getting In: My reviewers had no complaints. One wrote that she made it on her first attempt.

Getting There: Durham is usually a one-week destination of a three-week Great Britain University Programme Schedule. Flights originating in the United States may land at London's Gatwick or Heathrow Airport, or Manchester, Prestwick in Glasgow, Dublin, or Shannon.

ENGLAND, SCOTLAND, AND WALES

Various combinations are available for 3-week programs. The following are a sampling of those available.

London—London School of Economics

Courses of Study: Roman London: A Look at the Relics of 400 Years of Roman Rule; The Age of Elegance: 18th-Century English Art; Elizabethan London; Chaucer's London; Pepys's London; 2,000 years of London History

Quality of Instructors: All of the professors are learned scholars and stimulate the students' interest. Faculty for programs in London are members of King's College, Queen Mary College, and individual specialists.

Environment: Only crowd lovers should visit London, a city of great ethnic diversity with a unique character and sense of tradition. Contemporary London earns its reputation from its pubs, double-deckers, bobbies, and the amusing hats on the palace guards.

Rosebery Hall is ideally located for window shopping in Picadilly, discovering the National Gallery or British Museum, strolling through Hyde Park, or photographing the changing of the guard at Buckingham Palace. This location offers easy access to the Underground or to three bus lines. Wellington Hall, used for some London programs, is within walking distance of Tate Gallery, Buckingham Palace, and Westminster Abbey as well as the Victoria Underground Station for trains and buses.

Housing: Depending on the program selected, Elderhostelers may be housed in either Roseberry or Wellington Hall. Elderhostelers in Rosebery Hall have single rooms with communal bathroom facilities. One of my reviewers complained, "Rosebery Hall in

Elderhostelers enjoying free time, London, England (Photo: Mae Woods Bell)

London was the least attractive accommodation of the six Elderhostels I've attended." But a friend, a frequent hosteler in Great Britain, has risen to the defense of Rosebery! She writes, "Rosebery is spartan, but it is carpeted, the rooms are good size, and it has a pub for socializing, elevators, a laundromat, a kitchen and fridge on each floor, and a charming courtyard with flower beds."

Wellington Hall has been refurbished since its original use as a residence hall for theology students of King's College. It has three floors of rooms with no lifts. "Like living in a fairly new apartment house."

Food: On average, it's good in all three locations, where local specialties are served. In London that means Yorkshire pudding. Don't forget to try fish-and-chips wrapped in newspaper, and a relaxing midafternoon tea with crustless tea sandwiches. "Rosebery Hall serves what may be the best meals on the Elderhostel circuit," while Wellington Hall's meals are "nothing to write home about."

Unique Attributes: The Saga guide who accompanies the group is proficient; he handles luggage, arranges all side trips, purchases tickets to the theater, and tries to run interference when problems arise.

London has a vibrant entertainment scene. The theaters near Leicester Square are easily reached on the Underground or in London taxis, which have witty, well-informed drivers. Curtain time is early in London, and you'll sit in "the stalls," not in the orchestra. Window shopping on Regent Street or Bond Street in London is a not-to-be- missed treat, and if time permits, take a guidebook and find the London of Sherlock Holmes, Charles Dickens, or Geoffrey Chaucer. If you choose to spend some time shopping in Harrods famous department store, you may rub elbows with the Queen of England, since she is reputed to be Harrods most illustrious client.

Shortcomings: "Almost too much crammed into three weeks." "This is a great trip for the vigorous traveler." Many Elderhostelers complain that the bathrooms in Rosebery are inconveniently located. My friend writes, "True, the bathrooms are down a long hall, but they are clean, tiled, and relatively modern." As for Wellington, "some people may not like the neighborhood, but Sadler Welles is nearby—so how bad can it be?" And remember, nobody comes to London for the weather!

Getting In: Be smart—book early! However, the proliferation of programs in Great Britain has eased the registration problems. All nine of my groups of evaluators were accepted on the first try.

Getting There: The cost of the three-week package includes a round-trip, regularly scheduled jet flight from gateway cities in the United States to London / Heathrow Airport.

Glasgow—University of Strathclyde

Courses of Study: Glasgow and the Clyde; Glasgow—European City of Culture; Scottish Heritage: Food, Drink, Culture; Scottish Heritage: Great Scots; Tracing Your Scottish Roots; Literature from Ballads: Burns and Scott to the Twentieth Century

Looking over Bodmin Moor (Photo: Mae Woods Bell)

Quality of Instructors: Professors are from the Continuing Education Centre of the university. One outstanding professor knows how to enliven the learning. "He illustrated his lectures with exhibits of native costumes and samples of food."

Environment: Bustling, industrial Glasgow, Scotland's largest city, is at the heart of the region of Strathclyde. It is not nearly as romantic as the Scotland of Sir Walter Scott's novels, but one is apt to see sheep grazing on the hillsides. Glasgow is a city enjoying a renaissance. It has thrown off its reputation as a sooty city of slums and crowded tenements, and in 1990 it was designated the "European City of Culture." Many masterpieces of Victorian architecture remain; the Glasgow School of Art is a notable example of the city's Victorian heyday.

The University of Strathclyde has a cluster of modern high-rise buildings near the cathedral, "in a questionable neighborhood."

Housing: Murray Hall is a beautiful modern building located on the grounds of the university in the heart of Glasgow. There is no lift, but the accommodations are rated very pleasant and comfortable in a fairly new building. "Almost fit for a king." Single rooms are available and bathrooms are shared.

Food: Porridge for breakfast, cock-a-leekie soup and haggis for dinner, followed by Scottish flummery for dessert. "Wholesome and plentiful Scottish dishes."

Unique Attributes: Glasgow is rich in museums and galleries, has fine music, ballet, and theater, and is well stocked with shops. Highland Scots are very friendly people and travelers find them always ready to engage in conversation, particularly in the shops and on the buses. Strathclyde is just a short bus ride from town.

A day in Edinburgh visiting Burns country and Burrell and Kelvin museums is reported as one of the highlights of the Glasgow program for hostelers whose program does not include a week in Edinburgh.

Shortcomings: One panelist, a very level headed, much-traveled hosteler, has sworn off Saga travel arrangements. "They destroyed Glasgow for us. . .2.25 hours in a monstrous bus in London. . . 4 hours in the airport. . .terrible planning." Another couple expressed concern about the "questionable neighborhood." There was a break-in at their dorm, "but that shouldn't deter anyone—it's too good to miss."

Getting In: "We had no trouble. This was part of our first choice."

Getting There: "All taken care of by the Saga guide."

Edinburgh—Queen Margaret College

Courses of Study: Early Scotland: Picts and Scots; Historic Edinburgh; Scottish Art and Architecture; Scottish Clans and Families; The Scottish Nation; Scottish Discoveries and Inventions

Quality of Instructors: Excellent. Four-star.

Environment: Some admirers cite Edinburgh as the most beautiful city in northern Europe. It is also noted as a major center of European learning. Cobbled streets rise and twist up to its crown, the top of Castle Rock, where the great fortress of Edinburgh commands a view of the surrounding region just as it did in medieval times. Queen Margaret College stands on a 24-acre site in a residential area 4 miles from the center of the city.

James M. Barrie's home, Scotland (Photo: Mae Woods Bell)

Housing: Accommodations are on the first or second floor in single rooms, with a sink in each room. Described as pleasant and adequate.

Food: "Poor." Just basic necessities are served.

Unique Attributes: A highlight of everyone's trip seems to be the visit to Edinburgh Castle and an opportunity to enjoy theater within the mighty fortress. The day finishes with an entertaining display of dancers in traditional dress accompanied by the skirl of bagpipes. Some Elderhostelers have been lucky enough to be in Edinburgh during the annual festival, when the city throbs with music, dance, drama, and the wail of more bagpipes. "The crowds coming and going are good fun."

Shortcomings: One problem noted repeatedly in the Great Britain programs is the "time wasted and misused in Saga scheduling." There is very poor planning at the beginning and the end of the trip, to and from airports, lack of porterage, and so forth.

Getting In: No difficulty.

Getting There: Internal travel is arranged through Saga.

Bangor—University College of North Wales

Courses of Study: Welsh Music and Song: Welsh Heritage; Celts and Their Culture

Quality of Instructors: The teaching is splendid.

Environment: Wales is famed for its bleak landscape, singing people, and unpronounceable names. Bangor is in the heart of the most scenic area of Wales where relics of both Celtic civilization and Roman occupation can be found. The Roman, Anglo-Saxon, and Norman influences can still be found in Roman gold mines, Arthurian legends, and Norman castles. Bangor is primarily a small university town.

Housing: Elderhostelers stay in single rooms in Plas Gwyn, a modern dormitory that does not have a lift for access to the upper floors. Rated as "adequate."

Food: Very simple fare. Traditional cooking relies a great deal on potatoes and onions. In Bangor, the natives catch and dine on fresh fish.

Unique Attributes: The program location on a hill above the town is very pleasant. The buildings overlook the strait, the gardens are nice, and the resident program coordinator is very efficient.

The romantic myth of Camelot and the Celtic legends still live in Wales. There aren't too many coal miners still singing on their homeward march from the collieries, but sheep roam freely in the meadows and the poetry of Dylan Thomas is recited in classrooms. The Welsh language is lovely and lyrical but very difficult for foreigners to master. This is not a problem since most everyone speaks English.

Shortcomings: The bathroom facilities are in dire need of repair. Reports cite only one of three shower stalls usable, stairs uncarpeted, and no central gathering place for group activities.

Getting In: "We called Boston because we were registering late."

Getting There: "Saga Tours looked after us from arrival to departure."

Ferryside — Ferryside Residential Educational Center

Courses of Study: Arthur and Merlin; Castles and Cathedrals; Introducing Wales; Looking at the Past; Welsh Folk Songs

Quality of Instructors: Superb.

Environment: Ferryside is a modern center, built just for educational purposes. "It is a very tiny, isolated, not attractive village . . . just a railroad station." It is on the southwest coast of Wales just 9 miles from Carmarthen, a lovely village perched on the Tywi River. Carmarthen is reputed to be the birthplace of the wizard, Merlin. In this valley of rural beauty, puffins and other sea birds perch on the sandy beaches while cattle, sheep, and long-maned ponies roam free on the lower slopes of the hills. On the nearby coast, high cliffs and thundering waterfalls can be found.

Housing: Spic and span modern facilities, which are seldom found in Great Britain programs. Single rooms are readily available.

Food: Great. "I learned to love the laver bread (made of seaweed), Welsh rarebit, and fresh fish." Cockles, similar to clams, are gathered from the river mouth in Ferryside. "Porridge every single morning!"

Unique Attributes: One reviewer wrote, "Ferryside was definitely the high point for everyone. The staff is excellent in all areas of service and the location is wonderfully picturesque." Another panelist, on her fifth international tour, said, "There's nothing to do in Ferryside, but we did have a trip somewhere most every day, and movies some evenings. I did take the bus to Carmarthen and liked riding through the hedgerows." Boating on the estuary is a popular pastime between classes and excursions.

Shortcomings: "No air-conditioning and no cold drinks on the buses. The deluxe Volvo buses are designed for sightseeing but have no ventilation. During a hot summer the travel is spoiled. For the longest journeys, we would prefer rail."

Getting In: Early registration is advised.

Getting There: There are innumerable Great Britain and Ireland Elderhostel programs and 51 departure cities in the United States. Flights from the U.S. are overnight, arriving in England or Ireland the following morning. Morning return flights permit arrival back in the U.S. on the same day.

FRANCE

Chevreuse—Château Meridon

Courses of Study: A variety of 3-week programs are given at this destination. One starts with ten days at the château, then continues in Belgium and the Netherlands with an emphasis on politics, economics, and social and cultural life of the people. Another program that takes place at the château deals with French cuisine, food production, and wine tasting. One program focuses on the arts in France, and another on meeting urban and rural people.

Quality of Instructors: Very good. The visiting lecturers are excellent.

Environment: The setting is very pleasant. The château is a large country house surrounded by acres of grassy park 20 miles from Paris. Built a hundred years ago to replicate an eighteenth-century castle with tower and winding staircase, it was the home of a Portuguese banker, not the residence of a feudal lord or French nobleman. Chevreuse is a small village that invites one to stroll through the early morning open-air markets, their stalls piled high with fresh produce, wild mushrooms, and exotic cheeses.

Housing: Varied from decent to excellent, say my reviewers. Some rooms share baths on the same floor, while others enjoy private baths. Sleeping rooms are on the second and third floors of the château and also in a renovated farmhouse and barn about 250 yards from the château. A fair number of single accommodations are available in the main house and in an auxiliary building just down the walk. There is a great divergence in room size determined solely by a toss of the dice. Hostelers make their own beds in the tradition of the Dutch Folk School.

Food: Ambrosia. All meals are cooked by the resident French chef. Program participants assist in clearing tables after meals.

Unique Attributes: The director has extensive knowledge of modern and classical architecture, painting, sculpture, and literature, as well as a special ability to share that knowledge. Much of the lecturing takes place on the bus as the group travels to field trip sites. Time is very well organized in these programs; they are crowded with things to do and see. Included are many thorough visits to Paris, off-the-beaten-path locations as well as the better-known attractions. Lectures are varied with excursions to places of general interest and informal discussions with natives in their homes, farms, and factories. Reviewers enjoyed staying in one location for three weeks of intensive living and learning. This program is designed and conducted by Scandinavian Seminars, Inc.

Shortcomings: One reviewer wrote, "No shortcomings; I spent every Saturday in Paris on my own." But some of the travelers in her group believed that the one-hour distance from Paris was a problem (particularly at night) although it was possible to taxi to the Metro station in St. Remy and get to Paris independently if one wished. There is little or no evening entertainment scheduled at the château, a weakness for some, while others found the days so full nothing further was needed.

Getting In: All European destinations are very popular and France one of the most desired. This château program is my reviewer's "number one pick of the lot" of twelve Elderhostels, both domestic and foreign. One panelist, on her second trip to the château, was suprised to have her registration accepted on relatively short notice.

Getting There: Fly to and from Paris from your gateway city in the United States with an airfare that permits a stay of up to 180 days.

Montpellier (week I of a 3-week program)— University of Montpellier III/Paul Valery

Courses of Study: Ancient Gaul to the Riviera

Quality of Instructors: Good to excellent teachers throughout the program.

Environment: Montpellier is a university town that attracts hordes of foreign students each summer to learn French in the university by the sea. It is a great city for walking; the old streets full of eighteenth- and nineteenth-century mansions have interesting courtyards, while the renovated place de la Comedie is a shopper's paradise of boutiques and bookstores.

Housing: Accommodations are provided in a small three star hotel near the university campus. The rooms are small, but they have private baths.

Food: The hotel chef is extraordinary! "Magnifique."

Unique Attributes: This program was reviewed by a friend who annually attends six or more Elderhostels, some in the states and some overseas. She was eager that I include her evaluation because this IST-organized program "was the best trip I ever took." The Musée Fabre, off the tree-lined esplanade, has an impressive collection of paintings, and the municipal theater presents drama and concerts year-round.

Shortcomings: "Problems can be found in this program only by people who are irritated by trifles."

Getting In: "Surprisingly easy." Springtime is evidently not as popular as it should be in France.

Getting There: These two- or three-week programs in France have a choice of New York, Chicago, Los Angeles, or San Francisco as gateway cities. Airfare permits participants a stay of up to 180 days.

Dijon (week 2 of 3)—
University of Burgundy

Courses of Study: Dukes, Châteaux, and Wine

Environment: Dijon, the wealthy capital of Burgundy, the lush agricultural area of France, lies 2½ hours south of Paris. Stately fourteenth- and fifteenth-century mansions, once owned by the dukes of Burgundy, are part of the well-restored old city. A gastronomic paradise, Dijon is synonymous with gourmet mustard, just as Burgundy symbolizes great red wine.

Housing: Elderhostelers are housed in a modest hotel in town. All rooms have private baths. Participants are transported to and from the university.

Food: Breakfast and dinner are served at the hotel throughout France while lunches are provided at the universities. Dijon chefs are renowned for their excellence. During field trips, hostelers dine in local restaurants where "even the simplest fare is lovingly prepared."

Unique Attributes: "Gaby and Guy, our guides in Dijon, made our trip just plain wonderful!" A good place to start a walking tour is the palace in the center of town—stroll to the art museums to enjoy splendid Flemish paintings, to Gothic and Renaissance churches with bell towers, and to an archaeological museum of medieval artifacts.

Shortcomings: Obviously, there are no shortcomings for Francophiles.

Caen (week 3 of 3)—University of Caen

Courses of Study: From William the Bastard to World War II D Day

Environment: The beautiful city of Caen has been completely rebuilt after being gutted in World War II. Modern architecture has been pleasantly interspersed with patches of green and the beautiful blue River Orne winds through its center. Caen is definitely a university town where students crowd the many small cafes that lead up the hill to the university. Unlike many French universities, this school has a well-defined campus.

Housing: "A rather grungy two-star hotel, with many flights of stairs." The accommodations were a bit down-at-the-heels.

Food: "From that first bite of flaky, fresh-baked croissant each morning to the last sip of sweetened demitasse in the evening, the trip is a great gastronomic treat."

Unique Attributes: "The lecturers and our guides, Chantal and Jacques, were marvelous." Wonderful examples of Romanesque architecture are preserved in Caen, with the ruins of William the Conqueror's château in the town center. Within its walls are two museums, an art museum and one exhibiting Norman peasant life. The city is proud of its churches that have outstanding stained-glass windows, modern replacements for those destroyed in WW II. As in all French university towns, there are beaucoup bars and discos for socializing and people watching.

Shortcomings: The hotel is a disappointment.

Getting There: "Air France is a gracious airline; the wine, the attentive service, flight maps and hot towels, and the charming stewards and stewardesses remind me of the way air travel used to be."

ISRAEL

Tel Aviv (week 1 of 3-week program)— Beit Berl University

Courses of Study: Israel, Holy Land to Three Major Faiths; Jews and Arabs in Israel; Israel—A Pluralistic Society; Flora and Fauna of Israel—A Diverse Sampling of Natural Phenomena

Roman aqueduct, Caesarea, Israel (Photo: Ellen M. Reardon)

Quality of Instructors: The professors are all excellent, effective teachers.

Environment: Israel is a country of some four million people jammed into space the size of Maryland. It is a land where the conflict between faith and reason still rages and the conflict of orthodoxy versus nationalism continues. Beit Berl's campus is reminiscent of a rural Israeli settlement. The pastoral setting encourages students to spend much time outdoors enjoying the green lawns, tropical flowers, and palm tree-lined paths.

Housing: On-campus housing is offered in a one-story dormitory building that contains double rooms, each with a private bathroom and shower.

Food: The food served in the cafeteria is good and plentiful. Jewish dietary laws are observed—milk and meat are not served at the same meal, which may or may not be noticeable until the cream substitute is offered with coffee. Tel Aviv is peopled primarily by descendants of Eastern European immigrants, and the cuisine reflects this influence. Israel is a melting pot, so other dietary influences can be found. These include recipes devised by Spanish Sephardic Jews, Arabs, the French, and North Africans.

Unique Attributes: "Extraordinarily well versed guides" lead the Elderhostelers on a broad variety of field trips and activities to illustrate the subjects being studied in the classroom. Synagogues, mosques, churches, and educational institutions are visited, as well as a Jewish kibbutz and an Arab settlement where discussions are held with Arab students.

Tel Aviv is a glittering city, home to the Israel Philharmonic and an active theater. Sidewalk cafes line broad boulevards in front of five-star hotels. Elderhostelers are treated to an evening at the theater in Tel Aviv. They are the only members of the audience supplied with earphones through which the Hebrew dialogue is instantaneously translated into English.

Shortcomings: Absolutely no shortcomings were noted.

Getting In: I would urge early booking, even though many Israel programs are filled by registration lottery. A very enthusiastic husband and wife wrote, "This was our first Elderhostel. All else is commentary."

Getting There: El Al Airlines is used for nonstop jet service from New York to Tel Aviv. Special add-on fares to New York from other United States cities are available, and the fare permits up to a two-month stay in Israel.

Jerusalem (week 2 of 3-week program)— Hebrew University

Courses of Study: Jerusalem in the Light of Archaeology; The Bible and the Land; Jerusalem, Past and Present; Art in Israel

Quality of Instructors: The professors are superb in this institution, Israel's first school of higher learning.

The Western Wall, Jerusalem, Israel (Photo: Ellen M. Reardon)

Environment: The university is located in the city of Jerusalem, the eternal city sacred to Christianity, Islam, and Judaism. It is a city of contrast: one can go from the Arab quarters where minarets pierce the sky above the mosques to the ultra-Orthodox district where men wear beards and long side-curls and the women are all modestly dressed. Jerusalem, a modern city of almost half a million inhabitants, has been continuously inhabited for five thousand years—a mind-boggling concept.

Housing: Among my panel of reviewers are Elderhostelers who stayed in both the Zohar Hotel and at the Beit Maiersdorf Faculty Club. The Zohar is a new hotel in a lovely neighborhood of Jerusalem overlooking the Judean Desert. It is fully air-conditioned and heated and has elevator service, and in addition, all rooms have private baths, telephones, and radios. The faculty club is located on the university's Mount Scopus campus. All guest rooms have the same niceties as the Zohar Hotel. Both the hotel and the faculty club received praise.

Food: One couple from the East Coast of the United States wrote, "Great food if you like chicken!" The influence of immigrants from the Middle East predominates in Jerusalem. Chick-peas ground into hummus bi tahini is a favorite appetizer.

Unique Attributes: "If you've never seen the Judean desert by moonlight, you still have a thrill in store for you." Elderhostelers who have been to Jerusalem before observed, "Now that safety has become a factor in big cities, we find a major advantage in Elderhosteling is traveling in a group of such high-caliber people." In years past, this couple traveled extensively throughout the Middle East alone.

By studying the sources and manifestations of the Arab-Israeli conflict firsthand, one gains a deeper understanding of how difficult it is to maintain civility and values in a country under siege. The program week in Jerusalem usually includes an opportunity to float in the Dead Sea and a visit to the Ein Gedi Nature Reserve where one can observe ibex leaping among the rocks and watch desert streams rush down the mountainside.

During the long Israeli summers, Jerusalem is the most comfortable spot in the country. The air is dry, and cool winds blow in from the Judean mountains.

Shortcomings: One pair of panelists would have preferred housing closer to the center of the city even though both facilities had easy and frequent public bus service into the city.

Getting There: From the beaches of Tel Aviv it's a 45-minute drive along a four-lane thruway to Jerusalem.

Haifa (week 3 of 3-week program)— University of Haifa

Courses of Study: Media and the Image of Israel; Political Processes in Israel; Dynamics of the Middle East Situation; Early Man in the Holy Land

Quality of Instructors: The faculty is superb.

Environment: The University of Haifa perches atop the crest of Mount Carmel with a breathtaking view of the coastline, Mount Hermon, and the Galilee. Haifa is the third largest city in Israel, situated only 40 kilometers from the Lebanese border. The country's largest concentration of heavy industry lies to the east of the city and heavy maritime traffic passes through its port. The sense of danger and perpetual conflict on the borders dominates this area. The reason Israel is burdened with astronomical defense costs is all too visible here.

Housing: Elderhostelers stay at the Kibbutz Beit Oren, an agricultural kibbutz, four miles from the university. Each double room has its own bathroom, and the guest houses have lounges, social halls, and a swimming pool.

Food: Homegrown fresh fruits and dairy products are served along with wonderful oranges, dates, persimmons, and wine pressed from grapes from their own vineyards.

Unique Attributes: Many of the early tenets of the kibbutzim have been altered, but the self-sufficient, communal agricultural society is still a unique Israeli phenomenon. Men and women still plow the fields side by side, and some children are raised communally. But drip irrigation has revolutionized Israeli agriculture, and the family takes a greater role in child rearing than in the past. Kibbutz members still share property and eat in a communal dining hall.

Southeast of Haifa, the ancient people, the Druzes, live in small villages. A visit to a Druze village is one of the Elderhostel field trips. Evenings at the Haifa Symphony and the Israeli Dance Theater are also arranged.

Shortcomings: None reported.

Getting In: According to the national registration department, all overseas programs are much in demand.

Getting There: See information on week number one of the Israel program.

Beersheva—Ben Gurion University of the Negev

Beersheva—Ben Gurion University of the Negev

Courses of Study: Ben Gurion: Vision and Achievement; Faces of a People; A Look at Communities in Israel; Man in the Desert

Quality of Instructors: "Superior. Teaching is done by outstanding scholars."

Environment: "Dramatic and inspiring." Beersheva, the capital of the still-virgin Negev, is in southern Israel. It is a land of striking contrasts: Bedouin caravans cross the desert; camel caravans stride down the city's main street; yet Beersheva is a developing modern city of 115,000. It is the only large city in the region, full of stone buildings erected by the Turks. At the core stands Ben Gurion University, named for Israel's first prime minister whose dream was to build a great university and cultural center in the desert. The university of stark futuristic buildings is internationally recognized for research.

Housing: Hostelers stay in a modest hotel in Beersheva—double rooms with private baths are air-conditioned and or heated. "Very good."

Food: "You wouldn't starve. Just adequate."

Unique Attributes: In some ways Beersheva is like a Wild West frontier town, but it has a fine orchestra and a legitimate theater company. Many visitors are intrigued by the site in the old town where Lawrence of Arabia was imprisoned in World War I. The weekly Bedouin market is a colorful and vital part of life in the Negev.

Shortcomings: The intensiveness of the program is tiring, and most of the participants are too stimulated to "miss anything."

Getting In: At this time, the Israel programs are not as heavily oversubscribed as they were a few years ago. "Just give it the old school try."

Getting There: See description of the Tel Aviv program.

ITALY

Sorrento — Trinity College, Hartford, Connecticut

Courses of Study: Volcanology; Neopolitan Music; Art and Archaeology of the Campania; Contemporary Italian Society; Twentieth-Century Italy

Quality of Instructors: One of my panelists, totally distracted by the sensual experience, wrote, "The lectures were interesting and well presented, but we couldn't concentrate."

Environment: Sorrento is a gorgeous resort city overlooking the clear, crystal blue water of the Bay of Naples. Tourists have long flocked to Sorrento and the nearby island of Capri to enjoy the physical beauty, significant history, and enchantment, all of which have been recorded in song. It is said that a visit to Sorrento is guaranteed to reawaken the sentimental memories of aging romantics.

Housing: Elderhostelers enjoy living in an excellent luxury hotel. The rooms, doubles with private baths, have accommodated an impressive list of illustrious guests—Milton, Goethe, Byron, Shelley, Scott, and Ibsen, to name a few. The hotel and its beautiful gardens are a short stroll from the city center.

Food: "Fabulous."

Unique Attributes: The splendid field trips to Mount Vesuvius, the Naples Opera House, Pompeii, the Sorrento Cathedral, and the Museum, as well as Positano and the Greek settlement of Cuma. Cuma is the site of the Grotto of the Sibyl immortalized by Virgil in the *Aeneid*. The Archeological Museum in Naples is reputed to be the most interesting of its type in the world. Frescoes, silverware, and artifacts prove the elegance of life in Pompeii before A.D. 79. This program includes many of the glories of Italy.

"To spend two weeks in the charming fishing village of Sorrento, with its snow-white stone houses scattered along the cliffs, is a lifelong dream come true." Unpacking once for a two-week sojourn is one of the enticements of this program.

"If you are brave, and have time to stay after the Elderhostel, rent a car and see Amalfi and the fabled Amalfi Drive!" This curving road twists precipitously along the crest of the rocky headland where every turn opens up a vista more beautiful than the last. "Just go!"

Shortcomings: "The Elderhostel leader was an excellent teacher but an uncaring person. Couldn't be bothered with people."

Getting In: No difficulties were experienced by our panelists.

Getting There: New York is the gateway city for all Italian destinations. The airfare used for these programs entitles travelers to stay on for a maximum of 21 days.

JAPAN

Kobe (week 1 of 3-week program)—YMCA

Courses of Study: Sense of Time and Communication—Comparison between America and Japan; Japanese Mind and Traditional Culture—Demonstrations of Chanoyu, Ikebana, Bonseki; Get to Know Kobe

Quality of Instructors: "Our instructors in Japan were some of the best of many years of Elderhosteling." Lectures and demonstrations in Kobe are given at the YMCA Kobe International Center.

Environment: Kobe is a major industrial city and has a busy port that serves as many as 10,000 ships a year. A large foreign population has made it very sophisticated and cosmopolitan. It is a twentieth-century city, with crowded shopping malls, fancy restaurants, and an active nightlife. Elderhostelers searching for either the exotic or the traditional will not find it here.

Housing: Hostelers reside at the Union Hotel in the downtown area. "Very good—all modern conveniences."

Food: "Very good at the hotel in Kobe." My reviewers were familiar with the classic Japanese food served in the United States—sushi, tempura, sukiyaki, and the Japanese white wine, sake.

Unique Attributes: "Meeting and exchanging views with the Japanese people." "There were at least fifty people in each city who were all most anxious to know how Americans think and feel about social problems, how we treat our elderly, and the economic impact of Japan on our current economy and standard of living."

Shortcomings: None.

Getting In: "It was smooth as silk, with no hitches."

Getting There: Los Angeles is the gateway city for all Elderhostel programs in Japan. The 9½-hour flight is long and trying. Because of time differences, jet lag and fatigue are inevitable. Try to rest and relax as much as possible on the plane.

Kyoto (week 2 of 3-week program)— Doshisha University

Courses of Study: Japanese History; Japanese Religion and Culture; Japanese Women Today; U.S.-Japan Economic Relations

Quality of Instructors: Courses are taught by excellent professors from Doshisha University and a woman researcher from Kobe College.

Environment: Kyoto is the city that best exhibits the contrast of the ancient Japan with an emerging modern city. Because the city was Japan's capital for more than ten centuries, its history is full of contradictions, war and peace, famine and prosperity. It remains the cradle of traditional Japanese culture, where women still wear kimonos and geishas still entertain.

Housing: Accommodations are provided in the Kansai Seminar House— comfortable double rooms with private baths on the second floor or rooms with shared bath facilities on the third floor.

Food: "Not too great. . . almost peasant food." All traditional Japanese meals include a bowl of hot, freshly cooked white rice.

Unique Attributes: All classes are conducted in the morning so afternoons are free to explore the Nijo castle, a Buddhist Temple, and the Kyoto Museum's collection of 8,000 works of art including archaeological artifacts and lacquer ware or to stroll along the canal and perhaps see the cherry blossoms. "We got very close to civilians who were as anxious to know about us as we were to know about them."

Shortcomings: At the Kansai Seminar House hostelers are subjected to some religious regulations. These do not cause any real friction.

Getting There: Elderhostelers travel from Kobe to Kyoto by bus.

Nagoya (week 3 of 3-week program)— Kobe College

Courses of Study: The Chubu Region—History and Geography; Art and Crafts in the Chubu Region

Quality of Instructors: The schedule in Nagoya emphasizes much one-on-one exchange of ideas and opinions through field trips and lecture / demonstrations. Guides and lecturers are effective communicators.

Environment: Nagoya, in the central region of Japan and the country's fourth largest city, is not particularly attractive architecturally. Its 2.2 million people are prosperous, engaged in high-tech automobile and aircraft manufacturing, textiles, tools, and food processing. It is a newly rebuilt city, much admired by urban planners for its grid design.

Housing: Accommodations are at the Nagoya Daiichi Hotel, a commercial hotel near the railroad station.

Food: Traditional Japanese food is served at the hotel every evening. "Very good native delicacies."

Unique Attributes: The hotel is located within walking distance of the Nagoya International Center, a base for international exchange activities. The side trips in Nagoya are particularly interesting, "especially the full-day visit to the Toyota automobile factory, with part of the day spent with the Toyota Volunteer Group who provided much entertainment. A great social afternoon."

Getting There: The group travels from Kyoto to Nagoya on the "Super Express Hikari 228" bullet train, a ride of 43 minutes. This train is three times faster than a bus would be. Sayonara.

KENYA

Nairobi and Masai Mara National Reserve (1 week in Nairobi and a 4-day safari at Masai Mara)—U.S. International University

Courses of Study: The academic program in Nairobi is orientational; lectures cover native customs, educational systems, economics, African art and culture, and wildlife conservation. Field trips complement the lectures. The safari at Masai Mara is conducted by professsional guides and faculty whose evening lectures follow all-day excursions on the finest big game reserve in Kenya.

Quality of Instructors: "Only fair. The personalities are interesting even when the information is sketchy. The native guides on safari are splendid."

Group leader and Elderhostelers at Art and Cultural Center near Nairobi (Photo: Ethel Booth)

Environment: Kenya, the most popular safari destination, has been immortalized once by Teddy Roosevelt and then by Isak Dinesen in *Out of Africa*, her affectionate portrait of life on a 4,000-acre coffee plantation. The book describes a country of wide-branching mimosa trees, meandering riverbeds, sunfilled days, and cold nights. Kenya is famous for the Serengeti migration of wildebeest and zebra, colorful Masai tribes, and dramatic landscapes. One and a half million of Kenya's twenty million people live in Nairobi, a city where most western goods and services can be found. In the Masai language, Nairobi means "place of cool waters." The campus and hotel are some distance from downtown in 5 acres of lovely gardens.

Housing: In Nairobi, Elderhostelers stay at the Hotel Jacaranda, a "moderately good" facility that has twin-bedded rooms and private baths. On safari, accommodations are at the Fig Tree Camp in comfortable tents, romantic, yet equipped with inside plumbing. Some of the zipper-flapped tents have their own porches. "Service is amiable."

Food: "Better the week in Nairobi than on safari. Great generous English and American breakfasts." Meals are usually buffet-style with many choices. There are good restaurants in Nairobi and delightful musical entertainment at dinner in the Masai Mara dining room.

Unique Attributes: "A fascinating place. I loved the week in Nairobi, where we visited the National Museum, a tea plantation, the central Municipal Market of produce and curios, the National Park, and the Karen Blixen home, all places many safaris miss," my reviewer wrote. In Nairobi National Park, scores of long-necked giraffes pace within view of the high-rise buildings of Kenya's capital. The Masai Mara is a northern extension of the Serengeti Plains, a paradise for big game spotters, ornithologists, and photographers. The Elderhostelers make daily excursions in microvans with retractable roofs; occupants can sight elephants, leopards, buffalo, or giraffes galloping across the plain at 35 miles per hour.

Shortcomings: "In retrospect, we might have enjoyed more free time, but perhaps not. Most participants were enthusiastic about the whole trip."

Getting In: This adventure is not oversubscribed.

Getting There: New York is the only gateway city, and airfare permits a stay of up to 30 days. "Kenya Airways is not too great," my reviewer commented.

MEXICO

Oaxaca—Southern Illinois University

Courses of Study: Spanish Language and Hispanic Culture (a two-week program)

Quality of Instructors: The Southern Illinois teachers are competent, not inspiring.

Environment: Oaxaca, the capital of the state of Oaxaca is situated in the deep southern portion of Mexico, 315 miles south of Mexico City. It's a center of high-quality native crafts, particularly weaving and embroidery done in bright primary colors on simple backlooms; women dye, card, and spin their own wool. The city, with a current population of 100,000 people, was founded in 1522 by a group of Spanish soldiers. The laid-back atmosphere of the mostly Indian population is vastly different from bustling Mexico City. Architecture is predominately Spanish Colonial, with many buildings built of the local pale green stone.

Housing: My reviewers found the accommodations in the small hotel adequate. The hotel is in the heart of the city across the street from the central park. Each double occupancy room has its own bath. Single rooms are available upon request.

Food: "Mundane," was the comment of one panelist. The program tuition does not include the noon meal; only breakfast and dinner are served to participants.

Unique Attributes: Since the Spanish language is here to stay as a regional language, this course offers an excellent opportunity for one to practice language skills, see basic Mexican life, and absorb a smattering of Mexican history, arts, cinema,and culture. Nearby are unusual examples of pre-Columbian ruins and artifacts.

In Oaxaca, one can see the continuing grandeur of a 3,000-year-old civilization. The main feature of Oaxaca is the weekly market held each Saturday—vendors dressed in striped serapes and brilliantly colored rebozos hawk their wares on the cobblestone streets. Straw-hatted men, hidden behind mounds of red and green chilies, sell hand-embroidered blouses and hangings. It's a city of bell-ringing churches and shady trees.

Shortcomings: The class is too large and accepts individuals with such a wide range of ability and experience that the language instruction becomes too slow for the more advanced members of the group. One panelist found two weeks in Oaxaca "too long."

Getting In: This is a much sought after destination. "Getting in is very difficult; I didn't make it until my third try," was the complaint of one reviewer.

Getting There: Individuals need to make their own travel arrangements to Oaxaca. Mexico's two national airlines, Aeromexico and Mexicana Airlines have connecting daily flights through Guadalajara or Mexico City. One can also reach Oaxaca on an overnight train from Mexico City. The Pan-American Highway from Mexico City is currently being improved by the Mexican government.

PORTUGAL

Braga—Centro Apostólico do Sameiro

Courses of Study: Architectural Splendor from Religion; 20th-Century Portugal

Shepherd and his flock in Portugal (Photo: Barbara L. Silvers)

Quality of Instructors: Very somber but excellent.

Environment: The Centro Apostólico is a small, private school affiliated with the Catholic church. The modern buildings of the school command a spectacular view of Braga, capital of the northern province of Minho. The influence of the church predominates in this city. It is said that Braga's archbishops have been known to wield greater power than the king. Braga attracts many pilgrims visiting the shrine of Bom Jesus. It is the home of Holy Week processions and colorful religious festivals during which the villagers sing and dance through the streets.

Housing: Elderhostelers stay in very comfortable twin-bedded rooms with private bath facilities. Many rooms also have balconies.

Food: Delicious, round loaves of country bread, hot out of the wood-burning oven, fresh seafood, and very sweet desserts are just part of the fare.

Unique Attributes: The ambience of Portugal is colorful and lively, and this province of Minho is considered the most vivacious. Romanesque jewels and adorned columns in the churches, brilliant reds and blues of the regional costumes of the peasant women, and paper flowers all contribute to the festival atmosphere. Trellises of grapes are everywhere, winding between gardens, edging the rooftops of the white cottages, and built against the almond and fig trees. Elderhostelers visit palaces, churches, and Viana do Castelo at the mouth of the River Lima on the Atlantic Ocean.

Shortcomings: No complaints other than the overlong bus rides.

Getting In: The Spain / Portugal programs are very popular.

Getting There: Overnight trans-Atlantic flights from the United States fly to either Spain or Portugal. Apex fares allow for a stay of 180 days. Cost of the flight and program vary according to the gateway city chosen.

S P A I N

Madrid, Granada, Córdova, Segovia, and Barcelona—University of Madrid, University of Córdova, University of Barcelona

Courses of Study: The Moorish Period in Spain; Catalán Culture; Great Painters of the Twentieth Century; Granada—A Study of a Historic City; The Inquisition in Spain; The Spanish Masters

Quality of Instructors: My reviewers reported all instructors either excellent or outstanding.

Environment: A beautiful country full of magic moments and castles sitting on the highest hills. From the sight of Picasso's *Guernica*

The Spanish countryside (Photo: Barbara L. Silvers)

hanging in the Prado Museum in Madrid to the cave dwellings in Granada, this Saga-organized study adventure includes a heavy dose of history, monuments, and castles. Madrid is a handsome city of palaces and plazas; Segovia is an ancient city: Barcelona is the mecca for Spanish artists; Cordova is the site of the Maimonides memorial; Granada is home to the tombs of Ferdinand and Isabella in the Royal Chapel of the cathedral.

Housing: The accommodations received both yeas and nays. "Mediocre to superb," was reported by one traveler; "good in hotels but wonderful in homestays," wrote another. Do not expect single rooms on homestays. One reviewer was assigned an Elderhostel roommate on homestay in Segovia.

Food: "Usually very good but very different from the usual American diet." "Inconsistent," commented one hosteler. The colorful "tapa bars" that line the streets are a great way to sample local specialties, tasty sardine treats, or other nibbles in olive oil. Both lunch and dinner hour in Spain are much later than is customary in the United States, and the pace of dining is leisurely.

Spain

Unique Attributes: Too many to enumerate. All my reviewers were on two- or three-week programs and spent one week in each destination. The social homestay week in Segovia was the highlight of one Elderhosteler's journey to Spain. "Before you go," she wrote, "learn as much Spanish language as you can; it will enhance your experience immeasurably. Do not expect everyone in Spain to speak English!" She particularly enjoyed accompanying her hostess to market, to visit old churches, and to the public square.

Other highlights include guided tours to the fourteenth-century Alhambra in Granada, where you tour the great Moorish palace and luxurious garden with some 20,000 other visitors per day; a day as guests of the mayor in Santa Fe de Granada; the working Roman Aqueduct in Segovia; and viewing collections of the work of Catalonian artists Pablo Picasso, Joan Miró, and Salvador Dali in Barcelona. Whether driving through fields of sunflowers or earthy-smelling vineyards, or viewing the dramatic vistas of the snow-capped Pyrenees, travelers will find the countryside rich with unexpected pleasures.

Shortcomings: The bus travel between cities is long and arduous, and the roads narrow and curvy. All my evaluators complained about the length of the bus rides.

Getting In: Early registration is recommended.

Getting There: Apex airfare for Spain and Portugal programs permits a stay of 180 days. All flights from gateway cities in the United States are routed through New York City for overnight flights to Madrid, Barcelona, or Lisbon. "Vaya con Dios."

TURKEY

Two separate programs are offered in Turkey: Crossroads of Civilizations focuses on on the art, history, and ancient civilizations, and Turkey's Silk Road, a program that follows the northwestern routes of the silk traders, examines the influences of religion, customs, and folklore on life in Turkey today.

Istanbul (week I of 3-week program, Crossroads of Civilizations)— The University of Istanbul in conjunction with Saga Holidays, Ltd.

Courses of Study: The Byzantine Civilization and the Ottoman Empire and the Arts

Quality of Instructors: "Less than excellent."

Environment: Elderhostel classes are held in the heart of this city of intrigue, beauty, and mystery; a city that is now struggling with twentieth-century problems of bumper to bumper traffic, water shortages, crowding, and chaos.

Turkey is a large Middle Eastern country situated between the Black Sea and the Mediterranean. In 1923, the first president of the Republic replaced the fez, the veil, and the harem with industry. Kemal Ataturk modernized the political, social, and religious life of Turkey, but for Americans, Istanbul is still an exotic travel experience. Remember, many women still wear traditional garb in this country, so visitors should dress modestly.

Housing: Hostelers are accommodated in the Klas Hotel, a good tourist class establishment a short walk from the classrooms. The hotel has elevator service and provides a separate lounge for the Elderhostelers' use.

Food: "Excellent for our taste," wrote my panel members. The couple who submitted this review of the Turkey Elderhostel are not only veteran hostelers but have been journeying to this Middle Eastern republic since 1959. "We particularly love the sweet, thick Turkish coffee."

Quality of Instructors: In Istanbul, Elderhostelers visit the 500-year-old indoor bazaar where turbaned Moorish merchants eagerly await the tourists. They observe suppliants at prayer in the renowned Blue Mosque with its slender minarets and see the fabulous jewel collection in the sultan's Topkapi Palace and the splendid Byzantine mosaics in the Haghia Sophia Museum. "The color, sounds, and smells of the trip are memorable."

Shortcomings: Most of us have a smattering of Romance languages —French, Italian, or Spanish remembered from high school or college—but the Turkish language is thoroughly unfamiliar. This adds a dimension of distance and exoticism to the excursion. "Some hostelers found the language barrier a problem; we couldn't decipher street signs, menus, or newspapers, but the friendliness and hospitality of our teachers, hosts, and the people compensated for this difficulty."

Getting In: The popularity of this program is well deserved.

Getting There: Elderhostelers depart from one of many gateway cities in the United States and fly to Istanbul for the first seven nights of the program. They return to Istanbul for the last night before departing for home.

Ankara and Aksaray in Cappodocia (week 2 of 3)—University of Ankara

Courses of Study: The Hittite and Phrygian Arts and the Valley of Cappodocia

Quality of Instructors: The faculty of Turkish history and arts is excellent. In Cappodocia, lectures are held in an outdoor amphitheater.

Environment: Ankara, the capital of Turkey is a modern city of almost two million inhabitants. Gleaming skyscrapers and elegant residences vie with squatters' shacks that huddle on the fringe of the city. The streets throb with heavy traffic (pugnacious taxi drivers are reminiscent of New York City) while in the pastoral plains to the east, shepherds tend their flocks of sheep. The region of Cappodocia holds a unique place in Turkish history that dates back to the arrival of the Hittites in 1700 B.C. Folklore explains that the terrain was an invading army turned to stone, but modern geology describes the area as consisting of volcanic rock.

Housing: In Ankara, Elderhostlers stay in the Evkuran Hotel in twin-bedded rooms with private baths. This nice tourist class hotel has elevator service, and is situated a short distance from the lecture rooms. In Aksaray in the Cappodocia region hostelers stay in the Agacli Motel. My reviewers found this motel excellent and raved about the lovely gardens.

Unique Attributes: In Ankara, one becomes sensitive to Turkey's precarious location, geographically bridging Europe and Asia. In Cappodocia, until recently, peasants inhabited old cave dwellings that date back to 3000 B.C. Elderhostelers also visit a labyrinth of underground cities tunneled into the rock, where ancient tribes hid from invading armies. Once upon a time, camel caravans plodded through Cappodocia.

Getting There: From Istanbul the group boards an air-conditioned coach for the ride to Ankara. After five nights in Ankara, they reboard the bus for the trip to Aksaray where they spend nights six and seven of week number two.

Ephesus (week 3 of 3)—
Aegean University at Izmir

Courses of Study: The Civilization of Western Anatolia

Quality of Instructors: The professors from the archaeological section of Aegean University are excellent.

Environment: Izmir (near Seljuk) is a port on the Aegean Sea. The ancient archaeological sites of Western Anatolia reveal the myriad influences on Turkey's history—influences of Persians, Greeks, Romans, Byzantines, Armenians, and Kurds. Although 99 percent of Turks practice the Islamic religion, the conflicting forces and ideologies of its ethnic history have created a country that is an intriguing amalgamation of cultures.

✦

Ephesus, founded between 1600 and 1500 B.C., is now being reconstructed to its former splendor after being excavated by archaeologists. The multifaceted history of Ephesus includes Greek, Roman, and barbarian invaders, as well as destruction by Mongols and Christians in the Crusades.

Housing: The AK hotel in Seljuk is a very simple, walk-up building. The hike up to the third and fourth floors requires a healthy heart. The accommodations are in twin-bedded rooms with private bath facilities. The hotel, in a village just 3 kilometers from the program site, is ideally located for visiting the other archaeological sites of the region.

Unique Attributes: Elderhostel classes are held in the old Seljukie baths, now converted into a conference hall belonging to the Ephesus Museum. The hotel, museum, and lecture rooms are all conveniently located near one another. A field trip to the ancient city of Troy on a fertile plain in Asia Minor brings to mind the legends of Homer's *Iliad* and *Odyssey*. In the sacred city of Ephesus, Elderhostelers visit the Temple of Diana, one of the seven wonders of the world.

Getting There: Elderhostelers arrive in Izmir on a Turkish Airlines flight from Ankara. The trip from Ephesus back to Istanbul is made in modern air-conditioned buses. The flight back to the United States is on a regularly scheduled airline with brief stops en route.

Kayseri and Konya (week 1 of 3-week program, Turkey's Silk Road)—University of Istanbul and Seljuk University

Courses of Study: Influences from the Seljuk Period and the Mysticism of Mevlana

Quality of Instructors: Varies with the professors' command of English. "In Konya, excellent, but in Kayseri, we had some difficulty understanding the lectures." "Our tour guide was very fluent in English."

Environment: The cities of Kayseri and Konya are in Anatolia, an area settled by nomadic Turkish shepherds about 1100 B.C. The land probably reminded them of central Asia, semiarid with rolling steppes and numerous streams, perfect for their flocks. Both Kayseri and Konya are currently growing at a remarkable pace, fueled by the wealth of agriculture and light industry. They are modern cities with wide blocks of apartment houses and bustling traffic, but at the heart of each city is an old town with a fortress dating back to Roman times.

Housing: Kayseri accommodations are in the Yukseller Hotel at Urgup in Cappodocia and in Konya in the Hotel Sema just outside the city center. Both hotels were rated "good and comfortable."

Food: "Not gourmet but satisfactory." Tasty, simple meals are the rule.

Unique Attributes: Kayseri is in Cappodocia, an area favored by tourists, between the Black Sea and the Tauros Mountains. Once the heart of the Hittite Empire, it is now a hotbed of crafty rug dealers, the center of the country's booming textile industry. Hostelers see the many Seljuk archaeological treasures now in the museums.

Konya, standing alone on a plateau like a caravan stopping place, is the heart of Turkey's present-day "breadbasket." A hill in the center of town contains bones of Bronze Age men and women. A never-to-be-forgotten experience is witnessing the worship ceremony of the Mevlevi Dervishes. The whirling ritual dance is done to the haunting music of small drums.

Bursa (week 2 of 3)—
University of Istanbul and University of Bursa

Courses of Study: Influences from the Ottoman Periods and Folklore Characters; Ottoman Arts and Modern Turkish Life

Quality of Instructors: The group had some difficulty understanding the instructor.

Environment: Bursa lies not far from the Sea of Marmara in the foothills of Turkey's tallest mountain, Ulu Dag, once called Mount Olympus. Bursa is really two cities—the present-day industrial center of Turkish automobile manufacture, and behind it the proud old quiet city. Bursa was the first Ottoman capital, a sacred city and spa once used by the Roman Caesars. Marble hints of the Roman Empire can still be found in the walls of old houses. The new Bursa has become the most luxurious city in Turkey, and elegant hotels have been built around the hot mineral springs.

Housing: En route to Bursa, Elderhostelers stay in Kutahya in a small hostelry that overlooks the town square, and in Bursa at the Vildiz Hotel. "Good."

Food: My panelists reported the cuisine as somewhere between strange and so-so.

Unique Attributes: At the center of the old city is a thirteenth-century Great Mosque with a magnificent fountain at its hub and a spectacular silhouette of 20 domes. Bursa is also the silk center of Turkey; in the Koza Han (*koza* means silk cocoon) one may buy silk cloth, rugs, or scarves and some of the finest leather in the country. One never forgets Bursa because of the lovely turquoise color characteristic of the town, caused by the predominance of bright, iridescent blue and green tiles. "The historical significance of Turkey is not only as a meeting place of East and West but also the important role it played in the development of Christianity as we know it today."

Shortcomings: Some participants found the food very strange and the language difficult. "This is a very poor country. . . not a trip for hostelers looking for resort life."

Getting In: My reviewers wrote, "This program was our second choice in Turkey, but it turned out to be the better choice as we saw more of the interior and gained a better insight of the real Turkey."

Getting There: "Saga Holidays made all the transportation arrangements and did a thorough job." Allaha Ismarladik!

Istanbul (week 3 of 3)—
University of Istanbul

See the description in the "Crossroads of Civilization" program, above.

Looking Ahead

Any movement that is growing 17 to 20 percent a year must be doing something right. And it is. Elderhosteling is feeding the insatiable appetites of its members by constantly expanding its network of program destinations. The Costa Rican program reviewed here was brand-new in 1990. And after long negotiations with the Soviet Ministry of Education and Bureau of Tourism, programs have been developed in the Soviet Union. Bicycle adventures in England, France, and the Netherlands have been created for hostelers with the courage and endurance to pedal 25 to 35 miles a day. New programs are opening in Zagreb, Yugoslavia, in the jungles of the Brazilian Amazon, in Lapland, and in the mountains of Nepal.

The movement has also developed its own repertoire of insider jokes. There's the yarn about the Lothario who has attended over 100 hostels in search of romance. Program directors have been alerted to his not-so-scholarly pursuit. My own favorite anecdotes are those that appeared in a 1984 *Time* magazine article. A professor at Rollins described Elderhostelers as people "refreshingly different and quite willing to look at the professor and say, 'Now Sonny, you don't have this straight.'" The article continued with the story of the teacher at the University of Northern Colorado who was using the bombing of Pearl Harbor as an example of poor communications when she was challenged by an Elderhosteler in the class who turned out to be a retired air force general. These humorous tales are the exceptions; as a rule, hostelers are very attentive, polite students.

Looking Ahead

In addition to being "refreshingly different," we are referred to as the nation's most potent constituency. Because seniors swing great weight on Capitol Hill and vote in record numbers, many teachers like to preach a bit of their favorite gospel to us. Conservationists get in a few licks about urban sprawl, environmentalists call our attention to acid rain, historians with a special point of view use the lectern to try to proselytize their audiences and sway some votes.

This movement is also addictive. I recently met a woman from Boston who had attended her first Elderhostel in September. When I interviewed her in August, eleven months later, she was on her fourteenth! Perhaps "looking ahead" is an odd concept for people with more past than future, but the words symbolize the Elderhostel movement.

Happy hosteling,
Mildred L. Hyman

Other Books from John Muir Publications

Adventure Vacations: From Trekking in New Guinea to Swimming in Siberia, Bangs 256 pp. $17.95

Asia Through the Back Door, 3rd ed., Steves and Gottberg 326 pp. $15.95

Belize: A Natural Destination, Mahler and Wotkyns 304 pp. $16.95

Buddhist America: Centers, Retreats, Practices, Morreale 400 pp. $12.95

Bus Touring: Charter Vacations, U.S.A., Warren with Bloch 168 pp. $9.95

California Public Gardens: A Visitor's Guide, Sigg 304 pp. $16.95

Catholic America: Self-Renewal Centers and Retreats, Christian-Meyer 325 pp. $13.95

Costa Rica: A Natural Destination, Sheck 280 pp. $15.95 (**2nd ed.** available 3/92 $16.95)

Elderhostels: The Students' Choice, 2nd ed., Hyman 304 pp. $15.95

Environmental Vacations: Volunteer Projects to Save the Planet, Ocko 240 pp. $15.95 (**2nd ed.** available 2/92 $16.96)

Europe 101: History & Art for the Traveler, 4th ed., Steves and Openshaw 372 pp. $15.95

Europe Through the Back Door, 9th ed., Steves 432 pp. $16.95 (**10th ed.** available 1/92 $16.95)

Floating Vacations: River, Lake, and Ocean Adventures, White 256 pp. $17.95

Great Cities of Eastern Europe, Rapoport 240 pp. $16.95

Gypsying After 40: A Guide to Adventure and Self-Discovery, Harris 264 pp. $14.95

The Heart of Jerusalem, Nellhaus 336 pp. $12.95

Indian America: A Traveler's Companion, 2nd ed., Eagle/Walking Turtle 448 pp. $17.95

Mona Winks: Self-Guided Tours of Europe's Top Museums, Steves and Openshaw 456 pp. $14.95

Opera! The Guide to Western Europe's Great Houses, Zietz 280 pp. $18.95

Paintbrushes and Pistols: How the Taos Artists Sold the West, Taggett and Schwarz 280 pp. $17.95

The People's Guide to Mexico, 8th ed., Franz 608 pp. $17.95

The People's Guide to RV Camping in Mexico, Franz with Rogers 320 pp. $13.95

Ranch Vacations: The Complete Guide to Guest and Resort, Fly-Fishing, and Cross-Country Skiing Ranches, 2nd ed., Kilgore 396 pp. $18.95

The Shopper's Guide to Art and Crafts in the Hawaiian Islands, Schuchter 272 pp. $13.95

The Shopper's Guide to Mexico, Rogers and Rosa 224 pp. $9.95

The Shopper's Guide to Art and Crafts in the Hawaiian Islands, Schuchter 272 pp. $13.95

The Shopper's Guide to Mexico, Rogers and Rosa 224 pp. $9.95

Ski Tech's Guide to Equipment, Skiwear, and Accessories, edited by Tanler 144 pp. $11.95

Ski Tech's Guide to Maintenance and Repair, edited by Tanler 160 pp. $11.95

A Traveler's Guide to Asian Culture, Chambers 224 pp. $13.95

Traveler's Guide to Healing Centers and Retreats in North America, Rudee and Blease 240 pp. $11.95

Understanding Europeans, Miller 272 pp. $14.95

Undiscovered Islands of the Caribbean, 2nd ed., Willes 232 pp. $14.95

Undiscovered Islands of the Mediterranean, Moyer and Willes 232 pp. $14.95

Undiscovered Islands of the U.S. and Canadian West Coast, Moyer and Willes 208 pp. $12.95

A Viewer's Guide to Art: A Glossary of Gods, People, and Creatures, Shaw and Warren 144 pp. $10.95

2 to 22 Days Series
Each title offers 22 flexible daily itineraries that can be used to get the most out of vacations of any length. Included are not only "must see" attractions but also little-known villages and hidden "jewels" as well as valuable general information.

22 Days Around the World, 1992 ed., Rapoport and Willes 256 pp. $12.95

2 to 22 Days Around the Great Lakes, 1992 ed., Schuchter 192 pp. $9.95

22 Days in Alaska, Lanier 128 pp. $7.95

2 to 22 Days in the American Southwest, 1992 ed., Harris 176 pp. $9.95

2 to 22 Days in Asia, 1992 ed., Rapoport and Willes 176 pp. $9.95

2 to 22 Days in Australia, 1992 ed., Gottberg 192 pp. $9.95

22 Days in California, 2nd ed., Rapoport 176 pp. $9.95

22 Days in China, Duke and Victor 144 pp. $7.95

2 to 22 Days in Europe, 1992 ed., Steves 276 pp. $12.95

2 to 22 Days in Florida, 1992 ed., Harris 192 pp. $9.95

2 to 22 Days in France, 1992 ed., Steves 192 pp. $9.95

2 to 22 Days in Germany, Austria, & Switzerland, 1992 ed., Steves 224 pp. $9.95

2 to 22 Days in Great Britain, 1992 ed., Steves 192 pp. $9.95

2 to 22 Days in Hawaii, 1992 ed., Schuchter 176 pp. $9.95

22 Days in India, Mathur 136 pp. $7.95

22 Days in Japan, Old 136 pp. $7.95

22 Days in Mexico, 2nd ed., Rogers and Rosa 128 pp. $7.95

2 to 22 Days in New England, 1992 ed., Wright 192 pp. $9.95

2 to 22 Days in New Zealand, 1991 ed., Schuchter 176 pp. $9.95

2 to 22 Days in Norway, Sweden, & Denmark, 1992 ed., Steves 192 pp. $9.95

2 to 22 Days in the Pacific Northwest, 1992 ed., Harris 192 pp. $9.95

2 to 22 Days in the Rockies, 1992 ed., Rapoport 192 pp. $9.95

2 to 22 Days in Spain & Portugal, 1992 ed., Steves 192 pp. $9.95

22 Days in Texas, Harris 176 pp. $9.95

22 Days in Thailand, Richardson 176 pp. $9.95

22 Days in the West Indies, Morreale and Morreale 136 pp. $7.95

Parenting Series

Being a Father: Family, Work, and Self, *Mothering* Magazine 176 pp. $12.95

Preconception: A Woman's Guide to Preparing for Pregnancy and Parenthood, Aikey-Keller 232 pp. $14.95

Schooling at Home: Parents, Kids, and Learning, *Mothering* Magazine 264 pp. $14.95

Teens: A Fresh Look, *Mothering* Magazine 240 pp. $14.95

"Kidding Around" Travel Guides for Young Readers
Written for kids eight years of age and older.

Kidding Around Atlanta, Pedersen 64 pp. $9.95

Kidding Around Boston, Byers 64 pp. $9.95

Kidding Around Chicago, Davis 64 pp. $9.95

Kidding Around the Hawaiian Islands, Lovett 64 pp. $9.95

Kidding Around London, Lovett 64 pp. $9.95

Kidding Around Los Angeles, Cash 64 pp. $9.95

Kidding Around the National Parks of the Southwest, Lovett 108 pp. $12.95

Kidding Around New York City, Lovett 64 pp. $9.95

Kidding Around Paris, Clay 64 pp. $9.95

Kidding Around Philadelphia, Clay 64 pp. $9.95

Kidding Around San Diego, Luhrs 64 pp. $9.95

Kidding Around San Francisco, Zibart 64 pp. $9.95

Kidding Around Santa Fe, York 64 pp. $9.95

Kidding Around Seattle, Steves 64 pp. $9.95

Kidding Around Spain, Biggs 108 pp. $12.95

Kidding Around Washington, D.C., Pedersen 64 pp. $9.95

Environmental Books for Young Readers
Written for kids eight years and older.

The Indian Way: Learning to Communicate with Mother Earth, McLain 114 pp. $9.95

The Kids' Environment Book: What's Awry and Why, Pedersen 192 pp. $13.95

Rads, Ergs, and Cheeseburgers: The Kids' Guide to Energy and the Environment, Yanda 108 pp. $12.95

"Extremely Weird" Series for Young Readers
Written for kids eight years of age and older.

Extremely Weird Bats, Lovett 48 pp. $9.95

Extremely Weird Frogs, Lovett 48 pp. $9.95

Extremely Weird Primates, Lovett 48 pp. $9.95

Extremely Weird Reptiles, Lovett
48 pp. $9.95
Extremely Weird Spiders, Lovett
48 pp. $9.95

Quill Hedgehog Adventures Series

Written for kids eight years of age
and older. Our new series of green
fiction for kids follows the adventures of Quill Hedgehog and his
Animalfolk friends.

**Quill's Adventures in the Great
Beyond,** Book 1, Waddington-
Feather 96 pp. $5.95
Quill's Adventures in Wasteland,
Book 2, Waddington-Feather
132 pp. $5.95
**Quill's Adventures in Grozzie-
land,** Book 3, Waddington-Feather
132 pp. $5.95

Other Young Readers Titles

**Kids Explore America's Hispanic
Heritage,** edited by Cozzens
112 pp. $7.95 (avail. 2/92)

Automotive Repair Manuals

**How to Keep Your VW Alive, 14th
ed.,** 440 pp. $21.95
How to Keep Your Subaru Alive
480 pp. $21.95
**How to Keep Your Toyota Pickup
Alive** 392 pp. $21.95
**How to Keep Your Datsun/Nissan
Alive** 544 pp. $21.95

Other Automotive Books

**The Greaseless Guide to Car
Care Confidence: Take the Terror
Out of Talking to Your Mechanic,**
Jackson 224 pp. $14.95

**Off-Road Emergency Repair &
Survival,** Ristow 160 pp. $9.95

Ordering Information

If you cannot find our books in your
local bookstore, you can order
directly from us. Please check the
"Available" date above. If you send
us money for a book not yet available, we will hold your money until
we can ship you the book. Your
books will be sent to you via UPS
(for U.S. destinations). UPS will not
deliver to a P.O. Box; please give us
a street address. Include $3.25 for
the first item ordered and $.50 for
each additional item to cover shipping and handling costs. For airmail within the U.S., enclose $4.00.
All foreign orders will be shipped
surface rate; please enclose $3.00
for the first item and $1.00 for each
additional item. Please inquire
about foreign airmail rates.

Method of Payment

Your order may be paid by check,
money order, or credit card. We
cannot be responsible for cash
sent through the mail. All pay-
ments must be made in U.S. dollars drawn on a U.S. bank. Canadian postal money orders in U.S.
dollars are acceptable. For VISA,
MasterCard, or American Express
orders, include your card number,
expiration date, and your signa-
ture, or call (800) 888-7504. Books
ordered on American Express
cards can be shipped only to the
billing address of the cardholder.
Sorry, no C.O.D.'s. Residents of
sunny New Mexico, add 5.875%
tax to the total.

Address all orders and inquiries to:
John Muir Publications
P.O. Box 613
Santa Fe, NM 87504
(505) 982-4078
(800) 888-7504